"The ideas in Beatriz Preciado's pornosophical gem are a thousand curious fingers slipped beneath the underpants of conventional thinking. Teach the sex scenes in your seminars, and read the flights of theory aloud to your latest lover amid a tangle of sweaty sheets."

—SUSAN STRYKER, author of
THE TRANSGENDER STUDIES READER

"*Testo Junkie* is unlike anything I've ever read. Beatriz Preciado has produced a volume of work that goes far beyond memoir to create an entirely new way of understanding not only the history of sex, gender, and the body, but of life as we have come to know it. Powerful and disturbing in the most pleasurable way."

—DEL LAGRACE VOLCANO, author of
FEMMES OF POWER

"Beatriz Preciado offers an exhilarating and sometimes shattering portrait of how gender shapes the ways we live and fuck and grieve and fight and love. *Testo Junkie* is a fearless chronicle of the gender revolution currently in progress. Anyone who has a gender—or has dispensed with one—should read this book."

—GAYLE SALAMON, author of
ASSUMING A BODY

"Inventive, daring, and blindingly lucid, Beatriz Preciado opens a new branch of philosophical practice. Driven by a flair for technological adventure and the uncommon ability to craft somatic and political fiction, *Testo Junkie* probes the limits of textual trafficking, gender-hacking, and the different regimes of prosthetic imposition that govern our existence. This book is not for the faint of philosophical heart!"

—AVITAL RONELL, author of *CRACK WARS*

TESTO JUNKIE

BEATRIZ PRECIADO

SEX, DRUGS, AND BIOPOLITICS IN THE PHARMACOPORNOGRAPHIC ERA

TRANSLATED FROM THE FRENCH BY BRUCE BENDERSON

THE
FEMINIST PRESS
AT THE CITY UNIVERSITY
OF NEW YORK
NEW YORK CITY

CONTENTS

INTRODUCTION

This book is not a memoir. This book is a testosterone-based, voluntary intoxication protocol, which concerns the body and affects of BP. A body-essay. Fiction, actually. If things must be pushed to the extreme, this is a somatopolitical fiction, a theory of the self, or self-theory. During the time period covered by this essay, two external transformations follow on each other in the context of the experimental body, the impact of which couldn't be calculated beforehand and cannot be taken into account as a function of the study; but it created the limits around which writing was incorporated. First of all, there is the death of GD, the human distillation of a vanishing epoch, an icon, and the ultimate French representative of a form of written sexual insurrection; almost simultaneously, there is the tropism of BP's body in the direction of VD's body, an opportunity for perfection—and for ruin. This is a record of physiological and political micromutations provoked in BP's body by testosterone, as well as the theoretical and physical changes incited in that body by loss, desire, elation, failure, or renouncement. I'm not interested in my emotions insomuch as their being mine, belonging only, uniquely, to me. I'm not interested in their individual aspects, only in how they are traversed by what isn't mine. In what emanates from our planet's history, the evolution of living species, the flux of economics, remnants of technological innovations, preparation for wars, the trafficking of organic slaves and commodities, the creation of hierarchies, institutions of punishment and repression, networks of communication and surveillance, the random overlapping of market research groups, techniques and blocs of opinion, the biochemical transformation of feeling, the production and distribution of pornographic images. Some will read this text as a manual for a kind of gender bioterrorism on a molecular scale. Others will see in it a single point in a cartography of extinction. In this text, the reader won't come to any definitive conclusion about the truth of my sex, or predictions about the world to come. I present these pages as an account of theoretical junctions, molecules, affects, in order to leave a trace of a political experiment that lasted 236 days and nights and that continues today under other forms. If the reader sees this text as an uninterrupted series of philosophical reflections, accounts of hormone administration, and detailed records of sexual practices without the solutions provided by continuity, it is simply because this is the mode on which subjectivity is constructed and deconstructed.

Question: If you could see
a documentary on a philosopher,
on Heidegger, Kant, or Hegel,
what would you like to see in it?

Jacques Derrida's answer:
For them to talk about their sex life.
. . . You want a quick answer?
Their sex life.†

† Jacques Derrida. *Derrida*, directed by Kirby Dick and Amy Ziering Koffman. (New York: Zeitgeist Video, 2003), DVD.

1. YOUR DEATH

October 5: Tim tells me you've died. He's crying. He loves you. However, in your last books, you didn't treat him with generosity. He says, "It's William." He's crying, repeats, "It's William, it's William. We found him dead in his new apartment in Paris. We don't know. It happened two days ago, on the third. We just don't know."

Until now, no one was aware of your death. You rotted for two days in the same position in which you had fallen. It's better like that. No one came to bother you. They left you alone with your body, the time necessary for abandoning in peace all that misery. I cry with Tim. It can't be.

I hang up, and the first thing I do is call VD—I don't know why. We've seen each other twice. Once, alone. You're the one who pushes me to dial her number. You listen to our conversation. Your mind unfurls and forms an electromagnetic layer from which our words flow. Your ghost is a wire transmitting our voices. As we talk about your death, her voice awakens the life in me. *The strongest is his voice, I think,*[1] you were saying. I don't dare cry when talking with her. I hang up, and then I cry, alone. Because you didn't want to keep living and because, as your godfather would say, "a dead poet writes no more."[2]

---

1. Guillaume Dustan, *Nicolas Pages* (Paris: Editions Balland, 1999), 17.
2. Michel Houellebecq, *Rester vivant et autres textes* (Paris: Librio, 1997), 19.

That same day, a few hours later, I put a fifty-milligram dose of Testogel on my skin, so that I can begin to write this book. It isn't the first time. This is my usual dose. The carbon chains, O-H3, C-H3, C-OH, gradually penetrate my epidermis and travel through the deep layers of my skin until they reach the blood vessels, nerve endings, glands. I'm not taking testosterone to change myself into a man or as a physical strategy of transsexualism; I take it to foil what society wanted to make of me, so that I can write, fuck, feel a form of pleasure that is postpornographic, add a molecular prostheses to my *low-tech* transgender identity composed of dildos, texts, and moving images; I do it to avenge your death.

VIDEOPENETRATION

> *I'd rather go blind than to see you walk away.*
> —ETTA JAMES

8:35 p.m. Your spirit comes through the window and darkens the room. I turn on all the lights. Put a blank cassette in the video camera and screw the camera to the tripod. I check the framing. The image is smooth and symmetrical; the black leather couch forms a horizontal line at the bottom of the frame. The white wall easily follows that line, but without creating any feeling of volume or relief. Play. I move to the sofa. Off camera, on the coffee table, I've left electric clippers, a small mirror, a sheet of white paper, a plastic bag, a bottle of hypoallergenic glue for use on the face, a dose of fifty milligrams of testosterone in gel form, a tube of lubricant, anal-dilator gel, a harness with a realistic rubber dildo (9½ x 1½ in.), a realistic black silicone dildo (9¾ x 2½ in.), a black ergonomic one (5½ x ¾ in.), a razor and shaving cream, a plastic basin filled with water, a white towel, and one of your books, the first, the sublime one, the beginning and end of everything. I walk into the frame. Get undressed, but not completely. Keep my black tank top on. As if for surgery, I expose only those organs on which the instruments will be working. I stand the mirror up on the table. I plug in the electric clippers. A sharp, high-pitched sound, the voice of a cyberchild trying to get out of the motor, spitting in the face of the past. I adjust the blades of the comb to a width of one centimeter. Your spirit sends me a discrete sound of approval. I sit on the couch, and one half of my face—looking expressionless, centerless— appears in the mirror: my short black hair; contact lenses, whose edges create a thin halo around the iris; patchy skin; very white in places and flecked with bright pink in others. I was labeled a woman, but that's imperceptible in the partial image reflected in the mirror. I begin shaving my head, starting at the front and moving backward, then from the middle toward the left, then toward the right. I bend forward so that the locks drop onto the table. I open the plastic bag and slide the hair into it. Turn off the machine and adjust the comb to zero. I place a sheet of white paper on the table, then turn the clippers back on and move them again over my entire head. Short, very thin hairs rain onto the white paper. When my head is completely smooth, I unplug the machine. I fold the sheet of paper in two, so that the hairs collect at the center, forming a uniform line. A line of black cocaine. I'm doing up a line of hair. It's almost the same high. I open the jar of glue and add a streak of it above my upper lip with the moistened brush, then take a strand of hair between my fingers and set it along the streak of glue until it sticks perfectly to the skin of my face. A fag's mustache. I check myself out in the mirror. My eyes have the same halo around the iris. Same face, skin. Identical yet unrecognizable. I look into the camera, curl back my lip to show my teeth, the way you do it. It's your gesture.

The silver package containing a fifty-milligram dose of testosterone in gel form is the same size as a small packet of sugar. I rip into the aluminum-coated paper; out comes a thin, cold, transparent gel that disappears immediately into the skin of my left shoulder. A cool vapor remains, like a memory of icy breath, the kiss of a snowwoman.

I shake the can of shaving cream, deposit a ball of expanding white lather on my palm, then cover the hairs of my pubes, the lips of my vulva and the skin surrounding my anus with it. I dip the blade in water and begin to shave. Hairs and cream float to the surface. A few splashes fall onto the couch or the floor. This time I don't cut myself. When all the skin on my crotch has been shaved, I rinse off and dry. Slip on the harness and buckle the straps at the side of each hip. In front of me, the dildo is super erect, forming a right angle with the line of my vertebral column. The dildo belt is high enough to allow me to see two very distinct orifices when I bend down.

I coat my hands with transparent gel and pick up the two dildos. I rub, lubricate, warm them, one in each hand, then one against the other, like two giant cocks twisting against each other in a gay porn film. I know the camera is filming because I can see the red light blinking. I dangle my silicone cock over the paragraphs tattooed across the pages of *Dans ma chambre*.[3] It's your gesture. The dildo conceals part of the page, creating a barrier that allows certain words to be read and hides others: "We laughed. He went with me in the car. I looked at him. His hand signaled me before / night fell. I know that I would have had to / I'll never be in love with him. But how wonderful it was that he loved me. It was good."[4]

Next I slide the dildos into the openings at the lower part of my body. First, the realistic-looking one, then the ergonomic one, which goes into my anus. It's always easier for me to put something into my anus, which is a multidimensional space without any bony edges. This time, it's the same. On my knees, I turn my back to the camera, the tips of my feet and my head pressing against the floor, and hold my arms behind me so that they can manage the two dildos in my orifices.

You're the only one who could read this book. In front of this camera, "for the first time I'm tempted to make a self-portrait for you."[5] Design an image of myself as if I were you. *Do you in drag*. Cross-dress into you. Bring you back to life with this image.

---

3. *In My Room*, the first novel of French gay writer Guillaume Dustan.—Trans.
4. Dustan, *Nicolas Pages*, 155.
5. Hervé Guibert, *L'Image fantôme* (Paris: Editions de Minuit, 1981), 5.

From this moment on, all of you are dead. Amelia, Hervé, Michel, Karen, Jackie, Teo, and You. Do I belong more to your world than I do to the world of the living? Isn't my politics yours; my house, my body, yours? Reincarnate yourselves in me, take over my body like extraterrestrials took over Americans and changed them into living sheaths. Reincarnate yourself in me; possess my tongue, arms, sex organs, dildos, blood, molecules; possess my girlfriend, dog; inhabit me, live in me. Come. *Ven.* Please don't leave. *Vuelve a la vida.* Come back to life. Hold on to my sex. Low, down, dirty. Stay with me.

This book has no other reason for being outside the margin of uncertainty existing between me and my sex organs, all imaginary, between three languages that don't belong to me, between the alive you and the dead you, between my desire to carry on your line and the impossibility of restoring your sperm, between your eternal and silent books and the flood of words that are in a hurry to come out of my fingers, between testosterone and my body, between V and my love for V. Looking into the camera again: "This testosterone is for you, this pleasure is for you."

I don't watch the mini-DV I just filmed. I don't even number it. I put it into its transparent red case and write on the label:

October 3, 2005. DAY OF YOUR DEATH.

The preceding and following days are marked by my ritual of testosterone administration. It's a home protocol; it would even be a secret and private one if each of these administrations weren't being filmed and sent anonymously to an Internet page on which hundreds of transgender, mutating bodies all over the planet are exchanging techniques and know-how. On this audiovisual network, my face is immaterial, my name of no significance. Only the strict relationship between my body and the substance is a cult object, an object of surveillance. I spread the gel over my shoulders. First instant: the feeling of a light slap on the skin. The feeling changes into one of coldness before it disappears. Then, nothing for a day or two. Nothing. Waiting. Then, an extraordinary lucidity settles in, gradually, accompanied by an explosion of the desire to fuck, walk, go out everywhere in the city. This is the climax in which the spiritual force of the testosterone mixing with my blood takes to the fore. Absolutely all the unpleasant sensations disappear. Unlike speed, the movement going on inside has nothing to do with agitation, noise. It's simply the feeling of being in perfect harmony with the rhythm of the city. Unlike with coke, there is no distortion in the perception of self, no logorrhea or any feeling of superiority. Nothing but the feeling of strength reflecting the increased capacity of my muscles, my brain. My body is present to itself. Unlike with speed and coke, there is no immediate comedown. A few days go by, and the movement inside calms, but the feeling of strength, like a pyramid revealed by a sandstorm, remains.

How can I explain what is happening to me? What can I do about my desire for transformation? What can I do about all the years I defined myself as a feminist? What kind of feminist am I today: a feminist hooked on testosterone, or a transgender body hooked on feminism? I have no other alternative but to revise my classics, to subject those theories to the shock that was provoked in me by the practice of taking testosterone. To accept the fact that the change happening in me is the metamorphosis of an era.

2. THE PHARMACOPORNOGRAPHIC ERA

I was born in 1970. The automobile industry, which had reached its peak, was beginning to decline. My father had the first and most prominent garage in Burgos, a Gothic city full of parish priests and members of the military, where Franco had set up the new symbolic capital of fascist Spain. If Hitler had won the war, the new Europe would have been established around two obviously unequal poles, Burgos and Berlin. At least, that was the little Galician general's dream.

Garage Central was located on rue du General Mola, named after the soldier who in 1936 led the uprising against the Republican regime. The most expensive cars in the city, belonging to the rich and to dignitaries of the Franco regime, were kept there. In my house there were no books, just cars. Some Chrysler Motor Slant Sixes; several Renault Gordinis, Dauphines, and Ondines (nicknamed "widows' cars," because they had the reputation of skidding on curves and killing husbands at the wheel); some Citroën DSs (which the Spanish called "sharks"); and several Standards brought back from England and reserved for doctors. I should add the collection of antique cars that my father had put together little by little: a black "Lola Flores" Mercedes, a gray, pre-1930s Citroën with a traction engine, a seventeen-horsepower Ford, a Dodge Dart Swinger, a 1928 Citroën with its "frog's ass," and a Cadillac with eight cylinders. At the time, my father was investing in brickyard industries, which (like the dictatorship, coincidentally) would begin to decline in 1975 with the gas crisis. In the end, he had to sell his car collection to make up for the collapse of the factory. I cried about it. Meanwhile, I was growing up like a tomboy. My father cried about it.

During that bygone yet not-so-long-ago era that we today call Fordism, the automobile and mass-produced suburban housing industries synthesized and perfected a specific mode of production and consumption, a Taylorist temporal organization of life characterized by a sleek polychrome aesthetic of the inanimate object, a way of conceiving of inner space and urban living, a conflictual arrangement of the body and the machine, a discontinuous flow of desire and resistance. In the years following the energy crisis and the decline of the assembly line, people sought to identify new growth sectors in a transformed global economy. That is when "experts" began talking about biochemical, electronic, computing, or communications industries as new industrial props of capitalism . . . But these discourses won't be enough to explain the production of added value and the metamorphosis of life in contemporary society.

It is, however, possible to sketch out a new cartography of the transformations in industrial production during the previous century, using as an axis the political and technical management of the body, sex, and identity. In other words, it is philosophically relevant today to undertake a *somato-political*[1] analysis of "world-economy."[2]

From an economic perspective, the transition toward a third form of capitalism, after the slave-dependent and industrial systems, is generally situated somewhere in the 1970s; but the establishment of a new type of "government of the living"[3] had already emerged from the urban, physical, psychological, and ecological ruins of World War II—or, in the case of Spain, from the Civil War.

How did sex and sexuality become the main objects of political and economic activity?

Follow me: The changes in capitalism that we are witnessing are characterized not only by the transformation of "gender," "sex," "sexuality," "sexual identity," and "pleasure" into objects of the political management of living (just as Foucault had suspected in his biopolitical description of new systems of social control), but also by the fact that this management itself is carried out through the new dynamics of advanced technocapitalism, global media, and biotechnologies. During the Cold War, the United States put more money into scientific research about sex and sexuality than any other country in history. The application of surveillance and biotechnologies for governing civil society

1. I refer here to Foucault's notion *"somato-pouvoir"* and *"technologie politique du corps."* See Michel Foucault, *Surveiller et punir: Naissance de la prison* (Paris: Gallimard, 1975), 33–36; see also Michel Foucault, *"Les rapports de pouvoir passent à l'intérieur du corps,"* in *La Quinzaine Littéraire*, 247 (1er–15 janvier 1977): 4–6.

2. Here I draw on the well-known expression used by Immanuel Wallerstein in *World-Systems Analysis: An Introduction* (Durham, NC: Duke University Press, 2004).

3. Michel Foucault, *"Du gouvernement des vivants* (1979–1980)," Leçons du Collège de France, 1979–1980, in *Dits et Ecrits*. (Paris: Gallimard, 1974), 4: 641–42.

started during the late 1930s: the war was the best laboratory for molding the body, sex, and sexuality. The necropolitical techniques of the war will progressively become biopolitical industries for producing and controlling sexual subjectivities. Let us remember that the period between the beginning of World War II and the first years of the Cold War constitutes a moment without precedent for women's visibility in public space as well as the emergence of visible and politicized forms of homosexuality in such unexpected places as, for example, the American army.[4] Alongside this social development, American McCarthyism—rampant throughout the 1950s—added to the patriotic fight against communism the persecution of homosexuality as a form of antinationalism while at the same time exalting the family values of masculine labor and domestic maternity.[5] Meanwhile, architects Ray and Charles Eames collaborated with the American army to manufacture small boards of molded plywood to use as splints for mutilated appendages. A few years later, the same material was used to build furniture that came to exemplify the light design of modern American disposable architecture.[6] During the twentieth century, the "invention" of the biochemical notion of the hormone and the pharmaceutical development of synthetic molecules for commercial uses radically modified traditional definitions of normal and pathological sexual identities. In 1941, the first natural molecules of progesterone and estrogens were

4. Allan Bérubé, *Coming Out Under Fire: The History of Gay Men and Women in World War Two* (New York: The Free Press, 1990).

5. John D'Emilio, *Sexual Politics, Sexual Communities: The Making of a Homosexual Minority in the United States, 1940–1970* (Chicago: University of Chicago Press, 1983).

6. See Beatriz Colomina, *Domesticity at War* (Cambridge, MA: MIT Press, 2007), 29.

obtained from the urine of pregnant mares (Premarin) and soon after synthetic hormones (Norethindrone) were commercialized. The same year, George Henry carried out the first demographic study of "sexual deviation," a quantitative study of masses known as *Sex Variants*.[7] The Kinsey Reports on human sexual behavior (1948 and 1953) and Robert Stoller's protocols for "femininity" and "masculinity" (1968) followed in sexological suit. In 1957, the North American pedo-psychiatrist John Money coined the term "gender," differentiating it from the traditional term "sex," to define an individual's inclusion in a culturally recognized group of "masculine" or "feminine" behavior and physical expression. Money famously affirms that it is possible (using surgical, endocrinological, and cultural techniques) to "change the gender of any baby up to 18 months."[8] Between 1946 and 1949 Harod Gillies was performing the first phalloplastic surgeries in the UK, including work on Michael Dillon, the first female-to-male transsexual to have taken testosterone as part of the masculinization protocol.[9] In 1952, US soldier George W. Jorgensen was transformed into Christine, the first transsexual person discussed widely in the popular press. During the early 50s and into the 60s, physician Harry Benjamin systematized the clinical use of hormonal molecules in the treatment of "sex change" and

7. Jennifer Terry, *An American Obsession: Science, Medicine, and Homosexuality in Modern Society* (Chicago: The University of Chicago Press, 1999), 178–218.

8. John Money, Joan Hampson, and John Hampson, "Imprinting and the Establishiment of Gender Role," *Archives of Neurology and Psychiatry* 77 (1957): 333-36.

9. Harold Gillies and Raph Millard J., *The Principles and Art of Plastic Surgery* (Boston: Little Brown, 1957), 385-88; Michael Dillon, *Self. A Study in Ethics and Endocrinology* (London: Heinemann, 1946); for a larger historical survey see also: Berenice L. Hausman, *Changing Sex, Transsexualism, Technology, and the Idea of Gender* (Durham, North Carolina: Duke University Press, 1995), 67.

defined "transsexualism," a term first introduced in 1954, as a curable condition.[10]

The invention of the contraceptive pill, the first biochemical technique enabling the separation between heterosexual practice and reproduction, was a direct result of the expansion of endocrinological experimentation, and triggered a process of development of what could be called, twisting the Eisenhower term, "the sex-gender industrial complex."[11] In 1957, Searle & Co. commercialized Enovid, the first contraceptive pill ("the Pill") made of a combination of mestranol and norethynodrei. First promoted for the treatment of menstrual disorders, the Pill was approved for contraceptive use four years later. The chemical components of the Pill would soon become the most used pharmaceutical molecules in the whole of human history.[12]

The Cold War was also a period of transformation of the governmental and economic regulations concerning pornography and prostitution. In 1946, elderly sex worker and spy Martha Richard convinced the French government to declare the "*maison closes*" illegal, which ended the nineteenth-century governmental system of brothels in France. In 1953, Hugh Hefner founded *Playboy*, the first North American "porn" magazine to be sold at newspaper stands, with a photograph of Marilyn Monroe naked as the

10. Whereas homosexuality was withdrawn from the *Diagnostic and Statistical Manual of Mental Disorders* (DSM) in 1973, in 1983, gender identity disorder (clinical form of transsexuality) was included in the DSM with diagnostic criteria for this new pathology.

11. President Eisenhower used the term "military-industrial complex" in his Farewell to the Nation speech of 1961.

12. Andrea Tone, *Devices and Desires. A History of Contraceptives in America* (New York: Hill and Wang, 2001), 203–31; Lara V. Marks, *Sexual Chemistry: A History of the Contraceptive Pill* (New Haven: Yale University Press, 2001).

centerfold of the first publication. In 1959, Hefner transformed an old Chicago house into the Playboy Mansion, which was promoted within the magazine and on television as a "love palace" with thirty-two rooms, becoming soon the most popular American erotic utopia. In 1972, Gerard Damiano produced *Deep Throat*. The film, starring Linda Lovelace, was widely commercialized in the US and became one of the most watched movies of all times, grossing more than $600 million. From this time on, porn film production boomed, from thirty clandestine film producers in 1950 to over 2,500 films in 1970.

If for years pornography was the dominant visual technology addressed to the male body for controlling his sexual reaction, during the 1950s the pharmaceutical industry looked for ways of triggering erection and sexual response using surgical and chemical prostheses. In 1974, Soviet Victor Konstantinovich Kalnberz patented the first penis implant using polyethylene plastic rods as a treatment for impotency, resulting in a permanently erect penis. These implants were abandoned for chemical variants because they were found to be "physically uncomfortable and emotionally disconcerting." In 1984 Tom F. Lue, Emil A. Tanaghoy, and Richard A. Schmidt implanted a "sexual pacemaker" in the penis of a patient. The contraption was a system of electrodes inserted close to the prostate that permitted an erection by remote control. The molecule of sildenafil (commercialized as Viagra© by Pfizer laboratories in 1988) will later become the chemical treatment for "erectile dysfunction."

During the Cold War years psychotropic techniques first developed within the military were extended to medical and recreational uses for the civil population. In the 1950s, the United States Central Intelligence Agency performed a series of experiments involving electroshock techniques as well as psychedelic and hallucinogen drugs as part of a program of "brainwashing," military interrogation, and psychological torture. The aim of the experimental program of the CIA was to identify the chemical techniques able to directly modify the prisoner's subjectivity, inflecting levels of anxiety, dizziness, agitation, irritability, sexual excitement, or fear.[13] At the same time, the laboratories Eli Lilly (Indiana) commercialized the molecule called Methadone (the most simple opiate) as an analgesic and Secobarbital, a barbiturate with anaesthetic, sedative, and hypnotic properties conceived for the treatment of epilepsy, insomnia, and as an anaesthetic for short surgery. Secobarbital, better known as "the red pill" or "doll," became one of the drugs of the rock underground culture of the 1960s.[14] In 1977, the state of Oklahoma introduced the first lethal injection composed of barbiturates similar to "the red pill" to be used for the death penalty.[15]

The Cold War military space race was also the site of production of a new form of technological embodiment.

13. On the use of chemicals for military purposes during the Cold War years see: Naomi Klein, "The Torture Lab," in *The Schock Doctrine* (New York: Penguin, 2007), 25-48.

14. Methadone became in the 70s the basic substitution treatment for heroine addiction. See: Tom Carnwath and Ian Smith, *Heroin Century* (New York: Routledge, 2002), 40–42.

15. The same method had already been applied in a Nazi German program called "Action T4" for "racial hygiene" that euthanatized between 75,000 and 100,000 people with physical or psychic disabilities. It was abandoned because of the high pharmacological cost; instead it was substituted by gas chambers or simply death caused by inanition.

At the start of the 60s, Manfred E. Clynes and Nathan S. Kline used the term "cyborg" for the first time to refer to an organism technologically supplemented to live in an extraterrestrial environment where it could operate as an "integrated homeostatic system."[16] They experimented with a laboratory rat, which received an osmotic prosthesis implant that it dragged along—a cyber tail. Beyond the rat, the cyborg named a new techno-organic condition, a sort of "soft machine"[17] (to use a Burroughs term) or a body with "electric skin" (to put it in Haus-Rucker & Co. terms) subjected to new forms of political control but also able to develop new forms of resistance. During the 1960s, as part of a military investigation program, *Arpanet* was created; it was the predecessor of the global Internet, the first "net of nets" of interconnected computers capable of transmitting information.

On the other hand, the surgical techniques developed for the treatment of "*les geules cassées*" of the First World War and the skin reconstruction techniques specially invented for the handling of the victims of the nuclear bomb will be transformed during the 1950s and 1960s into cosmetic and sexual surgeries.[18] In response to the threat inferred by Nazism and racist rhetoric, which claims that racial or religious differences can be detected in anatomical signs, "de-circumcision," the artificial reconstruction of foreskin, was one of the most practiced cosmetic surgery operations

---

16. M. E. Clynes and N. S. Kline, "Cyborgs and Space," in *Astronautics* (September, 1960).

17. William S. Burroughs, *The Soft Machine* (New York: Olympia Press, 1961).

18. Martin Monestier, *Les geules cassées, Les médecins de l'impossible 1914-18* (Paris: Cherche Midi, 2009).

in the United States.[19] At the same time, facelifts, as well as various other cosmetic surgery operations, became mass-market techniques for a new middle-class body consumer. Andy Warhol had himself photographed during a facelift, transforming his own body into a bio-pop object.

Meanwhile, the use of a viscous, semi-rigid material that is waterproof, thermally and electrically resistant, produced by artificial propagation of carbon atoms in long chains of molecules of organic compounds derived from petroleum, and whose burning is highly polluting, became generalized in manufacturing the objects of daily life. DuPont, who pioneered the development of plastics from the 1930s on, was also implicated in nuclear research for the Manhattan project.[20] Together with plastics, we saw the exponential multiplication of the production of transuranic elements (the chemical elements with atomic numbers greater than 92—the atomic number of Uranium), which became the material to be used in the civil sector, including plutonium, that had, before, been used as nuclear fuel in military operations.[21] The level of toxicity of transuranic elements exceeds that of any other element on earth, creating a new form of vulnerability for life. Cellulosic, polynosic, polyamide, polyester, acrylic, polypylene, spandex, etc., became materials used equally for body consumption and architecture. The mass consumption of plastic defined

19. Sander L. Gilman, "Decircumcision: The First Aesthetic Surgery," *Modern Judaism* 17, 3 (1997): 201–10. Maxell Matz, *Evolution of Plastic Surgery* (New York: Froben Press, 1946), 287–89.

20. Pap A. Ndiaye, *Nylon and Bombs: DuPont and the March of Modern America* (Baltimore: John Hopkins University, 2006).

21. See: Donna J. Haraway, *Modest_Witness@Second_Millennium. FemaleMan©Meets_ OncoMouse™: Feminism and Technoscience*, (New York: Routledge, 1997), 54.

the material conditions of a large-scale ecological transformation that resulted in destruction of other (mostly lower) energy resources, rapid consumption, and high pollution. The *Trash Vortex*, a floating mass the size of Texas in the North Pacific made of plastic garbage, was to become the largest water architecture of the twenty-first century.[22]

We are being confronted with a new kind of hot, psychotropic, punk capitalism. Such recent transformations are imposing an ensemble of new microprosthetic mechanisms of control of subjectivity by means of biomolecular and multimedia technical protocols. Our world economy is dependent on the production and circulation of hundreds of tons of synthetic steroids and technically transformed organs, fluids, cells (techno-blood, techno-sperm, techno-ovum, etc.), on the global diffusion of a flood of pornographic images, on the elaboration and distribution of new varieties of legal and illegal synthetic psychotropic drugs (e.g., bromazepam, Special K, Viagra, speed, crystal, Prozac, ecstasy, poppers, heroin), on the flood of signs and circuits of the digital transmission of information, on the extension of a form of diffuse urban architecture to the entire planet in which megacities of misery are knotted into high concentrations of sex-capital.[23]

These are just some snapshots of a postindustrial, global, and mediatic regime that, from here on, I will call *pharmacopornographic*. The term refers to the processes of a biomolecular (pharmaco) and semiotic-technical (porno-

---

22. Susan Freinkel, *Plastic: A Toxic Love Story* (Boston: Houghton Mifflin Harcourt, 2011).
23. See Mike Davis, "Planet of Slums," *New Left Review* 26 (April–March 2004).

graphic) government of sexual subjectivity—of which "the Pill" and *Playboy* are two paradigmatic offspring. Although their lines of force may be rooted in the scientific and colonial society of the nineteenth century, their economic vectors become visible only at the end of World War II. Hidden at first under the guise of a Fordist economy, they reveal themselves in the 1970s with the gradual collapse of this phenomenon.

During the second half of the twentieth century, the mechanisms of the pharmacopornographic regime are materialized in the fields of psychology, sexology, and endocrinology. If science has reached the hegemonic place that it occupies as a discourse and as a practice in our culture, it is because, as Ian Hacking, Steve Woolgar, and Bruno Latour have noticed, it works as a material-discoursive apparatus of bodily production.[24] Technoscience has established its material authority by transforming the concepts of the psyche, libido, consciousness, femininity and masculinity, heterosexuality and homosexuality, intersexuality and transsexuality into tangible realities. They are manifest in commercial chemical substances and molecules, biotype bodies, and fungible technological goods managed by multinationals. The success of contemporary technoscientific industry consists in transforming our depression into Prozac, our masculinity into testosterone, our erection into Viagra, our fertility/sterility into the Pill, our AIDS into tritherapy, without knowing which comes first: our

24. Ian Hacking, *Representing and Intervening: Introductory Topics in the Philosophy of Natural Science* (Cambridge, UK: Cambridge University Press, 1983); and Bruno Latour and Steve Woolgar, *La vie de laboratoire: La production des faits scientifiques* (Paris: La Découverte, 1979).

depression or Prozac, Viagra or an erection, testosterone or masculinity, the Pill or maternity, tritherapy or AIDS. This performative feedback is one of the mechanisms of the pharmacopornographic regime.

Contemporary society is inhabited by toxic-pornographic subjectivities: subjectivities defined by the substance (or substances) that supply their metabolism, by the cybernetic prostheses and various types of pharmacopornographic desires that feed the subject's actions and through which they turn into agents. So we will speak of Prozac subjects, cannabis subjects, cocaine subjects, alcohol subjects, Ritalin subjects, cortisone subjects, silicone subjects, heterovaginal subjects, double-penetration subjects, Viagra subjects, $ subjects . . .

There is nothing to discover in nature; there is no hidden secret. We live in a punk hypermodernity: it is no longer about discovering the hidden truth in nature; it is about the necessity to specify the cultural, political, and technological processes through which the body as artifact acquires natural status. The oncomouse,[25] the laboratory mouse biotechnologically designed to carry a carcinogenic gene, eats Heidegger. Buffy kills the vampire of Simone de Beauvoir. The dildo, a synthetic extension of sex to produce pleasure and identity, eats Rocco Siffredi's cock. There is nothing to discover in sex or in sexual identity; there is no *inside*. The truth about sex is not a disclosure; it is *sexdesign*. Pharmacopornographic biocapitalism does not produce *things*.

---

25. See Donna J. Haraway, "When Man™ is on the Menu," in *Incorporations(Zone 6)*, eds. Jonathan Crary and Sanford K. Winter (New York: Zone Books, 1992), 38–43.

It produces mobile ideas, living organs, symbols, desires, chemical reactions, and conditions of the soul. In biotechnology and in pornocommunication there is no object to be produced. The pharmacopornographic business is the *invention of a subject* and then its global reproduction.

MASTURBATORY COOPERATION

The theoreticians of post-Fordism (Virno, Hardt, Negri, Corsani, Marazzi, Moulier-Boutang, etc.) have made it clear that the productive process of contemporary capitalism takes its raw material from knowledge, information, communication, and social relationships.[26] According to the most recent economic theory, the mainspring of production is no longer situated in companies but is "in society as a whole, the quality of the population, cooperation, conventions, training, forms of organization that hybridize the market, the firm and society."[27] Negri and Hardt refer to "biopolitic production," using Foucault's cult notion, or to "cognitive capitalism" to enumerate today's complex forms of capitalist production that mask the "production of symbols, language, information," as well as the "production of

---

26. Some of the most influential analyses of the current transformations of industrial society and capitalism relevant to my own work are the following: Maurizio Lazzarato, *"Le concept de travail immaterial: la grande enterprise,"* *Futur Antérieur* 10 (1992); Antonella Corsani, *"Vers un renouveau de l'économie politique: anciens concepts et innovation théorique,"* *Multitudes* 2 (printemps 2000); Antonio Negri and Michael Hardt, *Multitude: guerre et démocratie à l'âge de l'empire* (Paris: La Decouverté, 2006); Yann Moulier-Boutang, *Le capitalisme cognitive: La nouvelle grande transformation* (Paris: Editions Ámsterdam, 2007).

27. Yann Moulier-Boutang, *"Eclats d'économie et bruits de lutte,"* *Multitudes* 2 (Mai 200): 7. See also Antonella Corsani, *"Vers un renouveau de l'économie politique."*

affects."[28] They call "biopolitical work" the forms of production that are linked to aids provided to the body, to care, to the protection of the other and to the creation of human relations, to the "feminine" work of reproduction,[29] to relationships of communication and exchange of knowledge and affects. But most often, analysis and description of this new form of production stops biopolitically at the belt.[30]

What if, in reality, the insatiable bodies of the multitude—their cocks, clitorises, anuses, hormones, and neurosexual synapses—what if desire, excitement, sexuality, seduction, and the pleasure of the multitude were all the mainsprings of the creation of value added to the contemporary economy? And what if cooperation were a *masturbatory cooperation* and not the simple cooperation of brains?

The pornographic industry is currently the great mainspring of our cybereconomy; there are more than a million and a half sites available to adults at any point on the planet. Sixteen billion dollars is generated annually by the sex industry, a large part of it belonging to the porn portals of the Internet. Each day, 350 new portals allow virtual access to an exponentially increasing number of users. If

28. Antonio Negri and Michael Hardt, *Multitude: guerre et démocratie à l'âge de l'empire* (Paris: Editions 10–18, DL, 2006), 135.

29. Ibid., 137. Cristian Marazzi, *The Violence of Financial Capitalism*, trans. Kristina Lebedeva and Jason Francis McGimsey (New York: Semiotext(e), 2011), op. cit.

30. Several trajectories in this direction come from the reflections in *Precarias a la Deriva*, by Anne Querrien and Antonella Corsani. See *Precarias a la Deriva, A la deriva por los circuitos de la precariedad feminina* (Madrid: Traficantes de Sueños, 2004); Antonella Corsani, *"Quelles sont les conditions nécessaires pour l'émergence de multiples récits du monde? Penser le revenu garanti à travers l'histoire des luttes des femmes et de la théorie feminist,"* Multitudes 27 (hiver 2007); Antonella Corsani, "Beyond the Myth of Woman: The Becoming-Transfeminist of (Post-)Marxism," trans. Timothy S. Murphy, *SubStance #112: Italian Post-Workerist Thought* 36, no. 1, (2007): 106–38; and Linda McDowell, "Life without Father and Ford: The New Gender Order of Post-Fordism," *Transactions of the Institute of British Geographers* 16, no. 4 (1991): 400–19.

it's true that the majority of these sites belong to the multinationals (Playboy, Hotvideo, Dorcel, Hustler . . .), the amateur portals are what constitute the truly emerging market for Internet porn. When Jennifer Kaye Ringley had the initiative in 1996 to install several webcams throughout her home that broadcast real-time videos of her daily life through her Internet portal, the model of the single transmitter was supplanted. In documentary style, JenniCams produce an audiovisual chronicle of sex lives and are paid for by subscription, similar to the way some TV stations operate. Today, any user of the Internet who has a body, a computer, a video camera, or a webcam, as well as an Internet connection and a bank account, can create a porn site and have access to the cybermarket of the sex industry. The autopornographic body has suddenly emerged as a new force in the world economy. The recent access of relatively impoverished populations all over the planet to the technical means of producing cyberpornography has, for the first time, sabotaged a monopoly that was until now controlled by the big multinationals of porn. After the fall of the Berlin Wall, the first people able to make use of this market were sex workers from the former Soviet bloc, then those in China, Africa, and India. Confronted with such autonomous strategies on the part of sex workers, the multinationals of porn have gradually united with advertising companies, hoping to attract cybervisitors by offering free access to their pages.

The sex industry is not only the most profitable market on the Internet; it's also the model of maximum profitability for the global cybernetic market (comparable only to financial speculation): minimum investment, direct sales of the product in real time in a unique fashion, the production of instant satisfaction for the consumer. Every Internet portal is modeled on and organized according to this masturbatory logic of pornographic consumption. If the financial analysts who direct Google, eBay, or Facebook are attentively following the fluctuations of the cyberporn market, it's because the sex industry furnishes an economic model of the cybernetic market as a whole.

If we consider that the pharmaceutical industry (which includes the legal extension of the scientific, medical, and cosmetic industries, as well as the trafficking of drugs declared illegal), the pornography industry, and the industry of war are the load-bearing sectors of post-Fordist capitalism, we ought to be able to give a cruder name to *immaterial labor*. Let us dare, then, to make the following hypothesis: the raw materials of today's production process are excitation, erection, ejaculation, and pleasure and feelings of self-satisfaction, omnipotent control, and total destruction. The real stake of capitalism today is the pharmacopornographic control of subjectivity, whose products are serotonin, techno-blood and blood products, testosterone, antacids, cortisone, techno-sperm, antibiotics, estradiol, techno-milk, alcohol and tobacco, morphine, insulin, cocaine, living human eggs, citrate of sildenafil (Viagra), and the entire material and virtual complex participating in the production of mental and psychosomatic states of excitation, relaxation, and discharge, as well as those of omnipotence and total control. In these conditions, money itself becomes an abstract, signifying psychotropic substance.

Sex is the corollary of capitalism and war, the mirror of production. The dependent and sexual body and sex and all its semiotechnical derivations are henceforth the principal resource of post-Fordist capitalism.

Although the era dominated by the economy of the automobile has been named "Fordism," let us call this new economy *pharmacopornism*, dominated as it is by the industry of the pill, the masturbatory logic of pornography, and the chain of excitation-frustration on which it is based. The pharmacopornographic industry is white and viscous gold, the crystalline powder of biopolitical capitalism.

Negri and Hardt, in rereading Marx, have shown that "in the course of the nineteenth and twentieth centuries, the global economy is characterized by the hegemony of industrial labor, even if, in quantitative terms, the latter remains minor in comparison to other forms of production such as agriculture."[31] Industrial labor was hegemonic by virtue of the powers of transformation it exerted over any other form of production.

Pharmacopornographic production is characteristic today of a new age of political world economy, not by its quantitative supremacy, but because the control, production, and intensification of narcosexual affects have become the model of all other forms of production. In this way, pharmacopornographic control infiltrates and dominates the entire flow of capital, from agrarian biotechnology to high-tech industries of communication.

In this period of the body's technomanagement, the

31. Antonio Negri and Michael Hardt, *Multitude* (Paris: Editions 10–18, DL, 2006), 133–34.

pharmacopornographic industry synthesizes and defines a specific mode of production and consumption, a masturbatory temporization of life, a virtual and hallucinogenic aesthetic of the living object, an architecture that transforms inner space into exteriority and the city into interiority and "junkspace"[32] by means of mechanisms of immediate autosurveillance and ultrarapid diffusion of information, a continuous mode of desiring and resisting, of consuming and destroying, of evolution and self-destruction.

POTENTIA GAUDENDI

To understand how and why sexuality and the body, the excitable body, at the end of the nineteenth century raided the heart of political action and became the objects of a minute governmental and industrial management, we must first elaborate a new philosophical concept in the pharmacopornographic domain that is equivalent to the force of work in the domain of classical economics. I call *potentia gaudendi*, or "orgasmic force," the (real or virtual) strength of a body's (total) excitation.[33] This strength is of indeterminate capacity; it has no gender; it is neither male nor female, neither human nor animal, neither animated nor inanimate. Its orientation emphasizes neither the fem-

32. For an elaboration of this idea, see Rem Koolhaas, "Junkspace," *October* 100 (Spring, 2002): 175–90.

33. My work here begins with the notion of "power of action or force of existing" elaborated by Spinoza and derived from the Greek idea of *dynamis* and its correlations in scholastic metaphysics; cf. Baruch Spinoza, *Éthique*, trans. Bernard Pautrat (Paris: Le Seuil, 1988); Gilles Deleuze, "Spinoza" (lecture, Université de Vincennes à Saint Denis, Université Paris 8, Paris, February 2, 1980).

inine nor the masculine and creates no boundary between heterosexuality and homosexuality or between object and subject; neither does it know the difference between being excited, being exciting, or being-excited-with. It favors no organ over any other, so that the penis possesses no more orgasmic force than the vagina, the eye, or the toe. Orgasmic force is the sum of the potential for excitation inherent in every material molecule. Orgasmic force is not seeking any immediate resolution, and it aspires only to its own extension in space and time, toward everything and everyone, in every place and at every moment. It is a force of transformation for the world in pleasure—"in pleasure with." *Potentia gaudendi* unites all material, somatic, and psychic forces and seeks all biochemical resources and all the structures of the mind.

In pharmacopornographic capitalism, the force of work reveals its actual substratum: orgasmic force, or *potentia gaudendi*. Current capitalism tries to put to work the *potentia gaudendi* in whatever form in which it exists, whether this be in its pharmacological form (a consumable molecule and material agency that will operate within the body of the person who is digesting it), as a pornographic representation (a semiotechnical sign that can be converted into numeric data or transferred into digital, televisual, or telephonic media), or as a sexual service (a live pharmacopornographic entity whose orgasmic force and emotional volume are put in service to a consumer during a specified time, according to a more or less formal contract of sale of sexual services).

Potentia gaudendi is characterized not only by its impermanence and great malleability, but also and above all by the impossibility of possessing and retaining it. *Potentia gaudendi*, as the fundamental energetics of pharmacopornism, does not allow itself to be reified or transformed into private property. I can neither possess nor retain another's *potentia gaudendi*, but neither can one possess or retain what seems to be one's own. *Potentia gaudendi* exists exclusively as an event, a relation, a practice, or an evolutionary process.

Orgasmic force is both the most abstract and the most material of all workforces. It is inextricably carnal and digital, viscous yet representational by numerical values, a phantasmatic or molecular wonder that can be transformed into capital.

The living pansexual body is the *bioport* of the orgasmic force. Thus, it cannot be reduced to a prediscursive organism; its limits do not coincide with the skin capsule that surrounds it. This life cannot be understood as a biological given; it does not exist outside the interlacing of production and culture that belongs to technoscience. This body is a technoliving, multiconnected entity incorporating technology.[34] Neither an organism nor a machine, but "the fluid, dispersed, networking techno-organic-textual-mythic system."[35] This new condition of the body blurs the traditional modern distinction between art, performance,

34. Haraway, *Modest_Witness*.
35. Donna J. Haraway, *Simians, Cyborgs, and Women: The Reinvention of Nature* (New York: Routledge, 1990), 219.

media, design, and architecture. The new pharmacological and surgical techniques set in motion tectonic construction processes that combine figurative representations derived from cinema and from architecture (editing, 3-D modeling, 3-D printing, etc.), according to which the organs, the vessels, the fluids (techno-blood, techno-sperm, etc.), and the molecules are converted into the prime material from which our pharmacopornographic corporality is manufactured. Technobodies are either not-yet-alive or already-dead: we are half fetuses, half zombies. Thus, every politics of resistance is a monster politics. Marshall McLuhan, Buckminster Fuller, and Norbert Wiener had an intuition about it in the 1950s: the technologies of communication function like an extension of the body. Today, the situation seems a lot more complex—the individual body functions like an extension of global technologies of communication. "Embodiment is significant prosthesis."[36] To borrow the terms of the American feminist Donna J. Haraway, the twenty-first-century body is a technoliving system, the result of an irreversible implosion of modern binaries (female/male, animal/human, nature/culture). Even the term *life* has become archaic for identifying the actors in this new technology. For Foucault's notion of "biopower," Donna J. Haraway has substituted "techno-biopower." It's no longer a question of power over life, of the power to manage and maximize life, as Foucault wanted, but of power and control exerted over a technoliving and connected whole.[37]

36. Ibid., 195.
37. Ibid., 204–30.

In the circuit in which excitation is technoproduced, there are neither living bodies nor dead bodies, but present or missing, actual or virtual connectors. Images, viruses, computer programs, techno-organic fluids, Net surfers, electronic voices that answer phone sex lines, drugs and living dead animals in the laboratory on which they are tested, frozen embryos, mother cells, active alkaloid molecules . . . display no value in the current global economy as being "alive" or "dead," but only to the extent that they can or can't be integrated into a bioelectronics of global excitation. Haraway reminds us that "cyborg figures—such as the end-of-the-millennium seed, chip gene, database, bomb, fetus, race, brain, and ecosystem—are the offspring of implosions of subjects and objects and of the natural and artificial."[38] Every technobody, including a dead technobody, can unleash orgasmic force, thus becoming a carrier of the power of production of sexual capital. The force that lets itself be converted into capital lies neither in *bios* nor in *soma*, in the way that they have been conceived from Aristotle to Darwin, but in *techno-eros*, the technoliving enchanted body and its *potentia gaudendi*. And from this it follows that biopolitics (the politics of the control and production of life) as well as necropolitics (the politics of the control and production of death) function as pharmacoporno politics, as planetary managements of *potentia gaudendi*.

Sex, the so-called sexual organs, pleasure and impotence, joy and horror are moved to the center of technopolitical management as soon as the possibility of drawing

38. Haraway, *Modest_Witness*, 12.

profit from orgasmic force comes into play. If the theorists of post-Fordism were interested in immaterial work, in cognitive work, in "non-objectifiable work,"[39] in "affective work,"[40] we theorists of pharmacopornographic capitalism are interested in sexual work as a process of subjectivization, in the possibility of making the subject an inexhaustible supply of planetary ejaculation that can be transformed into abstraction and digital data—into capital.

This theory of "orgasmic force" should not be read through a Hegelian paranoid or Rousseauist utopian/dystopian prism; the market isn't an outside power coming to expropriate, repress, or control the sexual instincts of the individual. On the other hand, we are being confronted by the most depraved of political situations: the body isn't aware of its *potentia gaudendi* as long as it does not put it to work.

Orgasmic force in its role as the workforce finds itself progressively regulated by a strict technobiopolitical control. The sexual body is the product of a sexual division of flesh according to which each organ is defined by its function. A sexuality always implies a precise governing of the mouth, hand, anus, vagina. Until recently, the relationship between buying/selling and dependence that united the capitalist to the worker also governed the relationship between the genders, which was conceived as a relationship between the ejaculator and the facilitator of ejaculation. Femininity, far from being nature, is the quality of the

39. Paolo Virno, "La multitude comme subjectivite," in *Grammaire de la multitude: pour une analyse des formes de vie contemporaines* (Paris: Éditions de l'éclat, 2002), 78–121.
40. Michael Hardt and Antonio Negri, *Multitudes*, 134.

orgasmic force when it can be converted into merchandise, into an object of economic exchange, into work. Obviously, a male body can occupy (and in fact already does occupy) a position of female gender in the market of sex work and, as a result, see its orgasmic power reduced to a capacity for work.

The control of orgasmic power (*puissance*) not only defines the difference between genders, the female/male dichotomy, it also governs, in a more general way, the technobiopolitical difference between heterosexuality and homosexuality. The technical restriction of masturbation and the invention of homosexuality as a pathology are of a pair with the composition of a disciplinary regime at the heart of which the collective orgasmic force is put to work as a function of the heterosexual reproduction of the species. Heterosexuality must be understood as a politically assisted procreation technology. But after the 1940s, the moleculized sexual body was introduced into the machinery of capital and forced to mutate its forms of production. Biopolitical conditions change drastically when it becomes possible to derive benefits from masturbation through the mechanism of pornography and the employment of techniques for the control of sexual reproduction by means of contraceptives and artificial insemination.

If we agree with Marx that "workforce is not actual work carried out but the simple potential or ability for work," then it must be said that every human or animal, real or virtual, female or male body possesses this masturbatory potentiality, a *potentia gaudendi*, the power to produce molecular joy, and therefore also possesses productive power without being consumed and depleted in the process. Until now, we've been aware of the direct relationship between the pornification of the body and the level of oppression. Throughout history, the most pornified bodies have been those of non-human animals, women and children, the racialized bodies of the slave, the bodies of young workers and the homosexual body. But there is no ontological relationship between anatomy and *potentia gaudendi*. The credit goes to the French writer Michel Houellebecq for having understood how to build a dystopian fable about this new capacity of global capitalism, which has manufactured the megaslut and the megaletch. The new hegemonic subject is a body (often codified as male, white, and heterosexual) supplemented pharmacopornographically (by Viagra, coke, pornography) and a consumer of pauperized sexual services (often in bodies codified as female, childlike, or racialized):

> "When he can, a westerner *works*; he often finds his work frustrating or boring, but he pretends to find it interesting: this much is obvious. At the age of fifty, weary of teaching, of math, of everything, I decided to see the world. I had just been divorced for the third time; as far as sex was concerned, I wasn't expecting much. My first trip was to Thailand, and immediately after that I left for Madagascar. I haven't fucked a white woman since. I've never even felt the desire to do so. Believe me," he added, placing a firm hand on Lionel's forearm, "you won't find a white woman with a soft, submissive, supple, muscular pussy anymore. That's all gone now."[41]

41. Michel Houellebecq, *Platform*, trans. Frank Wynne (New York: Random House, 2002), 80.

Power is located not only in the ("female," "childlike," or "nonwhite") body as a space traditionally imagined as pre-discursive and natural, but also in the collection of representations that render it sexual and desirable. In every case it remains a body that is always pharmacopornographic, a technoliving system that is the effect of a widespread cultural mechanism of representation and production.

The goal of contemporary critical theory would be to unravel our condition as pharmacopornographic workers/consumers. If the current theory of the *feminization of labor* omits the *cum shot*, conceals videographic ejaculation behind the screen of cooperative communication, it's because, unlike Houellebecq, the philosophers of biopolitics prefer not to reveal their position as customers of the global pharmacopornomarket.

In the first volume of *Homo Sacer*, Giorgio Agamben reclaims Walter Benjamin's concept of the "naked life" in order to define the biopolitical status of the subject after Auschwitz, a subject whose paradigm would be the concentration camp prisoner or the illegal immigrant held in a temporary detention center, reduced to existing only physically and stripped of all legal status or citizenship. To such a notion of the "naked life," we could add that of the pharmacopornographic life, or *naked technolife*; the distinctive feature of a body stripped of all legal or political status is that its use is intended as a source of production of *potentia gaudendi*. The distinctive feature of a body reduced to naked technolife, in both democratic societies and fascist regimes, is precisely the power to be the object of maximum pharmacopornographic exploitation. Identical codes of pornographic representation function in the images of the prisoners of Abu Ghraib,[42] the eroticized images of Thai adolescents, advertisements for L'Oréal and McDonald's, and the pages of *Hot magazine*. All these bodies are already functioning, in an inexhaustible manner, as carnal and digital sources of ejaculatory capital. For the Aristotelian distinction between *zōē* and *bios*, between animal life deprived of any intentionality and "exalted" life, that is, life gifted with meaning and self-determination that is a substrate of biopolitical government, we must today substitute the distinction between *raw* and *biotech* (biotechnoculturally produced); and the latter term refers to the condition of life in the pharmacopornographic era. Biotechnological reality deprived of all civic context (the body of the migrant, the deported, the colonized, the porn actress/actor, the sex worker, the laboratory animal, etc.) becomes that of the *corpus* (and no longer that of *homo*) *pornographicus* whose life (a technical condition rather than a purely biological one), lacking any right to citizenship, authorship, and right to work, is composed by and subject to self-surveillance and global mediatization. No need to resort to the dystopian model of the concentration or extermination camp—which are easy to denounce as mechanisms of control—in order to discover naked technolife, because it's at the center of postindustrial democracies, forming part of a global, integrated multimedia laboratory-brothel, where the control of the flow of affect begins under the pop form of excitation-frustration.

42. See Judith Butler, "Torture and Ethics fo Photography," in *Environment and Planning D: Society and Space*. 25, no. 6 (April 19, 2007): 951–66.

EXCITE AND CONTROL

The gradual transformation of sexual cooperation into a principal productive force cannot be accomplished without the technical control of reproduction. There's no porn without the Pill or without Viagra. Inversely, there is no Viagra or Pill without porn. The new kind of sexual production implies a detailed and strict control of the forces of reproduction of the species. There is no pornography without a parallel surveillance and control of the body's affects and fluids. Acting on this pharmacoporno body are the forces of the reproduction industry, entailing control of the production of eggs, techniques of programming relationships, straw collections of sperm, in vitro fertilization, artificial insemination, the monitoring of pregnancy, the technical planning of childbirth, and so on. Consequently, the sexual division of traditional work gradually disintegrates. Pharmacopornographic capitalism is ushering in a new era in which the most interesting kind of commerce is the production of the species as species, the production of its mind and its body, its desires and its affects. Contemporary biocapitalism at the same time produces and destroys the species. Although we're accustomed to speaking of a society of consumption, the objects of consumption are only the scintilla of a psychotoxic virtual production. We are consumers of air, dreams, identity, relation, things of the mind. This pharmacopornographic capitalism functions in reality thanks to the biomediatic management of subjectivity, through molecular control and the production of virtual audiovisual connections.

The pharmaceutical and audiovisual digital industry are the two pillars on which contemporary biocapitalism relies; they are the two tentacles of a gigantic, viscous built-in circuit. The pharmacoporno program of the second half of the twentieth century is this: control the sexuality of those bodies codified as woman and cause the ejaculation of those bodies codified as men. The Pill, Prozac, and Viagra are to the pharmaceutical industry what pornography, with its grammar of blowjobs, penetrations, and cum shots, is to the industry of culture: the jackpot of postindustrial biocapitalism.

Within the context of biocapitalism, an illness is the conclusion of a medical and pharmaceutical model, the result of a technical and institutional medium that is capable of explaining it discursively, of realizing it and of treating it in a manner that is more or less operational. From a pharmacopornopolitical point of view, a third of the African population infected with HIV *isn't really sick*. The thousands of seropositive people who die each day on the continent of Africa are precarious bodies whose survival has *not yet* been capitalized as bioconsumers/producers by the Western pharmaceutical industry. For the pharmacopornographic system, these bodies are *neither* dead *nor* living. They are in a prepharmacopornographic state or their life isn't likely to produce an ejaculatory benefit, which amounts to the same thing. They are bodies excluded from the technobiopolitical regime. The emerging pharmaceutical industries of India, Brazil, or Thailand are fiercely fighting for the right to distribute their antiretrovirus therapies. Similarly, if we are still waiting for the commercialization of a vaccine for malaria (a disease that was causing five million deaths a year on the continent of Africa), it is partly because the countries that need it can't pay for it. The same Western multinational companies that are launching costly programs for the production of Viagra or new treatments for prostate cancer would never invest in malaria. If we do not take into account calculations about pharmacopornographic profitability, it becomes obvious that erectile dysfunction and prostate cancer are not at all priorities in countries where life expectancies for human bodies stricken by tuberculosis, malaria, and AIDS don't exceed the age of fifty-five.[43]

In the context of pharmacopornographic capitalism, sexual desire and illness are produced and cultivated on the same basis: without the technical, pharmaceutical, and mediatic supports capable of materializing them, they don't exist.

We are living in a toxopornographic era. The postmodern body is becoming collectively desirable through its pharmacological management and audiovisual advancement: two sectors in which the United States holds—for the moment but, perhaps not for long—worldwide hegemony. These two forces for the creation of capital are dependent not on an economy of production, but on an *economy of invention*. As Philippe Pignare has pointed out, "The pharmaceutical industry is one of the economic sectors where the cost of research and development is very high, whereas the manufacturing costs are extremely low. Unlike in the automobile industry, nothing is easier than reproducing a drug and

---

43. Michael Kremer and Christopher M. Snyder, "Why Is There No AIDS Vaccine?" (Research Paper, Washington, DC: The Brookings Institution, June 2006).

guaranteeing its chemical synthesis on a massive scale, but nothing is more difficult or more costly than inventing it."[44] In the same way, nothing costs less, materially speaking, than filming a blowjob or vaginal or anal penetration with a video camera. Drugs, like orgasms and books, are relatively easy and inexpensive to fabricate. The difficulty resides in their conception and political dissemination.[45] Pharmacopornographic biocapitalism does not produce things. It produces movable ideas, living organs, symbols, desires, chemical reactions, and affects. In the fields of biotechnology and pornocommunication, there are no objects to produce; it's a matter of *inventing* a subject and producing it on a global scale.

44. Philippe Pignarre, *Le grand secret de l'industrie pharmaceutique* (Paris: La Découverte, 2004), 18.

45. Maurizio Lazzarato, *Puissance de l'invention: La Psychologie économique de Gabriel Tarde contre l'économie politique* (Paris: Les Empêcheurs de Penser en Rond, 2002).

3. TESTOGEL

*As always I'm inside writing, simultaneously the scientist and
the rat he's ripping open to study.*

—HERVÉ GUIBERT

A few months before your death, Del, my master gender
hacker, gives me a box of thirty packets of fifty-
milligram testosterone in gel form. I keep them in a glass
box for a long time, as if they were dissected scarabs, poison bullets extracted from a corpse, fetuses of an unknown
species, vampire teeth capable of flying at your throat just
for your having looked at them. During this period, I spend
my time with my trans friends. Some are taking hormones
as part of a protocol to change sex, and others are fooling
with it, self-medicating without trying to change their gender legally or going through any psychiatric follow-up. They
don't identify with the term *gender dysphorics* and declare
themselves "gender pirates," or "gender hackers." I belong
to this latter group of testosterone users. We're *copyleft*[1]
users who consider sex hormones free and open biocodes,
whose use shouldn't be regulated by the state or comman-
deered by pharmaceutical companies. When I decide to

1. A play on the word "copyright."—Trans.

take my first dose of testosterone, I don't talk about it to anyone. As if it were a hard drug, I wait until I'm alone in my home to try it. I wait for nightfall. I take a packet out of the glass box, which I close immediately, to be sure that today, for my first time, I'll take one, and only one, dose. I've barely started, yet I'm already behaving as if I were an addict of an illegal substance. I hide, keep an eye on myself, censure myself, exercise restraint. The following evening, almost at the same time, I take a second fifty-milligram dose. On the third day, the third dose. During these days and nights, I'm writing the text that will go with Del's last book of photos. I don't speak to anyone, just write. As if writing were the only accurate witness of this process. All the others are going to betray me. I know they're going to judge me for having taken testosterone. Some, because I'm going to become a man among men, because I was doing well as a girl. Others, because I took testosterone outside the aegis of a medical protocol, without wanting to become a man, because I used testosterone like a hard drug, like any other, and gave bad press to testosterone at the very moment when the law is beginning to integrate transsexuals into society, to guarantee reimbursement from the state health service for the drugs and operations.

Writing is the place where my secret addiction resides, at the same time as the stage on which my addiction seals a pact with the multitude. On the fourth night, no sleep. I'm lucid, energetic, wide awake, like I was the first night I had sex with a girl, when I was a kid. At four in the morning, I'm still writing, without the slightest sign of fatigue. Sitting in front of the computer, I feel the muscles of my back innervated by a cybernetic cable that starts at the surface of the city and grows in length, passing through my skull to connect with the planets most distant from Earth. At six in the morning, after ten hours of not moving from my chair, of drinking only water, I get up and go out with my dog, Justine, for a walk in the city. It's the first time I leave my home at six in the morning without a precise destination, on an autumn day. The bulldog is puzzled; she doesn't like to go out so early, but she follows. I need to breathe the air of the city, to leave the space of domesticity, to walk outside where I feel at home. I walk down rue de Belleville to the Chinese market; the African garbage collectors are building dikes with old rugs to change the course of the sewage. I wait for the Les Folies bar to open, have a coffee, wolf down two croissants, and return up the street. When I get home, I'm sweating. I notice my sweat has changed. I collapse onto the couch and watch i-Télé, the news only, and for the first time in three days I fall into a deep sleep drenched in that testosterone sweat, next to Justine.

CHEMICAL STRUCTURE
OF TESTOSTERONE

TESTOSTERONE METABOLISM

CHOLESTEROL
↓
PREGNENOLONE $\xrightarrow{3\beta-HSD}$ PROGESTERONE
↓ ↓
DHEA $\xrightarrow{3\beta-HSD}$ ANDROSTENEDIONE
↓
3α-ADIOL ← 5α-DHT ← ─ [TESTOSTERONE]
↓ ↓
3α-ADIOL ESTRADIOL

SHOOT

The testosterone I'm taking has the brand name Testogel. It was produced by Besins Laboratories in Montrouge, France. Here is the description of this drug from the package insert:

> TESTOGEL 50 mg is a transparent or slightly opalescent and colorless gel packaged in 5-gram sachets. It contains testosterone, a naturally secreted male hormone. This drug is recommended for illnesses related to a deficiency of testosterone. Before beginning a treatment with TES-TOGEL, a deficiency in testosterone must be established by a series of clinical signs (decline of secondary sexual characteristics, changes in physical constitution, asthenia, a decrease in libido, erectile dysfunction, etc.). This drug has been prescribed to you for your own use and must not be given to others.
>
> Attention: TESTOGEL should not be used by women.

Safety Instructions for Users of TESTOGEL 50 mg, gel in sachets:
Possible transference of testosterone.

Failing to follow recommended safety instructions may cause the transfer of testosterone onto another individual during intimate and prolonged cutaneous contact with the area to which the gel has been applied. This transfer can be avoided by covering the area of application with clothing or by showering before all contact.

The following safety instructions are advised:

Wash hands with water and soap after applying the gel.

Cover the area of application with clothing once the gel has dried.

Shower before all intimate contact.

For those individuals not being treated with TESTOGEL 50:
In case of contact with an unwashed or uncovered area of application, immediately wash with soap and water skin that may have been subjected to a transfer of testosterone.

Consult a physician if the following symptoms appear: acne, changes in pilosity.

It is preferable to wait approximately six hours between application of the gel and showering or bathing. However, washing occasionally one to six hours after application of the gel should not significantly change the course of treatment.

To guarantee the safety of one's female partner, the patient is advised to observe a prolonged interval of time between application of the gel and the period of contact, to wear a T-shirt over the site of application during the period of contact, or to shower before any sexual activity.

I am reading the Testogel package insert, realizing that I'm holding a manual for microfascism, at the same time as I'm worrying about the possible immediate or side effects of the molecule on my body. The laboratory assumes that the testosterone user is a "man" who isn't producing enough androgen naturally and who, obviously, is heterosexual (the safety instructions concerning the cutaneous transfer of testosterone allude to a female partner). Does this notion of a man refer to the chromosomal (XY), genital (possessing a penis and well-differentiated testicles), or legal (the specification "Sex: M" appearing on one's ID card) definition? If the administration of synthetic testosterone is prescribed for cases of testosterone deficiency, when and according to what criteria is it possible to affirm that a body is deficient? Does an examination of my clinical symptoms indicate a lack of testosterone? Isn't it the case that my beard has never grown and that my clitoris does not exceed a centimeter and a half? What would the ideal size and degree of erectility of a clitoris be? And what about the political signs? How can we measure them? Be that as it may, in order to legally obtain a dose of synthetic testosterone, it is necessary to stop defining yourself as a woman. Even before the effects of the testosterone are apparent in my body, the condition for the possibility of administering the molecule to me is having renounced my female identity. An excellent political tautology. Like depressions or schizophrenia, masculinity and femininity are pharmaco-pornographic fictions retroactively defined in relationship to the molecule with which they are treated. The category *depression* does not exist without the synthetic molecule of serotonin, the same way that clinical masculinity does not exist without synthetic testosterone.

I decide to keep my legal identity as a woman and to take testosterone without subscribing to a sex change protocol. It's a bit like biting the dick that's raping you, the pharmacopornographic system's dick. Obviously, such a position is one of political arrogance. If I'm able to take such a liberty at this time, it's because I don't need to go out and look for work, because I'm white, because I have no intention of having a bureaucratic relationship to the state. My decision does not enter into conflict with the position of all the transsexuals who've decided to sign a contract with the state for changing sex in order to have access both to the molecule and to legal identity as a male.[2] Actually, my gesture would lack strength were it not for the legions of silent transsexuals for whom the molecule, the protocol, and the change of legal identity are essential. All of us are united by the same carbon chains, by the same invisible gel; without them, none of this would have any meaning.

This drug is reserved for the use of the adult male.
Suggested dosage is 5 g of gel (equivalent to 50 mg of testosterone) once a day, to be applied at the same time, preferably in the morning. The physician will adapt the doses according to the needs of the patient, without exceeding

2. On March 1, 2007, the Spanish government acknowledged the request of the transsexual lobbies to have access to a legal change of sex (a change of name on identification cards) without being obliged to undergo surgery. However, this law requires the hormonal and social transformation of the individual during a period of at least two years as a condition for legally changing sex (in reality, the terms changing name or changing gender would be more precise). The measure is currently being criticized by various transsexual and transgender movements in Spain.

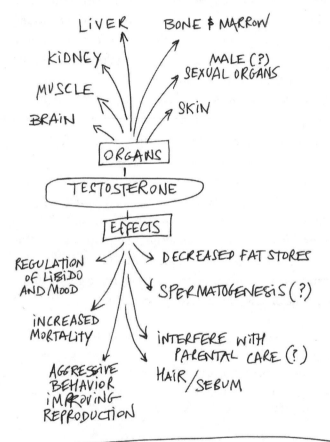

LIVER

KIDNEY

MUSCLE

BRAIN

BONE & MARROW

MALE (?) SEXUAL ORGANS

SKIN

ORGANS

TESTOSTERONE

EFFECTS

REGULATION OF LIBIDO AND MOOD

DECREASED FAT STORES

SPERMATOGENESIS (?)

INCREASED MORTALITY

INTERFERE WITH PARENTAL CARE (?)

AGGRESSIVE BEHAVIOR iMPROVING REPRODUCTION

HAIR/SEBUM

Scientific discourse about TESTOSTERONE

10 g of gel per day. Use the product on clean, dry and healthy skin and apply a thin coating on the shoulders, arms or abdomen without rubbing. Once a sachet has been opened, all its contents should be applied immediately to the skin. Allow to dry 3 to 5 minutes before dressing. Wash hands with soap and water after application. Do not apply in the area of the genitals (penis and testicles); due to its high alcohol content, the gel can cause irritations at the site of application.

Respect the directions for use indicated by your physician.
If you have accidentally exceeded the proper dose of TESTOGEL mg, consult your physician.

The leaflet doesn't supply instructions for hormonal therapy for the changing of sex. Undoubtedly, in such a case, the doses must be different. The only mention of potential addiction to testosterone is this discreet reference: "Consult your physician if you've exceeded the prescribed dose of Testogel." I take a mental inventory of all my friends who are taking more than fifty milligrams a day: HJ, PP, RZ, FU, KB, BS . . . I won't be able to claim that I didn't know.

If you've forgotten to take your TESTOGEL 50 mg, gel in sachets:
Do not take a double dose to compensate for this oversight.

Possible side effects of TESTOGEL 50 mg, gel in sachets:
Like all active substances, TESTOGEL 50 mg, gel in sachets, can produce side effects. Cutaneous reactions at the site of application, such as irritation, acne, dry skin, have been

observed. TESTOGEL can cause headaches, alopecia (hair loss), a feeling of pressure in mammary areas accompanied or not by pain, changes in the prostate, alteration of blood composition (increase of red blood cells and lipids in the blood), cutaneous hypersensitivity, and itching. Other side effects that have been observed during oral or injectable testosterone treatment include hypertrophy of the prostate (a benign increase in size of prostate), progression of undetected cancer of the prostate, pruritus (itching) anywhere on the body, reddening of the face or neck, nausea, icterus (yellow coloration of the skin and mucous membranes), increase of libido (sexual desire), depression, nervousness, muscle pains, changes in electrolyte balance (content of salt in the blood), oligospermia (decrease in number of spermatozoa), frequent or prolonged erections.

Certain clinical signs, such as irritability, nervousness, weight gain, or too frequent or persistent erections, may indicate that the effects of this substance are too powerful. Speak about this with your physician, who will adjust your daily dose of TESTOGEL.

Use by athletes and women:

Athletes and women should be warned that this product contains an active ingredient that is likely to produce a positive result in antidoping screenings.

Athletes *and* women? Must one detect a hidden syllogism here according to which all athletes are men, or must one understand that women, even if they are athletic, always remain women more than athletes? This is one way of tracing a political boundary when it comes to testosterone use. Actually, it's a warning to athletes *and* to women that testosterone can be considered to be an illegal stimulant. Outside the law. For women, whether they're athletic or not, taking testosterone is a form of doping.

Keep this leaflet. You may need to reread it.

The list of undesirable side effect may be long, but I'm placing a limit on cultural paranoia, and I put the leaflet in a file intended for the following: "T. Research." I certainly will need to reread it.

Testogel, says the medical leaflet, is not in any case to be given to an individual for whom it has not been prescribed (for example, the way Del has given it to me, as I've given it to King E., as King E. has given it to V. King, etc.), a condition that is common to the majority of drugs: antibiotics, antivirals, corticoids, and so on. In the case of testosterone, controls over "passage of the substance" seem more complicated, not only because it is liable to be sold on the black market and consumed without a prescription, but especially because Testogel applied to one body can "pass" imperceptibly onto another body through skin contact. Testosterone is one of the rare drugs that is spread by sweat, from skin to skin, body to body.

How can such trafficking—the microdiffusion of minute drops of sweat, the importing and exporting of vapors, such contraband exhalations—be controlled, surveyed; how to prevent the contact of crystalline mists, how to control the transparent demon's sliding from another's skin toward mine?

RENDEZVOUS WITH T

Paris, November 25, 2005. I'm waiting until ten in the evening to take a new dose of Testogel. I've taken a shower so that I don't have to wash myself after applying it. I've set out a blue work shirt, a tie, and black trousers to take Justine out for a walk afterward. I haven't felt any change since yesterday. I'm waiting for the effects of T., without knowing exactly what they'll be or how or when they'll become apparent. I've spent the last two hours on Skype talking with Del; we've been choosing the photos that will be published in his new book, *Sex Works*. I prefer the ones taken in public places, like that series from the S&M scene at Scott's Bar in the early 1980s. Three bodies are getting it on in the bathrooms, which have paneled walls: two lesbians with their clothes on are busy with a third, half-naked body. They're using a black leather switch to whip an ass that's been offered to them, someone leaning against a door with a plaid shirt rolled up around the neck and Levis 501 at the knees. In this series, the lens varies its point of view, getting nearer and farther from skin, objects, seeking out or evading glances, showing or hiding the affects that are produced. One of the photos disregards the main scene to focus on the geometric patterns of the tiles. Scott's Bar was a lesbian cathedral; the arrangement of its secret signs outlines the labyrinth of a Sapphic Chartres, shows the path of a pleasure that has never yet been experienced. Then the lens returns to the bodies. In the middle ground of the shot, a butch and a femme, who are nude, are rummaging through the shirts hanging in a makeshift wardrobe. Bill, the perfect embodiment of butch, is in the foreground: short hair, a fifties rocker look, smooth face, a cigarette dangling slightly downward from the left side of the mouth, a small name tag around the neck (the graininess of the black-and-white photo makes it impossible to make out the details); a black leather jacket over a naked torso, nothing underneath except the hump of a stuffed white jockstrap and a studded black belt from which hangs a bunch of sparkling keys. To the left, a slender butch is leaning a shaved head against a fire extinguisher. We talk only about the photos, even though it was Del who gave me the packets of Testogel. I don't tell him that I'm hanging up in order to take my dose. I just tell him I have to hang up. He manages to keep me on a few minutes more by paying me compliments, and I'm late for my ten o'clock rendezvous with T. A minute later, there I am: I've opened the silver packet, and the cool, transparent gel has disappeared under the skin of my arms. All that's left is a cool whiff of mint that draws my shoulders up toward the sky.

No drug is as pure as testosterone in gel form. It's odorless. However, the day after I take it, my sweat becomes sickly sweet, more acidic. The smell of a plastic doll heated by the sun comes from me, apple liqueur abandoned at the bottom of a glass. It's my body that is reacting to the molecule. Testosterone has no taste or color, leaves no traces. The testosterone molecule dissolves into the skin as a ghost walks through a wall. It enters without warning, penetrates without leaving a mark. You don't need to smoke, sniff, or inject it or even swallow it. It's enough to bring it near my skin, and its mere proximity to the body causes it to disappear into and become diluted in my blood.

4. HISTORY OF TECHNOSEXUALITY

The discontinuity of history, body, power: Foucault describes the transformation of European society in the late eighteenth century from what he calls a "sovereign society" into a "disciplinary society," which he sees as a shift away from a form of power that determines and ritualizes death toward a new form of power that technically plans life based on population, health, and the national interest. *Biopouvoir* (biopower) is his way of referring to this new form of productive, diffuse, sprawling power. Spilling beyond the boundaries of the legal realm and punitive sphere, it becomes a force of "somato-power" that penetrates and composes the body of the modern individual. This power no longer plays the role of a coercive law through a negative mandate but is more versatile and welcoming, taking on the form of "an art of governing life," an overall political technology that is transformed into disciplinary architectures (prisons, barracks, schools, hospitals, etc.), scientific texts, statistical tables, demographic calculations, how-to manuals, usage guidelines, schedules for the regulation of reproduction, and public health projects. Foucault underlined the centrality of sex and of sexuality in this modern art of government. The biopower processes of the feminine body's hysterization, children's sexual pedagogy, the regulation of procreative conduct, and the psychiatrization of the pervert's pleasures will be to Foucault the axes of this project that he characterized with some degree of irony as a process of sexual modernization.[1]

In keeping with the intuitions of Michel Foucault, Monique Wittig, and Judith Butler, I refer to one of the dominant forms of this biopolitical action, which emerged with disciplinary capitalism, as *sexopolitics*.[2] *Sex*, its truth, its visibility, and its forms of externalization; *sexuality* and the normal and pathological forms of pleasure; and *race*, in its purity or degeneracy, are three powerful somatic fictions that have obsessed the Western world since the eighteenth century, eventually defining the scope of all contemporary theoretical, scientific, and political activity. These are somatic fictions, not because they lack material reality but because their existence depends on what Judith Butler calls the performative repetition of processes of political construction.[3]

Sex has become such a part of plans for power that the discourse on masculinity and femininity, as well as techniques of normalizing sexual identity, have turned into governmental agents of the control and standardization of life. Hetero- and homosexual identities were invented in 1868, inside a sphere of empiricism, taxonomic classification, and psychopathology. Likewise, Krafft-Ebing created an encyclopedia of normal and perverse sexualities where

1. Michel Foucault, *Histoire de la sexualité: La volonté de savoir* (Paris: Gallimard, 1976), 136–39; see also Michel Foucault, *Naissance de la biopolitique: Cours au collège de France, 1978–1979* (Paris: Seuil, 2004).

2. Beatriz Preciado, "Multitudes Queer," *Multitudes* 12 (printemps 2003): 17–25.

3. Judith Butler, *Gender Trouble: Feminism and the Subversion of Identity* (New York: Routledge, 1990).

sexual identities became objects of knowledge, surveillance, and judicial repression.[4] At the end of the nineteenth century, laws criminalizing sodomy spread throughout Europe. "Sexual difference" was codified visually as an anatomical truth. The fallopian tubes, Bartholin's gland, and the clitoris were defined as anatomical entities. One of the elemental political differences of the West (being a man or a woman) could be summed up by a banal equation: whether one had or did not have at birth a penis that was a centimeter and a half long. The first experiments in artificial insemination were accomplished on animals. With the help of mechanical instruments, interventions were made in the domain of the production of female pleasure; whereas, on the one hand, masturbation was controlled and prohibited, on the other, the female orgasm was medicalized and perceived as a crisis of hysteria.[5] Male orgasm was mechanized and domesticated through the lens of a budding pornographic codification . . . Machinery was on the way. The body, whether docile or rabid, was ready.

We could call the "sexual empire" (if we can be allowed to sexualize Hardt and Negri's rather chaste catchword)[6] that biopolitical regime that uses sex, sexuality, and sexual identity as the somato-political centers for producing and governing subjectivity. Western disciplinary sexopolitics at

---

4. Richard von Krafft-Ebing, *Psychopathia Sexualis: The Classic Study of Deviant Sex* (New York: Arcade, 1998).

5. For a visual history of hysteria see Georges Didi-Huberman, *Invention of Hysteria: Charcot and the Photographic Iconography of the Salpetriere* (Cambridge, MA: MIT Press, 2004); for a history of the technologies of the hysteric body see Rachel P. Maines, *The Technology of Orgasm: "Hysteria," Vibrators and Women's Sexual Satisfaction* (Baltimore: John Hopkins University Press, 2001).

6. Antonio Negri and Michael Hardt, *Empire* (Paris: Exils, 2000).

the end of the nineteenth and during a good part of the twentieth century boils down to a regulation of the conditions of reproduction or to those biological processes that "concern the population." For the sexopolitics of the nineteenth century, the heterosexual is the artifact that will rake in the most success for government. The *straight mind*, to borrow an expression developed by Monique Wittig in the 1980s to designate heterosexuality— taken not as a sexual practice but as a political regime[7]—guarantees the structural relationship between the production of sexual identity and the production of certain body parts (to the detriment of others) as reproductive organs. One important task of this disciplinary work will consist of excluding the anus from circuits of production and pleasure. In the words of Deleuze and Guattari, "The first organ to suffer privatization, removal from the social field, was the anus. It was the anus that offered itself as a model for privatization, at the same time that money came to express the flows' new state of abstraction."[8] The anus as a center of production of pleasure (and, in this sense, closely related to the mouth or hand, which are also organs strongly controlled by the sexopolitical campaign against masturbation and homosexuality in the nineteenth century) has no gender. Neither male nor female, it creates a short circuit in the division of the sexes. As a center of primordial passivity and a perfect locale for the abject, positioned close to waste and shit, it serves as the universal black hole into which rush genders, sexes, identities, and capital. The West has

7. Monique Wittig, *La Pensée straight* (Paris: Balland, 2001), 65–76.
8. Gilles Deleuze and Félix Guattari, *Anti-Oedipus* (London: Continuum, 2004), 157.

designed a tube with two orifices: a mouth that emits public signs and an impenetrable anus around which it winds a male, heterosexual subjectivity, which acquires the status of a socially privileged body.

2 STRAIGHT SOMATIC FICTIONS

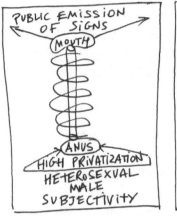 

Until the seventeenth century, the sexual epistemology of the sovereign regime was dominated by what the historian Thomas Laqueur calls "a system of similarities"; female sexual anatomy was set up as a weak, internalized, degenerate variation of the only sex that possessed an ontological existence, the male.[9] The ovaries were considered to be internal testicles and the vagina to be an inverted penis that served as a receptacle for male sex organs. Abortion and infanticide, practices of the time, weren't regu-

9. Thomas Laqueur, *Making Sex: Body and Gender from the Greeks to Freud* (Cambridge, MA: Harvard University Press, 1992), 63–108.

lated by the legal apparatus of the state but by different economic-political micropowers to which pregnant bodies found themselves affixed (the tribe, the feudal house, the paterfamilias . . .). Two hierarchically differentiated social and political expressions divide the surface of a "monosexual" model: "man," the perfect model of the human, and "woman," a reproductive receptacle. In the sovereign regime, masculinity is the only somatic fiction with political power. Masculinity (embodied within the figures of the king and the father) is defined by necropolitical techniques: the king and the father are those who have the right of giving death. Sex assignment depended not only on the external morphology of the organs but, above all, on reproductive capacity and social role. A bearded woman who was capable of pregnancy, of putting a child into the world and nursing it, was considered a woman, regardless of the shape and size of her vulva. Within such a somato-political configuration, sex and sexuality (note that the term *sexuality* itself wouldn't be invented until 1880) do not yet amount to categories of knowledge or techniques of subjectivization that are likely to outdo the political segmentation that separates the slave from the free man, the citizen from the metic, or the lord from the serf. Differences between masculinity and femininity remain, as well as between several modes of the production of sexual pleasure, but these do not yet determine the crystallizations of sexopolitical subjectivity.

Beginning in the eighteenth century, a new, visual sexopolitical regime that depends on a "system of oppositions" rather than on "similarities" takes form. It maps out a new sexual anatomy, in which the female sex ceases to be an inversion or interiorization of the male sex and becomes an entirely different sex whose forms and functions proceed from their own anatomical logic. According to Thomas Laqueur, the invention of what could be called the aesthetic of sexual (and racial) difference is needed to establish an anatomical-political hierarchy between the sexes (male, female) and the races (white, nonwhite) in the face of upheavals resulting from movements of revolution and liberation that are clamoring for the enlargement of the boundaries of the public spheres for women and foreigners. It is here that anatomical truth functions like a legitimization of a new political organization of the social field.[10]

The change that will give birth to the disciplinary regime begins with the political management of syphilis, the advent of sexual difference, the technical repression of masturbation, and the invention of sexual identities.[11] The culmination of these rigid and cumbersome technologies of the production of sexual identity will come in 1868 with the pathologizing of homosexuality and the bourgeois normalization of heterosexuality. From then on, abortion and postpartum infanticide will be subject to surveillance and punished by law. The body and its products will become the property of the male/husband/father and, by extension, the state and God.

Inside this system of recognition, any corporal divergence from the norm (such as the size and form of the sex organs, facial pilosity, and the shape and size of the breasts)

10. Ibid., 149–92.
11. See Thomas Laqueur, *Solitary Sex: A Cultural History of Masturbation* (New York: Zone Books, 2003).

will be considered a monstrosity, a violation of the laws of nature or a perversion, a violation of moral law. As sexual difference is elevated to a category that is not only natural but even transcendental (going beyond historical and cultural contexts), differences between homosexuality and heterosexuality appear as both anatomical and psychological, and so do the differences between sadism, masochism, and pedophilia; between normalcy and perversion. Considered simple sexual practices until this moment, they become identities and conditions that must be studied, recorded, hounded, hunted, punished, cured. Each body, as Foucault tells us, becomes an "individual to correct."[12] Invented as well are the child masturbator and the sexual monster. Under this new epistemological gaze, the bearded woman becomes either an object of scientific observation or a fairground attraction in the new urban agglomerate. This double shift toward medico-legal surveillance and mediatic spectacularization, intensified as it is by digital and data-processing techniques and communication networks, will become one of the characteristics of the pharmacopornographic regime, whose expansion begins in the middle of the twentieth century.

The sexopolitical devices that develop with the nineteenth-century aesthetics of sexual difference and sexual identities are mechanical, semiotic, and architectonic techniques to naturalize sex. And here we can list a loose collection of the resulting phenomena: the atlas of sexual anatomy, treatises on optimizing natural resources com-

---

12. Michel Foucault, *Les anormaux: cours au Collège de France (1974–1975)* (Paris: Seuil, 1999), 53.

mensurate with the growth of population, legal texts on the criminalization of transvestism or sodomy, the tying of little girls' masturbating hands to their beds, irons for forcing apart the legs of young hysterics, silver nitrate photographic prints that engrave images of the dilated anus of passive homosexuals, straitjackets immobilizing the uncontrollable bodies of masculine women . . . These devices for the production of sexual subjectivity take the form of a political architecture *external* to the body. Their systems have a firm command of orthopedic politics and disciplinary exoskeletons. The model for these techniques of subjectivization, according to Foucault, could be Jeremy Bentham's architecture for the prison-factory (panopticism, in particular), the asylum, or the military barracks. If we think about devices of sexo-political subjectivization, then we must also speak about the expansion of a network of "domestic architecture." These extensive, intensive, and, moreover, intimate architectural forms include a redefinition of private and public spaces, the management of sexual commerce, but also gynecological devices and sexual orthopedic inventions (the corset, the speculum, the medical vibrator), as well as new media techniques of control and representation (photography, film, incipient pornography) and the massive development of psychological techniques for introspection and confession.

If it is true that Foucault's analysis up to this point, although not always chronologically exact, seems to have great critical acuity, it is no less true that his analysis loses intensity the closer it gets to contemporary society. Foucault neglected the emergence of a group of profound transformations of technologies of production of the body and subjectivity that progressively appeared beginning with World War II. They force us to conceptualize a third regime of subjectivization, a third system of knowledge-power that is neither sovereign nor disciplinary, neither premodern nor modern. In the postscript to *A Thousand Plateaus*, Deleuze and Guattari, inspired by William S. Burroughs, use the term "control society"[13] to name this "new monster" of social organization that is a by-product of biopolitical control. Adding notions inspired by both Burroughs and Bukowski, I shall call this the "pharmacopornographic society." A politically programmed ejaculation is the currency of this new molecular-informatic control.

After World War II, the somato-political context of the body's technopolitical production seems dominated by a series of new technologies of the body (biotechnology, surgery, endocrinology, genetic engineering, etc.) and representation (photography, cinema, television, internet, video games, etc.) that infiltrate and penetrate daily life like never before. These are biomolecular, digital, and broadband data-transmission technologies. This is the age of soft, featherweight, viscous, gelatinous technologies that can be injected, inhaled—"incorporated." The testosterone that I use is a part of these new gelatinous technologies.

These three regimes of production of sexual bodies and subjectivities should not be understood as mere historical periods. The disciplinary regime didn't erase the sovereign necropolitical techniques. Likewise, the pharmacoporno-

13. Gilles Deleuze, "Post-scriptum sur les sociétés de contrôle," in *Pourparlers* (Paris: Minuit, 1990), 241.

graphic regime has not totally obliterated biopolitical disciplinary techniques. Three different and conflicting power regime techniques juxtapose and act upon the body producing our contemporary subject and somatic fiction.

In disciplinary society, technologies of subjectivization controlled the body externally like orthoarchitectural apparatuses, but in the pharmacopornographic society, the technologies become part of the body: they dissolve into it, becoming *somatechnics*.[14] As a result, the body-power relationship becomes tautological: technopolitics takes on the form of the body and is incorporated. One of the first signs of the transformation of the somato-power regime in the mid-twentieth century was the electrification, digitalization, and molecularization of these devices for the control and production of sexual difference and sexual identities. Little by little, orthopedic-sexual and architectural disciplinary mechanisms were absorbed by lightweight, rapid-transmission microcomputing, as well as by pharmacological and audiovisual techniques. If architecture and orthopedics in the disciplinary society served as models for understanding the relation of body to power, in the pharmacopornographic society, the models for body control are microprosthetic: now, power acts through molecules that incorporate themselves into our immune system; silicone takes the shape of our breasts; neurotransmitters alter our perceptions and behavior; hormones produce their systemic

---

14. In the early 2000s, a group of academics at Macquarie University, including Susan Stryker, coined the term "somatechnics" to highlight the complex relationship between body and technology. Technology does not add upon a given body, but rather it is the very means by which corporeality is crafted.

effects on hunger, sleep, sexual arousal, aggressiveness, and the social decoding of our femininity and masculinity.

We are gradually witnessing the miniaturization, internalization, and reflexive introversion (an inward coiling toward what is considered intimate, private space) of the surveillance and control mechanisms of the disciplinary sexopolitical regime. These new soft technologies of microcontrol adopt the form of the body they control and become part of it until they are inseparable and indistinguishable from it, ending up as techno-soma-subjectivities. The body no longer inhabits disciplinary spaces but is inhabited by them. The biomolecular and organic structure of the body is the last hiding place of these biopolitical systems of control. This moment contains all the horror and exaltation of the body's political potential.

WESTERN SEXUAL EPISTEMOLOGY

SOVEREIGN REGIME ——— XVIII ——— DISCIPLINARY REGIME

⟨FOUCAULT + LAQUEUR⟩

⟨FOUCAULT + LAQUEUR⟩

NECROPOLITICAL POWER

BIOPOLITICS of SEX

"ONE-SEX" MODEL

"TWO-SEX" MODEL

SYSTEM of SIMILARITIES

SYSTEM of DIFFERENCES

MAN/MASCULINITY

Invention of sexual difference as anatomical DIMORPHISM

CONFLICT

AND

STRATEGIC ALLIANCE

Technologies of production of truth

MYTH
RELIGION
THEOLOGY

REPRESSION of MASTURBATION

INVENTION of HETEROSEXUALITY and HOMOSEXUALITY (1868)

INVENTION of SEX AS NATURE

TECHNOLOGIES of PRODUCTION of TRUTH

SCIENCE

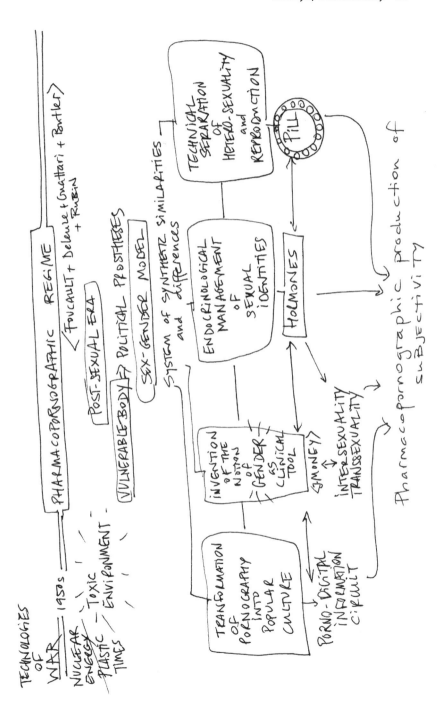

TECHNOLOGIES OF WAR — 1950s — PHARMACOPORNOGRAPHIC REGIME ⟨Foucault + Deleuze (Guattari + Butler) + Rubin⟩

NUCLEAR ENERGY — Toxic — PLASTIC — ENVIRONMENT — TIMES

POST-SEXUAL ERA

VULNERABLE BODY ⟹ POLITICAL PROSTHESES

SEX-GENDER MODEL

SYSTEM OF SYNTHETIC SIMILARITIES and DIFFERENCES

TECHNICAL SEPARATION OF HETERO-SEXUALITY and REPRODUCTION

ENDOCRINOLOGICAL MANAGEMENT OF SEXUAL IDENTITIES

PILL

HORMONES

INVENTION OF THE NOTION OF GENDER AS CLINICAL TOOL

⟨MONEY⟩

INTERSEXUALITY TRANSSEXUALITY

TRANSFORMATION OF PORNOGRAPHY INTO POPULAR CULTURE

PORNO-DIGITAL INFORMATION CIRCUIT

Pharmacopornographic production of SUBJECTIVITY

5. IN WHICH THE BODY OF VD BECOMES AN ELEMENT IN AN EXPERIMENTAL CONTEXT

I'd seen her twice before you died, but never with you. The first time, it was for the release of *Baise-Moi*; the second, five years later, five days before your death, was September 27, 2005, at the Lydia Lunch concert at Divan du Monde, in Paris. And it was my body, a biopower prosthesis, a micro-excitable platform of resistance that fell in love. This is how it happened.

Spring 2000. Under pressure from an organization of the extreme Right, the Council of State of the Socialist government decides to revoke the distribution permit allowing the showing of the film *Baise-Moi* in theaters. Terrified by their own addiction to pornography and by the potential visibility of their flaccid cocks, a federation of censors attacks the film as a way of saying "no to pornography." They prevent its distribution, prohibit it in all movie theaters, and confine it to distribution in DVD.

In reality, they are saying no to the only feminism that could save us, a kind of feminism that has the potential to turn pharmacopornographic hegemony upside down. I go to a Parisian movie theater, the MK2 Odéon, where a small support group created by Catherine Breillat is expecting women directors. At the time, I've been working with various different queer groups that include lesbian rebels, fags who have had it up to here with the gay ghetto and "pink" buying power, trannies who can't take any more of the system of medical protocols. This is the beginning of queer politics in Europe, and like everything, when it begins, people come with a joyful, innocent vitality. For months I devote all my time to organizing what I think is an impending pansexual revolution: the crumbling of sexual identity into a multiplicity of desires, practices, and aesthetics, the invention of new molecular sensibilities, new forms of collective living . . . All of it seems possible, real, and inevitable at the time. Several of us queer activists meet at my place on rue Jean-Pierre Timbaud to put together two hundred photocopies of a leaflet; there's no money to create any more. The idea is to funnel the pornopolitical forces of the film into the queer faction, not because the two protagonists in *Baise-Moi* are lesbian or anything as banal as that, but because they destroy everything in their path, because they're Franco-Arab girls who finish off a crowd of white men at the same time that they get down with all the good-looking boys they encounter. Certainly, the fact that both are superhot is an asset to the queer cause.

I feel a bit ridiculous when I see VD for the first time, right outside the movie theater. My hands are full of photocopies to the extent that I can't even offer her one as I greet her. I'm impressed by her Nordic peasant arms, her decidedly warriorlike walk. V is stoned on alcohol, coke, speed, I suppose. Coralie, too, but I see them as very confident about what they're doing, capable of shutting up any ideologue at all from the extreme Right. They're two dogs without a master, barking at the pack of liberals who are denouncing the sexual violence of the protagonists in the film. When I tell them that Nadine and Manu are heroines for a potential queer revolution, they look at me expressionlessly. Nobody knows what the word *queer* means at this point in France. Mainlining gender, class, and race terrorism—now, that kind of thing speaks to them. Seeing her among these people, some of whom I know and others whom I don't, immediately gives me the desire to get it on with her. Wanting to get done by VD must be a widespread sentiment. I'm attracted to her, beyond any concrete reference to the fact that she is, apparently, heterosexual. Or maybe that's the reason, and for the pleasure of knowing that someday she'll stop being it to become the queen of the dykes and the boy-girls. I figure it has something to do with the title of her book and the actresses in the film, with their way of fucking everything that passes by. The feeling doesn't impress me and even makes me feel a bit ashamed because there's something in it that's an unconscious response to an advertising gimmick, as if the performative power of the words B-a-i-s-e-M-o-i (F-u-c-k-M-e)[1] had appealed immediately to my synthetic urge to fuck her. However, I don't understand exactly why it's *she* who attracts me. And not Coralie, with her beauty reminiscent of the half-Nazi great lady of an Asian brothel; or Raffaëlla, as hot-tempered and jumpy as a lesbian pit bull; or Karen, who lets the crowd fawn on her the way a queen of the sand slowly cleaves the waves of a choppy sea. They pull

---

1. This is a reference to *Baise-Moi*, the groundbreaking and controversial novel by Virginie Despentes. "*Baise-moi*" translates as *Fuck Me*, but the American edition (trans. Bruce Benderson, Grove Press, 2003) was re-entitled *Rape Me* by the publisher to avoid censorship problems in the United States. —Trans.

me toward her. They're her harem, her Amazons, her hot, irascible she-wolves, her lady's companions with looks that kill, her tattooed bodyguards, revolutionary sluts, but she's the one I want. What astonishes me is the certainty with which her presence strikes me. But I do nothing to get to her, I'm too busy with queer politics. I've just published the *Manifesto* in your series, and, despite its editorial peculiarity, it does well enough. I'm invited to every part of France, especially by gay and lesbian organizations, and I travel to more than twenty cities where presidents of gay or trans associations with Club Med names—like Women Together, Women on Track, Trans-formation, Rose-Colored Glasses, the Am(orous)zons, Sappho's Way, the Violets—welcome me . . . I also do presentations at big bookstores, but only on Gay Pride Day. A healthy dose of affirmative action. I don't make a penny from all these trips, the organizations take months to reimburse me for train travel, and I always end up paying something out of my own pocket. Ruin. But I learn to think in public, to love crowds, to receive their vast impersonal love. At the time, this is how I become involved with organizing drag king workshops; lectures on American feminism and queer theory; reading workshops about Butler, Foucault, and Derrida; seminars on the history of sexuality in the electronic age. I'm too involved for a sex life.

The problem is that when I meet her again, five years have passed. During this time, I've become distanced from queer politics and she has put a lot into a heterosexual company that's going bankrupt and in which she ends up losing everything. After the breakup with RS, and after K's death, VD "would really have liked to be mowed down, to have someone put a bullet in the back of her neck, to finish her off like an animal."[2] Will I be capable of giving her what she wants?

September 2005. Five days before your death. I walk into Le Divan du Monde, see her. She's blond now. She looks a lot younger than she did the first time, as if she'd traveled backward, toward her teenage years. She's standing near the stage with a camera. Her eyes reach me first, before her body. The movements of her fans, gathered together like a swarm of wasps, transform the entire theater into a vortex coming toward me. My hair is long. I've hidden a large part of my head under a black winter hat, as if I'm trying to keep my ideas from scattering or being visible to anyone on the outside. I'm a mess; but I'm masculine, which gives me confidence. We exchange shy kisses on the cheek; her smell is intense, animal. We speak a few words to each other. It's impossible for me to remember the details of that conversation. A few seconds of it remain in my brain, like fragments from a silent film. I know the following was said: "Now I'm a lesbian," and "I've wanted to make it with you since the first time I laid eyes on you."

We'll come together at a fractal moment, on the edge of a techno-Greek tragedy: she has just started to go out with girls, and I've started to take testosterone. She is becoming a lesbian; and, as for me, I'm becoming something other than a girl. She loves breasts, and I love cocks. But she's what I'm looking for. And I'm what she's looking for. She has the cock I need, and I have the breasts she wants. Each

2. Virginie Despentes, *Bye Bye Blondie* (Paris: Grasset & Fasquelle, 2004).

of these life vectors could have moved in a different direction, but they converged toward us and met here, exactly, under her skin and mine.

We see each other again two days after a Lydia Lunch concert. You're still alive. So I'm still unaware that the ground that supports us is about to be overturned. The future: your death, my addiction to testosterone, VD's love.

FIRST SEXUAL CONTRACT

Our first contract is very clear: she's the whore; I'm the transsexual. She takes me to a hotel in Pigalle. It's neither night nor day. A translucent winter evening. That day, as we enter our room, she pays me. She wants me to be her slave. She turns on the television, as if she's summoning witnesses to watch what is about to happen. Without losing any time, she says, "Tomorrow you'll get out of here before I wake up." She places her bag on the chair, gets undressed, then falls onto the bed. She stretches out her arms, arranging her body in the form of an S. I look at her, not knowing if I'm supposed to get undressed, too, or not. I don't take anything off. I lie down next to her. It's Saturday, and *Star Academy*[3] is about to get rid of a new victim. As if she were still wearing her clothes, she makes remarks about which participants she thinks might win. She favors the older contestant, the one wearing orange-colored shades, who's the

3. The French version of a reality show, in which the contestants are singers or other types of performers but also live in a boarding school called the Academy, where they receive coaching to compete against one another, with the goal of being chosen for a nationwide tour.—Trans.

most rock 'n' roll of all; she's betting on him. Meanwhile, I'm taking in the room, down to its last detail. I glance at her out of the corner of my eye. Under the randomly changing beams of the television, I can see the shape of the areolas of her nipples, allergy or eczema in the area of her solar plexus; the rest of her skin is very white, her bush short and slightly blond. Next I think of my own nipples under my sweater, my completely shaved pubes, a cut at my right side, the alchemy of the testosterone coursing through my blood. I take turns imagining myself with and without a cock, and the two images keep following each other like a game on a seesaw. But I know that the moment I get undressed, she'll see only one of these bodies. Being reduced to one fixed image frightens me. I keep my clothes on a few minutes more, so I can enjoy the double option a little longer. When I get undressed, she won't know whether or not I have an erection. For me, an erection is an obvious fact, to the same extent in a body without a cock as in a body with one.

Then she leans over me, takes control of my legs without touching my pelvis, climbs astride my waist without wasting any time on my chest. I stick my tongue out. She takes it with her mouth. When our lips are almost touching, my tongue sharpens like an arrow. Her mouth fucks my tongue, mounting it and descending rapidly. She has found my erection. At times, a lock of her blond hair becomes part of the mechanics. She gently pulls it aside with one hand, using the opportunity to fuck the point of my tongue by raising her head. She changes rhythm. My tongue comes out of my mouth, and she grabs hold of the muscle by folding her palm into the shape of a ring. Her fingernails are impeccably red; her movements precise, *full of class*. Our bodies turn in tandem, our pelvises drawn magnetically nearer, united and at the same time separated by the cloth of my trousers. Next, I'm the one who takes her mouth with my tongue. Again and again, until saliva drips onto her breasts. Our bodies turn again, rise upward slightly. My mouth follows the path of the saliva, descending all the way to her vulva. She moans like a hooker, "Chérie, chéri." I suck her while pulling her head backward at the same time. "Tomorrow, I'll leave when I feel like it, slut." The violet light from the television floods the room. I did say that to her, but actually, I'm afraid of her. Afraid she'll kick me out into the street in the middle of the night. Afraid she'll get up and begin bawling me out. Afraid that she'll rip out the electric sockets with her fingernails. During that time, she has stretched out her arms to cling to the head of the bed. She's ready to come. I get up and leave her like that, like a dismembered animal. I'm thinking of leaving now, to up my masculinity quotient. Instead I put on a harness with an 8½ inch x 1½ inch dildo. Then I come back to fuck her. And I do—for an amorphous period of time that is neither long nor short, until we both come, me first and then she, my whore. Then she falls asleep. I move my arms, feeling entirely helpless. I get up, wash my dildo in the bathroom, take off the harness to soap it up. The suds flow through my fingers. I rinse, then glue it to the tiling with the plunger, leaving that erect organ looking as if it has sprung from the wall, in case somebody comes for a visit. I'll put it away when it's completely dry. I go back into the room. She's sleeping, hasn't changed position; her eyelids are quivering, but her face is still. They just eliminated a blond teenager from *Star Academy*, and half the audience is shouting out in despair. I lie down next to her. Can't sleep. I'm waiting for dawn so I can leave. But I fall asleep unexpectedly: in my dream, I'm the one who's the whore, something I knew. When I get up the next morning she's already gone. I unfasten the dildo from the bathroom wall, get dressed, and leave the hotel.

ALPHA BITCHES

Up to this point, I can't say that my gender revolt has ever put me in the position of victim. Actually, my love affair with VD is the apex of a sexual career as a conquistador without a cock, which began in my very innocent childhood days. Since fifth grade I've gone out only with the *sexiest* girls of the class, and I don't feature relinquishing that status. When I was fourteen, my first psychoanalyst explained to me that, fundamentally, I want to arm-wrestle God. I don't see why, on behalf of my mental health, she insists that I relinquish my desire to fuck only those at the top of the femininity pyramid, the alpha bitches, the supersluts— a desire that she calls "megalomaniacal." She thinks this desire is excessive because I'm not a cis-male, who could simply call the same thing "self-esteem."

Since childhood I've had a fantastical construction worker's cock. I react to every piece of ass that moves. It doesn't really matter whether it's a cute chick or a mommy, a bourgeois or a peasant, a faggot, bride of Christ, lesbian, or slut. The reaction in my cerebral sex organ is immediate. All girls, the most beautiful, the most heterosexual, the ones waiting for a Prince Charming full of natural testosterone, are actually destined without knowing it to become bitches that my dildos penetrate. Until I was twelve, I went to an all-girl Catholic secondary school. A real lesbian paradise. The best of the little ones were for me. Before they'd even had the time to cross the street and meet the boys at the secondary school opposite, they'd already put their tongues in my mouth. They're mine. I should make it clear, however, that this gravitating of the female sex around me isn't due to my beauty. At the age of four I was diagnosed with a maxillofacial deformation that would become radically more pronounced during my adolescence, to the point of looking grotesque. With the years, I become a myopic monster who was dramatically skinny, had a pronounced jaw and arms and legs that were too long. But during a good part of my childhood and adolescence, obviously because of some unrevealed secret, girls feel attracted to me. They say they're not lesbians, moan and weep after they've let their breasts be fondled and taken off their panties in my room, then stop speaking to me. They denounce me to the teachers after shutting themselves up in the girls' room with me and asking me to tell them smutty stories. But they keep the letters that I send them, keep the little ceramic tiles on which I write their name with a pink marker. They fight like warriors possessed by trying to monopolize my attention on the playground. They're mine. Marked forever with the fire of the revolution. One day, when I'm ten, someone calls my home and says to my mother, "Your daughter is a dyke," then hangs up. From that moment on, my mother reads my notebooks, goes through my pockets, rummages every day through my wallet to make sure I'm not hiding anything weird. She changes into a private detective being hired by the heteropatriarchal regime to disable my novice activities in terrorism: surveillance and home inspections, interrogations, interdictions, detentions, censorship . . . Those are the sophisticated methods that the system puts at the disposal of a simple housewife from post-Franco Spain to root out the masculine desire living inside my girl's body.

My mother and I often argue. She asks me if I'm on drugs, if I'm sleeping with boys, if I'm taking the Pill, if I'm stealing the money that she hides in the linen cabinet between the sheets. I answer no to all her questions. She insists. Tells me that girls like me end up having abortions. That if my father finds out, he'll kill me. I say no to everything she suggests. She's taken in by her own lies. I think she's accusing me of being a whore to avoid facing what she already knows. She warns me that if I go out with guys from the ETA,[4] she'll tie me up and won't let me leave the house any more. She tortures me until I finally tell her. Simply. Like a confirmation of her worst fears. A lot worse than being any kind of whore, than going to bed with everybody, than having abortions. I've been terrorized, too. But after having resisted her unrelenting heterosexual surveillance system, I revel in this moment of truth. With icy cruelty I tell her: I like girls. And immediately after that, without giving her time to answer: I'm a lesbian, a dyke, butch; I'm a boy, and you didn't realize it. I don't want to wear the skirts you

---

4. ETA is the Basque nationalist and separatist organization in Spain.—Trans.

buy for me. I don't want those shoes. I don't want blouses with frills. I don't want hairpins. I don't want nightgowns. I don't want to grow my hair long. I don't want to wear a brassiere. I don't want to talk like a girl. I don't want to be in love, and I don't want to get married; I don't want to comb my dolls' hair. I don't want to be beautiful. I don't want to stay home evenings. I don't want you to treat me like a girl. I say: I'm a boy, get it?—and I lift my shirt, show her my nipples that dot a still flat chest—and I deserve the same respect my father gets.

I was born during the dictatorship in a small Spanish city dominated by Catholic Francoism; I was assigned the female gender; Spanish was made my maternal language; I was brought up to be a perfect little girl; I was given an expensive education and private lessons in Latin. In the words of Judith Butler, these are "forcible reiterations of the norm"[5] that shaped me.

Today I live in several metropolises (four to eight million inhabitants, counting their suburbs) in which I survive sexually and politically thanks to a network of underground microcommunities. My life consists of circulating among different places that are both centers of production of the dominant discourses and cultural peripheries. I travel among three languages that I think of neither as mine nor as foreign to me. I personify a dyke-transgender condition made up of numerous biocodes, certain of which are normative and others spaces of resistance and still others potential places for the invention of subjectivity. In any

5. See Judith Butler, *Bodies That Matter: On the Discursive Limits of Sex* (New York: Routledge, 1993), 232.

case, these are artificial environments, synthetic islands of subjectivization that overlay the dominant sexo-urban tissue.

Twenty years later, when I go back to the city where I was born to visit my parents, I sometimes run into girls that I loved during my childhood. They're married, have children, dye their hair natural colors, wear leather coats, and actively resist relaxing their neck muscles. They greet me with terrorized surprise. They say to me, "You haven't changed." I'm always the little guy they knew at the school for girls. On the other hand—and this goes for the most bourgeois as much as it does for the most working class— they've already lived the best years of their heterosexual life and are preparing to reach forty, with only the hope of a rejuvenation technique. Some are happy about having children or are justifying not having had them; others seem indifferent; some are still in love with their husbands, or pretend to be. But in a certain way, within a temporary rift, they are still my little girls, my bitches. They still have time for the revolution.

ADDICTION

I don't see her for several days. She writes me and tells me that it can't go on, that it isn't going to be possible, that after P, she can't begin another relationship like that, in which there is such a level of connection and everything flows as easily as water. On the fifth day without her, I take another dose of fifty milligrams of testosterone. That night,

I don't sleep. I get up several times to reread her emails. I filter them, examine them, read them as the medieval monks read the Bible. Find grace in deciphering them. *Quis potest fallere amantem?* I remain sitting there on the couch for hours, in the darkness, and I enter a state close to self-hypnosis. I notice that the last four doses of fifty milligrams are interacting for the first time, forming a chemical bond that is getting me high. The skin inside my mouth has become thicker. My tongue is like an erectile muscle. I feel that I could smash the window with my fist. I could leap to the balcony opposite and fuck my neighbor if she were waiting for me with her thighs spread. But this time, like an energizing biosupplement being activated within a female cultural agenda, the testosterone compels me to tidy up and clean my apartment, frenetically, all night long. For a start, a profound and efficient sorting. I make practically no noise. My movements are precise. Eyes, arms, and legs move forward and draw back successively: right, left, forward, back. In my library, I move all the piles of Foucault to the cyberpolitics shelf and arrange them under the letter *F*; I put the Tomatis back in its place, as well as two Eliases, two Bourdieus, the Jo Spence, a Ragan, three Haraways, a Virno, a stack of Butlers in three languages, two Davises, the Nina Roberts; I put the Lemebel first, and the photo of Pedro and Paco both disguised as Frida Kahlo, their wounded hearts united by transparent tubing; I throw the English translation of Flaubert in the garbage, go and get Houellebecq's *Rester vivant* from the bedroom to put it on my desk. I pick up all the chairs, move the couch, the bed, the TV table, and a chest in order to sweep and mop the floor with antibacterial soap. I become involved in a disinfecting process. Justine the bulldog doesn't follow me in my testosterone delirium. She stays on the bed, even when I lift it a foot off the floor to take out what's under it. In less than twenty-five minutes, I've done the entire apartment. It's 5:35 a.m. I open the windows. The night air comes in like a vampire blowing its breath directly into the channels of my neocortex. And, like the other times, I begin to feel again that uncontrollable desire to go out, to feel the city awaken under my feet. So I do.

This is the way several days of T go by.

Finally her answer arrives: "Come."

She takes me to the Terrasse Hotel to make me her whore. I'm completely high on testosterone. I've become witness to my own body's experiencing the opening of new cellular centers of reception and excitation, aggressiveness, strength. But this state isn't permanent. The weakness can attack at any moment: once again I can start feeling in love, fragile, and all with somatic certainty, without needing to lie to myself. We've barely made it through the entrance to the hotel when she heads for reception, gives them a pseudonym, opens her great-lady Chanel bag, takes out her credit card, and pays for everything in advance, including two Cokes and two Toblerone bars from the minibar, which we'll have later. I don't make the slightest gesture of wanting to pay. That's our contract: she pays, I fuck.

We walk up to the fourth floor. In the stairway she says to me, "I want to be able to eat you out right here, right away." Gets undressed without speaking. She touches her nipples, moaning. Her tattoos look like ink bas-reliefs on her alabaster skin. Come. Come. We're at the Terrasse Hotel in the eighteenth arrondissement, where she and CTT filmed the scene from *Baise-Moi* in which Karen and Raffaëlla dance together. Before this, on the beach, with the sea as a background and the car on the sand, Manu has said to Nadine, "I think we should stay together." While they dance, the lyrics of the music repeat, "It's to see what I want to see, it's to feel what I want to feel." This pleasure is unlike any other, even the pleasure of masturbating in front of the television or the pleasure of smoking; it's the pleasure of knowing that they'll stay together whatever happens. After this, they go out and steal credit cards, bump off a girl at a cash machine. On the way back, they choose two guys, go up to their room with them—the room where V and I are now fucking—and they watch each other, from one bed to the other, sharing the pleasure of getting penetrated at the same time.

That day, in the same room as Karen and Raff's, we screw naked for the first time. Her pelvis is glued to mine, her vulva connected to mine, our organs gnawing each other like the muzzles of two dogs that recognize each other. As we screw, I feel as if my entire political history, all my years of feminism, are moving directly toward the center of her body and flowing into it, as if her skin provided their only real niche. When I come, Wittig and Davis, Woolf and Solanas, La Pasionaria, Kate Bornstein, and Annie Sprinkle bubble up with me. She is covered with my feminism as if with a diaphanous ejaculation, a sea of political sparkles.

When I wake up later, her hand is inside me. Her entire body has become my cock, is emerging from my loins. But the veins of her arms have a lot more class than the veins of a biocock. I catch her arm between my two hands and rub it from top to bottom as if for a counter-sexual jerk-off. Then I go all the way back to her right shoulder, her neck, and push two fingers into her mouth. She sucks them, without taking her hand off my body. Pleasure follows this arrangement of forces, this hierarchy of functions whose stability is necessarily precarious. We go on like that until I come in her hand, until my hand comes in her mouth.

We leave the hotel. My elbows are burning. Fucking her is harder than factory work, harder than driving a truck loaded with nitroglycerine in a cowboy film. She tears off my skin, every time.

6. TECHNOGENDER

The invention of the category *gender* signaled a splitting off and became the source point for the emergence of the pharmacopornographic regime for producing and governing sexuality. Far from its being the creation of a feminist agenda, the notion of gender belongs to the biotechnological discourse that appeared in the US medical and therapeutic industries at the end of the 1940s. Gender and pharmacopornographic masculinity and femininity are artifacts that originated with industrial capitalism and would reach commercial peaks during the Cold War, just like canned food, computers, plastic chairs, nuclear energy, television, credit cards, disposable ballpoint pens, bar codes, inflatable mattresses, or telecommunications satellites.

In 1955, the child psychologist John Money, who treated "hermaphrodites" and "intersex babies," became the first to make use of the grammatical category of *gender* as a clinical and diagnosis tool. He would develop it with Anke Ehrhardt and Joan and John Hampson as part of a set of potential hormonal or surgical techniques to modify the bodies of babies born with genitals or chromosomes that medicine—relying on its visual and discursive criteria—

couldn't classify as strictly female or male.[1] To the rigid nineteenth-century categorizations of sex, John Money opposed the malleability of *gender*, using social and biochemical techniques. When he used *gender* as a name for "social role" or "psychological identity," he was essentially thinking of the possibility of using technologies (from hormones to social techniques, such as those employed in pedagogic and administrative institutions) to modify the body or to produce subjectivity intentionally in order to conform to a preexisting visual and biopolitical order, which was prescriptive for what was supposed to be a female or male human body.[2] In order to ensure that their external "sexual" development could be identified as feminine, newborns declared to be "intersex" because they possessed a "micropenis" (according to somato-political visual criteria) had it amputated, and their genitals were reconstructed in the form of a vagina, after which they received hormone-substitution therapy.[3] Intersex activists have pointed out the similarity between traditional non-Western cliterodectomy techniques and industrialized practices of genital mutilation on intersex bodies in the West.[4] Far as they were from the rigidity and exteriority of techniques of normalization

1. John Money, Joan G. Hampson, and John L. Hampson, "Imprinting and the Establishment of Gender Role," *Archives of Neurology and Psychiatry* 77, no. 3 (1957): 333–36, doi:10.1001/archneurpsyc.1957.02330330119019.

2. Joanne Meyerowitz, *How Sex Changed: A History of Transsexuality in the United States* (Cambridge, MA: Harvard University Press, 2002), 98–129.

3. Suzanne Kessler, "The Medical Construction of Gender: Case Management of Intersex Infants," *Signs: Journal of Women in Culture and Society* 16, no. 1 (1990); Suzanne Kessler and Wendy McKenna, *Gender: An Ethnomethodological Approach* (New York: John Wiley,1978).

4. Cheryl Chase, "Hermaphrodites with Attitude: Mapping the Emergence of Intersex Political Activism," in *The Transgender Studies Reader*, eds. Susan Stryker and Stephen Whittle (New York: Routledge, 2006), 300–14.

of the body of the architectonic and disciplinary systems at the end of the nineteenth century and beginning of the twentieth, the new biocapitalism's pharmacopornographic techniques of gender production were simultaneously invasive and minimal, penetrating and invisible, intimate and toxic, high tech and mutilating.

Like the Pill or the oncomouse, gender is a biotech industrial artifact. The technologies of gender, sex, sexuality, and race are the true economicopolitical sectors of pharmacopornism. They are technologies of production of somatic fictions. *Male* and *female* are terms without empirical content beyond the technologies that produce them. That being the case, the recent history of sexuality appears as a gigantic pharmacopornographic Disneyland in which the tropes of sexual naturalism are fabricated on a global scale as products of the endocrinological, surgical, agrifood and media industries.

Whereas Money tampered with the bodies of infants to force them into the categories of "male gender" or "female gender," Dr. Henry Benjamin administered estrogens and progesterone to a new kind of patient of state-managed medicine: an adult who claims not to identify with the gender that was assigned at birth. Curiously, the criteria for the assignment of gender, as well as those for its reassignment in cases of transsexuality, function according to two metaphysical models of the body that are nearly irreconcilable. On the one hand, the criteria for sex assignment that permit a decision regarding whether or not a body is "female" or "male" at the moment of birth (or in utero, using a sonogram) depend on a model of visual recognition that is supposedly empirical and in which the signifiers (chromosomes, size of the genitals, etc.) are cast as scientific truths. In this case, making a body visible implies that it is being assigned a male *or* female gender in a univocal and definitive way. This unveiling of gender depends on an optical ontology: the real is what you can see. On the other hand, the idea that posits a true "psychological sex" distinct from the one that has been assigned at birth—in other words, a subjective conviction of being a "man" or a "woman"— belongs to the model of radical invisibility, of the nonrepresentable, and this paradigm is close to that of the Freudian unconscious: an immaterial ontology. In this case, the real isn't accessible to the senses and is by definition what cannot be apprehended by empirical means. These two models can function together thanks to a single metaphysical axis that attaches them as it opposes them. It's necessary to imagine the biopolitical ideals of masculinity and femininity as transcendental essences from which are suspended aesthetics of gender, normative codes of visual recognition, and immaterial psychological convictions prompting the subject to proclaim itself male or female, heterosexual or homosexual, cis- or trans. However, the visual criteria that govern sex assignment at birth are not a biological event any more than are the psychological criteria that lead to the "inner" conviction of being a man or a woman: "Physical genitals are a construction of biological and scientific forms of life."[5] Penises and vaginas are biocodes of power-

5. Suzanne Kessler and Wendy McKenna, "Toward a Theory of Gender," in *The Transgender Studies Reader*, eds. Susan Stryker and Stephen Whittle (New York: Routledge, 2006), 173.

knowledge regimes. They are ideal regulators, biopolitical fictions that find their somatic support in individual subjectivity.[6] The pharmacopornographic sex-gender regime is the result of the unexpected alliance between the nineteenth-century naturalist metaphysics of sexual dimorphism, focused on heterosexual reproduction, and the rise of a hyperconstructivist medical and biotech industry in which gender roles and identities can be artificially designed.[7] Plato meets Money in the high-tech gender garage.

The hyperbolic production of the postwar medical discourse on gender is the sign of an epistemic crisis: the endless "nature versus nurture" debates of the 1950s–70s that involved John Money, David O. Caudwell, Robert Stoller, Henry Benjamin, Richard Green, or Milton Diamond remind us of sixteenth-century tricks on spheres and epicycles whose aim was to maintain the hegemony of the geocentric astronomical model. The proliferation of the clinical discourse on "true hermaphroditism," "pseudohermaphroditism," "intersexuality," "sexual incongruities," and "psychopathia transexualis,"[8] as well as the medical normalization of techniques of sex reassignment, genital mutilation of intersex babies, and surgical reconstruction of gender, are nothing other than desperate (and violent) measures to reinforce a shattered epistemology. In the 1950s, which were confronted with the political rise of feminism and with homosexuality, as well as with the desire

6. Judith Butler, "Doing Justice to Someone: Sex Reassignment and Allegories of Transsexuality," in *Undoing Gender* (New York: Routledge, 2004), 57–74.

7. See Butler, "Doing Justice."

8. See David O. Caudwell, "Psychopathia Transexualis", in *The Transgender Studies Reader*, eds. Susan Stryker and Stephen Whittle (New York: Routledge, 2006), 40–44.

of "transvestites," "deviants," and "transsexuals" to escape or transform birth sex assignment, the dimorphism epistemology of sexual difference was simply crumbling. Nineteenth-century disciplinary epistemology was grounded on the biopolitical imperative of the heterosexual reproduction of the nation's population. As Suzanne J. Kessler and Wendy McKenna put it, human bodies were "diagnosed" male or female at birth as potential "sperm and egg cell carriers."[9] But "sperm and egg cell carriers" were gaining new political agency over their reproductive power. Moreover, new techniques in the 1950s for reading genetic and chromosomal differences and measuring endocrinological levels introduced variables that could not be reduced to the epistemological framework of sexual dimorphism. Medical, biological, and political discourses were confronted with an infinite variability of bodies and desires (multiple chromosomal, gonadal, hormonal, external genital, psychological, and political variables) that could not be subsumed within the disciplinary imperative of heterosexual reproduction. John Money puts it this way:

> In human beings, the irreducible sex differences are that males impregnate, and females menstruate, gestate, and lactate. Otherwise, sexual dimorphism that is programmed into the brain under the influence of prenatal hormones appears to be not sex-irreducible, but sex-shared and threshold-dimorphic. A complete theory of the differentiation of all the constituents of masculinity or femininity of the gender identity role needs to be both

9. Kessler and McKenna, "Toward a Theory of Gender," in *The Transgender Studies Reader*, 180.

multivariable and sequential in type. It must be applicable to all the syndromes of hermaphroditism, and to the genesis of the gender identity role phenomena, including transvestism and transsexualism, as well as to the genesis of a heterosexual gender identity role.[10]

But in the late 1950s, males are no longer guaranteed to impregnate, females stop menstruating and gestating under the effects of the contraceptive pill, and lactation is provided by food industries instead of by female breasts. The heterosexual dimorphic regime of "sperm and egg cell carriers" is going awry.

Instead of collectively producing an alternative (multimorphic) epistemology for understanding bodies and desires, the 1950s medical, biological, and political discourses decided to directly intervene within the structures of living beings to artificially construct sexual dimorphism using surgical, prosthetic, and hormonal techniques supported by the pharmacological, medical, and food industries.[11] When the possibility of the technical construction of sexual difference is recognized as a point of departure, nature and identity are brought to the level of a somatic parody. Whereas the disciplinary system of the nineteenth century considered sex to be natural, definitive, unchangeable, and transcendental, pharmacopornographic gender seems to be synthetic, malleable, variable, open to transfor-

10. John Money, "Pediatric Sexology and Hermaphroditism," *Journal of Sex and Marital Therapy*, 11, no. 3 (1985): 139, doi: 10.1080/00926238508405440.

11. See Anne Fausto-Sterling, "The Five Sexes, Revisited," *Sciences* 40, no. 4 (July/August 2000): 18–23. Several biologists have recently called for a change to a non-dimorphic epistemology of sex-gender assignment.

mation, and imitable, as well as produced and reproduced technically.

Strangely, the medical and biotechnological dimensions of gender production were ignored within the "cultural" version of white feminism's constructivism, which reappropriated the notion of "gender" in order to recast it as an instrument of critical analysis of the oppression of women. Gender appears gradually in the anthropological or sociological texts of Margaret Mead or Ann Oakley as the social and cultural construction of sexual difference.[12] The feminist culturalist definitions of gender have been the source of two stumbling blocks whose disastrous effects are still at work in the current "politics of gender" that maintain that sex, an anatomical truth, is a biological given and therefore isn't subject to cultural construction, whereas gender specifically expresses the social, cultural, and political difference of *women* in a society and at a particular historical moment. In this context, there's nothing surprising about feminism's finding itself on a dead-end street of the essentialism/constructivism debates or regarding the politics of the state's facility in co-opting feminist rhetoric into an extensive program of sexual normalization and social control. Why didn't 1970s culturalist and constructivist feminists fight against clinical diagnosis, reassignment protocols for intersex bodies, normalizing biochemical and surgical technologies, and the binary regime within administrative systems? Intersex activist Cheryl Chase answers: "Intersexuals have had such difficulty generating

12. One of the first texts where this difference is clearly thematicized is Ann Oakley, *Sex, Gender and Society* (London: Maurice Temple Smith, Ltd., 1972). See also Christine Delphy, *L'Enemi principal*, vol. 2, *Penser le genre*, (Paris: Syllepse, 2001).

mainstream feminist support not only because of the racist and colonialist frameworks that situate cliterodectomy as a practice foreign to proper subjects within the first world, but also because intersexuality undermines the stability of the category of 'woman.'"[13]

Apart from claims coming from the intersex and transsexual movements, late 1980s queer theory represented the first critique of the use of the notion of gender within feminism itself. In the 1980s, Teresa de Lauretis and Judith Butler started to point out that second-wave feminism uncritically shared the very epistemological sex-gender framework it aimed to question. Lauretis claimed that feminist "theory" could not be evinced unless it examined its own critical foundations, political terms, linguistic practices, and practices of the production of visibility. Lauretis asked what the political subject produced by feminism as a discourse and practice of representation was. Stripped of all self-indulgence, her conclusion takes the form of an extremely lucid warning: feminism functions, or can function, as an instrument of normalization and political control when it reduces its subject to "women." Under the apparent neutrality and universality of the term *woman*, a host of vectors of production and subjectivity are hiding: sex, race, class, sexuality, age, ability, geopolitical or corporal difference, and so on. In Lauretian terms, the subject of feminism is inevitably *eccentric*; rather than coinciding with "women," it arises as a force of displacement, as a practice for the transformation of subjectivity.[14]

13. Chase, "Hermaphrodites," in *The Transgender Studies Reader*, 312.
14. Teresa de Lauretis, "Eccentric Subjects: Feminist Theory and Historical Consciousness," *Feminist Studies* 16, no. 1 (Spring 1990): 115–50.

In order to question the conflation of gender and woman, Teresa de Lauretis developed the notion of "technologies of gender."[15] For Lauretis, filmmaking devices—specific modes of recording, projection, montage, signification, and decoding—serve as a paradigm for conceiving of the production of gender and sexual subjectivity. This amounts to saying that the pharmacopornographic regime functions like a machine of somatic representation in which text, image, and the corporal spread through the interior of an expansive cybernetic circuit. According to Laurentis's semiotic-political interpretation, gender is the effect of a system of signification that includes modes of production and decoding of politically regulated visual and textual signs. The subject, who is simultaneously the producer and interpreter of these signs, is constantly involved in a corporal process of signification, representation, and self-representation. Transposing Foucault's critique of disciplinary power and Metz's cinematographic semiotics to feminism, Lauretis writes:

> It seemed to me that gender was not the simple derivation of anatomical/biological sex but a sociocultural construction, a representation, or better, the compounded effect of discursive and visual representations which I saw emanating from various institutions—the family, religion, the educational system, the media, medicine, or law—but also from less obvious sources: language, art, literature, film, and so on. However, the constructed-ness or discursive nature of gender does not prevent it from

15. See Teresa de Lauretis, *Technologies of Gender: Essays on Theory, Film, and Fiction* (Bloomington, IN: Indiana University Press, 1987).

having real implications, or concrete effects, both social and subjective, for the material life of individuals. On the contrary, the reality of gender is precisely in the effects of its representation; gender is realized, becomes "real" when that representation becomes a self-representation, is individually assumed as a form of one's social and subjective identity.[16]

Lauretis displaces the naturalized notion of "woman" with "gender" while translating the question of the "dialectics of oppression" into a multiplicity of "technologies." The issue of this conceptual difference between gender and woman, between "technologies of power" and "dialectics of oppression" isn't limited to nominal questions of translation or semantics. The issue directly concerns body technologies and devices of subjectification. This distinction has the potential to disrupt the entire grammar of feminism, and even the entire political history of the production of difference between the sexes. Whereas the feminism of the 1970s studied the sources of the oppression of women, Lauretis invites us to identify the functioning of a collection of technologies of gender, operating across bodies that produce not only differences of gender but also sexual, racial, somatic, class, age, disability, and other differences.

As a result, a new field of study has been established for feminism: the analysis of different *technologies of gender* that produce (always in a precarious, unstable way) bodies,

16. Teresa de Lauretis, "Gender Identities and Bad Habits," in *Actas del IV Congreso Estatal Insomnía sobre Identidad de Género vs. Identidad Sexual* (Castelló de la Plana, España: Publicacions de la Universitat Jaume I, 2008): 13–23.

subjects of enunciation and action. It goes without saying that research about these technologies of gender cannot, in any case, be reduced to a statistical or sociological study of women's situation in the different domains of production of bodies, discourses, and representations.[17] The issue no longer comes down to considering gender as a cultural force that comes to modify a biologically determined foundation (sex). Instead, it is subjectivity as a whole, produced within the techno-organic circuits that are codified in terms of gender, sex, race, and sexuality through which pharmacopornographic capital circulates.

With Lauretis, Judith Butler introduced the largest and most acute critique of both gender-sex epistemology and the grammar of feminism. For Butler, gender is a system of rules, conventions, social norms, and institutional practices that *performatively* produce the subject they claim to describe. Through a cross-referenced reading of Austin, Derrida, and Foucault, Butler reaches a consideration of gender in which it is no longer an essence or psychological truth, but a discursive, corporal, and performative practice by means of which the subject acquires social intelligibility and political recognition.[18] Today, this Butlerian analysis comes together with Donna J. Haraway's lessons for examining the semiotechnical dimension of this performative production: pushing the performative hypothesis further into the body, as far as its organs and fluids; drawing it into the cells, chromosomes, and genes.

17. Lauretis, *Technologies of Gender*.
18. See Butler's *Gender Trouble*, *Bodies That Matter*, and *Undoing Gender*.

The clinical notion of gender invented by Money sees it above all as an instrument of rationalization for a living being whose visible body is only one of the parameters. The invention of gender as an organizing principle was necessary for the appearance and development of a series of pharmacopornographic techniques for the normalization and transformation of living beings—a process that includes photographing "deviants," cellular diagnosis, hormonal analysis and therapy, chromosomal readings, and transsexual and intersexual surgery.

Photography, invented at the end of the nineteenth century, before the appearance and perfection of hormonal and surgical techniques, signaled a crucial stage in the production of the new sexual subject and its visual truth. Of course, this process of representation of the body had already begun in the seventeenth century with anatomical and pornographic drawings,[19] but it is photography that would endow this technical production of the materiality of the body with the merit of visual realism. Let us take the example of one of the classical images by Félix Nadar[20] representing "hermaphrodites" and "inverts": a body, named "X" in medical histories, appears in a supine position with legs spread, covered with a white slip that has been raised to the level of the chest, exposing the upper part of the pelvis. The genitals have been unveiled to the eyes of the camera by a hand coming from outside the frame. The image reveals its own process of discursive production. It shares its codes

19. Laqueur, *Making Sex*, 154–63.
20. Nadar photographed a "hermaphrodite" patient around 1860 at the behest of the French physician Armand Trousseau.

of representation with the pornography that appears at the same period; the doctor's hand hides and exhibits the genitals, thus establishing a power relationship between the subject and the object of representation. The face and, especially, the eyes of the patient have been effaced; the deviant cannot be the agent of his/her own representation. The truth of sex takes on the nature of a visual disclosure, a process in which photography participates like an ontological catalyst, making explicit a reality that wouldn't be able to emerge any other way.

A century later, in 1980, the anthropologist Susan Kessler will denounce the aesthetic codes (relying on the shape and form of the penis and the clitoris) that dominate medical protocol for the assignment of sex to newborns. Although the visual criteria for sex assignment may not seem to have changed very much since the end of the nineteenth century, the current technical possibilities of body modification are introducing substantial differences in the process of the assignment and production of femininity and masculinity in the pharmacopornographic era. The process of normalization (assignment, reassignment) that could be accomplished only by discursive or photographic representation in the past is now inscribed within the very structure of the living being by surgical, endocrinological, and even genetic techniques.

After World War II, human mapping in the West, characterized by sexual dimorphism and its classification of sexualities as normal or deviant, healthy or disabled, becomes dependent on the legal and commercial management of molecules essential to the production of phenotypes (external signs) that are culturally recognized as female or male (facial hair, size and shape of the genitals, voice register . . .), as well as on the technopolitical management of the reproduction of the species and on the pharmacological control of our immune systems and their resistance to aggression, illness, and death.

There have been several regimes of body production—political regimes for producing and reproducing human life on the planet, depending on the historical moment and the political, economic, and cultural context. Some lost their potential for subjectification (for example, matriarchy or Greek pedophilia) when the *political technoecologies* inside of which they functioned disappeared. Others are undergoing full mutation. This is the case with ours.

If the concept of gender has introduced a rift, the precise reason is that it represents the first self-conscious moment within the epistemology of sexual difference. From this point on, there is no going back; Money is to the history of sexuality what Hegel is to the history of philosophy and Einstein to the conception of space-time. It is the beginning of the end, the explosion of sex-nature, nature-history, time and space as linearity and extension. With the notion of gender, the medical discourse is unveiling its arbitrary foundations and its constructivist character, and at the same time opening the way for new forms of resistance and political action. When I bring up the idea of a rift introduced by the notion of gender, I'm not claiming to be referring to the passage from one political paradigm to a radically distinct other, or to an epistemological rupture that will give rise to a form of radical discontinuity. Rather,

I'm referring to a superimposition of strata in which different techniques of producing and managing life are interlacing and overlapping. The pharmacopornographic body is not passive living matter but a techno-organic interface, a technoliving system segmented and territorialized by different (textual, data-processing, biochemical) political technologies.

Let us examine, for example, the displacement of production of body hair from the disciplinary sex regime to the gender pharmacopornographic regime. In the sexodisciplinary system of the nineteenth century, the "bearded lady" was considered to be a monstrous abnormality, and her body was becoming visible within the spectacularized framework of circuses and freak shows. In the pharmacopornographic regime, "hirsutism" has become a clinical condition, making women potential clients of the medical system and consumers of manufactured molecules (specifically, Androcur, which is administered to neutralize testosterone production, but also insulin regulators), the purpose of which is not hormonal, but political, normalization. After 1961, hirsutism was measured by the Ferriman-Gallwey scale, which examines nineteen body areas (from sideburns to toes) to assess normal hair growth.[21] The Ferriman-Gallwey score establishes a correlation between

---

21. David Ferriman and J.D. Gallwey, "Clinical Assessment of Body Hair Growth in Women," *Journal of Clinical Endocrinology* 21, no. 11 (November 1961): 1440–7.

gender, ethnicity, and hair; for example, in a Caucasian woman a score of eight is regarded as indicative of androgen excess whereas in East Asian and Native American women a much lower score reveals hirsutism. According to the same clinical method, Ashkenazi Jews and Hispanic women are "high-risk ethnic groups."[22] Hirsutism becomes here a method to clinically assess race as much as gender. Biopolitical loop: femininity-body-hair-visibility, circus-hirsutism-Androcur-race-cosmetic-treatment-invisibility-femininity. Different "techniques of the body"[23] and visual frameworks produce different somato-political living fictions: formerly exhibited in the circus, the racialized pharmacopornographic hirsute body becomes the object of the plastic surgery clinic and the beauty salon and their techniques of hormonal regulation and electrolysis.

In the changing definitions of gender, there is no succession of models (sovereign, disciplinary, and pharmacopornographic) about to be supplanted historically by others, or any ruptures or radical discontinuities, but rather an interconnected simultaneity, a transversal effect of multiple somato-political models that compose and implement subjectivity according to various intensities, different indexes of penetration, and different degrees of efficiency.

22. Daniel A. Dumesic and Lauri A. Pasch, "Hirsutism: Bother or Burden? Developing a patient-centered management approach," *Sexuality, Reproduction & Menopause* 9, no. 3 (August 2011): 14.

23. Marcel Mauss, "Techniques du corps," in *Sociologie et anthropologie* (Paris: PUF, 2001). This article was originally published in *Journal de Psychologie*, 32, no. 3–4 (15 mars–15 avril, 1936). Paper presented at the Société de Psychologie on May 17, 1934.

If this is not the case, then how to explain the fact that, at the beginning of the twenty-first century, rhinoplasty is considered plastic surgery whereas vaginoplasty (the surgical construction of a vagina) and phalloplasty (the surgical construction of a penis) are considered sex change operations?[24] One could say that two clearly distinct regimes of power-knowledge traverse the body and that they construct the nose and the genitals according to different somato-political technologies. Whereas the nose is regulated by a pharmacopornographic power in which an organ is considered to be private property and merchandise, the genitals are still imprisoned in a premodern, sovereign, and nearly theocratic power regime that considers them to be the property of the state and dependent on unchanging transcendental law. But in the pharmacopornographic society, a conflicting multiplicity of power-knowledge regimes is operating simultaneously on different organs, tearing the body apart. We are not bodies without organs, but rather an array of heterogeneous organs unable to be gathered under the same skin. Those who survive the mutation that is happening will see their bodies moving into a new semiotechnical system and will witness the proliferation of new organs; in other words, they'll cease to be the bodies that they were before.

When it comes to such transformations of the living body, the outlines of the problem become clearer. Pharma-

---

24. See Dean Spade, "Mutilating Gender," in *The Transgender Studies Reader* eds. Susan Stryker and Stephen Whittle (New York: Routledge, 2006), 315–52.

copornographic gender is neither metaphor nor ideology; it can't be reduced to a performance: it is a form of political technoecology. The certainty of being a man or a woman is a somato-political biofiction produced by a collection of body technologies, pharmacologic and audiovisual techniques that determine and define the scope of our somatic potentialities and function like prostheses of subjectification. Gender is an operational program capable of triggering a proliferation of sensory perceptions under the form of affects, desires, actions, beliefs, and identities. One of the characteristic results of such a technology of gender is the production of inner knowledge about oneself, with a sense of a sexual self that appears to be an emotional reality that is evident to consciousness. "I am a man," "I am a woman," "I am heterosexual," "I am homosexual," "I am transsexual": these are units of specific knowledge about oneself, hard biopolitical nuclei around which it's possible to assemble an entire collection of discourses and performative practices.

We could call the "programming of gender" a psycho-political neoliberal modeling of subjectivity that potentiates the production of subjects that think of themselves and behave like individual bodies, aware of themselves as private organic spaces and biological properties with fixed identities of gender and sexuality. The prevailing programming of gender operates with the following premise: an individual = a healthy body = a sex = a gender = a sexuality = a private property. But constructing gender, as Butler has argued, always amounts to taking the risk of dismantling it. Producing gender implies a collection of

strategies of naturalization/denaturalization and identifi-
cation/disidentification. Drag king devices and hormonal
self-experimentation are only two of these derailment
strategies.

Within the pharmacopornographic regime, gender is
constructed in industrial networks of biopolitical materialization; it is reproduced and reinforced socially by its
transformation into entertainment, moving images, digital
data, pharmacological molecules, cybercodes. Pharmacopornographic female or male gender exists before a public
audience, as a somato-discursive construction of a collective nature, facing a scientific community or a network.
Technogender is a public, scientific, community network
biocode.

Ocytocin, serotonin, codeine, cortisone, the estrogens,
omeprazole, testosterone, and so on, correspond to the
group of molecules currently available for the manufacturing of subjectivity and its affects. We are technobiopo-
litically equipped to screw, reproduce the National Body,
and consume. We live under the control of molecular technologies, hormonal straitjackets intended to maintain
biopower: hyperestrogened bodies–rape–testosterone–
love–pregnancy–sex drives–abjection–ejaculation. And the
state draws its pleasure from the production and control of
our pornogore subjectivity.

The objective of these pharmacopornographic technologies is the production of a living political prosthesis: a body

that is compliant enough to put its *potentia gaudendi*, its total and abstract capacity for creating pleasure, at the service of the production of capital and the reproduction of the species. Outside such somato-political ecology of "sperm and egg carriers," there are neither men nor women, just as there is neither heterosexuality nor homosexuality, neither ableness nor disability.

Our contemporary societies are gigantic sexopolitical laboratories where the genders are produced. The body—each and every one of our bodies—is the invaluable enclave where transactions of power are ceaselessly carried out. My body = the multitude's body. Postwar white men and women are biotechnological beings belonging to the sexopolitical regime, whose goal is the production, reproduction, and colonial expansion of heterosexual human life on the planet.

Beginning in the 1940s, the new biopolitical ideals of masculinity and femininity were created under laboratory conditions. These artifacts (us) can't exist in a pure state, but only within our enclosed sexual *technoecosystems*. In our role as sexual subjects, we're inhabiting biocapitalist amusement parks. We are men and women of the laboratory, effects of a kind of politicoscientific bio-Platonism. We are strange biopolitical fictions because we are alive: we are simultaneously the effect of the pharmacopornographic power (*biopower*) regime and the potential for its defeat (*bioempowerment*).

Some semiotechnical codes of white heterosexual femininity belonging to the postwar pharmacopornographic political ecology:

Little Women, a mother's courage, the Pill, the hyperloaded cocktail of estrogens and progesterone, the honor of virgins, *Sleeping Beauty*, bulimia, the desire for a child, the shame of deflowering, *The Little Mermaid*, silence in the face of rape, *Cinderella*, the ultimate immorality of abortion, cakes and cookies, knowing how to give a good blowjob, bromazepam, the shame about not having done it yet, *Gone with the Wind*, saying no when you want to say yes, not leaving home, having small hands, Audrey Hepburn's ballet shoes, codeine, taking care of your hair, fashion, saying yes when you want to say no, anorexia, knowing in secret that the one you're really attracted to is your best friend, fear of growing old, the need to be on a diet constantly, the beauty imperative, kleptomania, compassion, cooking, the desperate sensuality of Marilyn Monroe, the manicure, not making any noise when you walk, not making any noise when you eat, not making any noise, the immaculate and carcinogenic cotton of Tampax, the certainty that maternity is a natural bond, not knowing how to cry, not knowing how to fight, not knowing how to kill, not knowing much or knowing a lot but not being able to say it, knowing how to wait, the subdued elegance of Lady Di, Prozac, fear of being a bitch in heat, Valium, the necessity of the G-string, knowing how to restrain yourself, letting yourself be fucked in the ass when it's necessary, being resigned, accurate waxing of the pubes, depression, thirst, little lavender balls that smell good, the smile, the living mummification of the smooth face of youth, love before sex, breast cancer, being a kept woman, being left by your husband for a younger woman . . .

Some semiotechnical codes of white heterosexual masculinity belonging to the postwar pharmacopornographic political ecology:
James Bond, soccer, wearing pants, knowing how to raise your voice, *Platoon*, knowing how to kill, knowing how to smash somebody's face, mass media, stomach ulcers, the precariousness of paternity as a natural bond, overalls, sweat, war (including the television version), Bruce Willis, Operation Desert Storm, speed, terrorism, sex for sex's sake, getting hard like Ron Jeremy, knowing how to drink, earning money, *Rocky*, Prilosec, the city, bars, hookers, boxing, the garage, the shame of not getting hard like Ron Jeremy, Viagra, prostate cancer, broken noses, philosophy, gastronomy, *Scarface*, having dirty hands, Bruce Lee, paying alimony to your ex-wife, conjugal violence, horror films, porn, gambling, bets, the government, the state, the corporation, cold cuts, hunting and fishing, boots, the tie, the three-day growth of beard, alcohol, coronaries, balding, the Grand Prix, journey to the Moon, getting plastered, hanging yourself, big watches, callused hands, keeping your anus squeezed shut, camaraderie, bursts of laughter, intelligence, encyclopedic knowledge, sexual obsessions, Don Juanism, misogyny, being a skinhead, serial killers, heavy metal, leaving your wife for a younger woman, fear of getting fucked in the ass, not seeing your children after the divorce, the desire to get fucked in the ass . . .

For a long time I believed that only people like me were really in deep shit. Because we aren't and will never be Little Women or James Bond heroes. Now I know that shit concerns all of us, especially Little Women and James Bond heroes.

THE TWILIGHT OF HETEROSEXUALITY

Monique Wittig with Michel Foucault. Judith Butler with Antony Negri. Angela Davis with Félix Guattari. Kate Bornstein with Franz Fanon. White heterosexual femininity is, above all, an economic function referring to a specific position within biopolitical relationships of production and exchange, and based on the transformation of sex work, the work of pregnancy, body care, and other unpaid activity within industrial capitalism.[25] This sexualized economy functions through what Judith Butler has called performative coercion:[26] by means of semiotechnical, linguistic, and corporal processes of regulated repetitions imposed by cultural conventions. It's impossible to imagine the rapid expansion of industrial capitalism without the slave trade, colonial expropriation, and the institutionalization of the heterosexual *dispositif* as a mode of transformation in surplus value of unpaid sexual services historically performed by women. It is reasonable to posit an unpaid debt for sex work that heterosexual men historically contracted with regard to women, in the same way that Western countries

25. Wittig, 58–59.
26. Judith Butler, *Gender Trouble*.

should be, according to Franz Fanon, forced to reimburse a colonial debt to colonized peoples.[27] If interest were applied to the debt for sexual services and colonial plundering, all women and colonized peoples on the planet would receive an annuity that would allow them to spend the rest of their lives without working.

Heterosexuality hasn't always existed. The contemporary transformation of capitalism entails a mutation of the sex-gender order. If we look attentively at the signs of technification and informatization of gender that emerge starting with World War II, we can even affirm that heterosexuality has been summoned to disappear one day. In fact, it is in the act of disappearing now. The postsexual era will then begin as a secondary effect of the pharmacoporno industry. This means that there will no longer be sexual relations between cis-males and cis-females and that the conditions of sexual production (production of bodies and pleasures) are drastically changing, that they will begin to resemble more and more closely the production of bodies and deviant pleasures, under the control of the same pharmacopornographic regulations. In other words, all forms of sexuality and production of pleasure, all libidinal and biopolitical economies are now subject to the same molecular and digital technologies of the production of sex, gender, and sexuality.

The normative premises of the nineteenth-century

27. Frantz Fanon, "De la violence," in *Les Damnés de la terre*, in *Oeuvres* (Paris: La Découverte, 2011), 503.

disciplinary sexual regime (continuity between sexuality and reproduction and pathologization of nonreproductive practices, including masturbation and homosexuality) were radically displaced with the invention of the Pill and the making of pornography into a branch of popular media industries that transformed masturbation into a source of production of capital. But the technoliving park of which we are part isn't completely coherent and integrated. The two poles of the pharmacopornographic industry (pharmaco and porno) function more in opposition than they do in tandem. Although the pornography industry as a whole works as cultural propaganda for the gender dimorphic regime (producing normative and idealized representations of heterosexual and homosexual practice, where sexuality equals penetration with a biopenis) and the political asymmetry between cis-males and cis-females is legitimized as based on anatomical differences (cis-male = biopenis; cis-female = biovagina), the pharmaceutical and biotechnical industries and the new techniques of assisted reproduction—even if they do continue to function in a heteronormative legal framework—are ceaselessly redesigning the frontiers between the genders and, as a whole, turning the economic, heterosexual, and political system into an obsolete means of management of subjectivity.

The dialectic between pharmaco and porno is already arising in the contradictions between various (low-tech or high-tech) biocodes of subjectivity coming from different regimes of production of the body. For example, families (whether heterosexual, homosexual, or monoparental) in which reproduction has been accomplished by in vitro fertilization with anonymous donor sperm continue to function in a politicolegal system in which the performative ideals of masculinity and kinship have not been challenged. Moreover, the biocodes of the production of subjectivity (both those that are semiotic and those that are pharmaceutical, from Viagra to testosterone, by way of the aesthetics of the gay body or sexual practices using synthetic organs) are circulating within the pharmacopornographic market without any possibility of controlling the processes of production of subjectivity that they are inducing. Thus, biocodes (language, ways of dressing, hormones, prostheses) that once belonged to feminine, masculine, heterosexual, homosexual, transsexual, or even genderqueer configurations can achieve means of expression that are denaturalized and offbeat and free of a sexual identity or a precise biopolitical subjectivity. A way of life or an identity agenda. The visual codes governing the transformed face of Courtney Love, a rock icon, are not at all different from those used to rejuvenate the face of the queen of Spain, the actress Pamela Anderson, Chen Lili (the transsexual woman who attempted to compete in the Miss Universe contest in 2004), or the lesbian star Ellen DeGeneres, or from those used in remodeling the face of an anonymous working-class cis-female who wins the right to participate in the American TV show *Extreme Makeover*. As a result, we are witnessing a horizontalization of the consumption of the techniques of production of the body that redistributes the differences between class, race, or sexual identities, between the culture of rock music, high society, and the porn industry. This pharmacopornographic shifting is a sign that normative white heterosexuality will soon be one body aesthetic among many others, a retro reproductive style that various future generations will be able to denigrate or exalt, a low-tech reproduction machine possibly exportable to other parts of the world (even an excuse for waging war against Muslim countries), but completely out of date and decadent in Western democratic post-Judeo-Christian societies.

Fifty years after the invention of the Pill, all sexual bodies are produced and become intelligible according to a common pharmacopornographic epistemology. There are not body biotechnologies that differ but the administrative systems that, as Dean Spade argues, sort and manage the access and use of those technologies, distributing life chances according to class, race, ability, gender, or sexuality.[28] Today, a cis-male can self-administer a testosterone-based hormonal complex to increase his athletic efficiency, and a teenager can have an implant placed under her skin that releases a composite of estrogens and progesterone for three years, acting as a contraceptive; a cis-female who claims to be a man can sign an agreement for a sex change and receive endocrinal therapy with a base of testosterone that makes it possible to grow a beard and mustache and increases muscularity; a cis-female of sixty may discover that more than twenty years of swallowing her high-strength contraceptive pill has caused kidney failure or breast cancer that she is supposed to treat with chemotherapy resembling what the victims of Chernobyl were

28. See Dean Spade, *Normal Life: Administrative Violence, Critical Trans Politics and the Limits of the Law* (New York: South End Press, 2011).

exposed to; a heterosexual couple can resort to in vitro fertilization after discovering that the male can't produce sperm mobile enough to fertilize the ovum of his partner because he has consumed too much tobacco and alcohol. The same testosterone that helps turn the wheels of the Tour de France serves to transform the bodies of F2M transsexuals . . . The question is, who has access to hormone treatments? According to which clinical diagnosis? How do class and race modify the distribution of and the access to technologies of production of gender?

All this suggests that a normative regime for segregated distribution of race, class, gender, sexuality, and ability coexists with the process of "becoming common"[29] of technologies of the production of body, gender, sex, race, and sexuality. From now on, the mutation will be impossible to stop.

In the middle of the Cold War, a new ontological-political distinction between "cis-" (a body that keeps the gender it was assigned at birth) and "trans" (a body availing itself of hormonal, surgical, prosthetic, or legal technologies to change that assignment) made its appearance. Henceforth, I will use the nomenclature *cis-* and *trans*, with the understanding that these two biopolitical gender statuses are technically produced. Both of them fall within the province of common methods of visual recognition, performative production, and morphological control. The difference between "cis-" and "trans" is enumerated as a function of resistance to the norm of the consciousness of those tech-

29. See the notion of "becoming common" in Antonio Negri and Michael Hardt, *Multitudes*, 142.

nical (pharmacopornographic) processes that produce somatic fictions of masculinity and femininity and as a function of scientific techniques and social recognition in public space. This implies no judgment about value: "trans" gender is neither better nor more political than "cis-" gender. It comes down to saying that, in ontopolitical terms, there are only technogenders. Photographic, biotechnological, surgical, pharmacological, cinematographic, or cybernetic techniques come to construct the materiality of the sexes *performatively*. Some transsexuals claim to have been born "imprisoned in the body of the opposite sex" and say that the technical mechanisms placed at their disposal by contemporary medicine are only a way of revealing their *true, authentic* sex. Others, like Kate Bornstein, Del LaGrace Volcano, or Susan Stryker,[30] affirm their status as *gender queers*, or gender deviants, and refuse any summons as man or woman, declaring them to be impositions of the norm. Del LaGrace Volcano puts it this way:

> As a gender variant visual artist I access "technologies of gender" in order to amplify rather than erase the hermaphroditic traces of my body. *I name myself.* A gender abolitionist. A part time gender terrorist. An intentional mutation and intersex by design, (as opposed to diagnosis), in order to distinguish my journey from the thousands of intersex individuals who have had their "ambiguous" bodies mutilated and disfigured in a misguided attempt at "normalization."[31]

30. Kate Bornstein, *Gender Outlaw: On Men, Women, and the Rest of Us* (New York: Routledge, 1994); Susan Stryker, "My Words to Victor Frankenstein Above the Village of Chamounix: Performing Transgender Rage," *GLQ: A Journal of Lesbian and Gay Studies* 1, no. 3 (1994): 227–54.

31. Del LaGrace Volcano, "Artist Statement," last modified September 2005, http://www.dellagracevolcano.com/statement.html.

One cannot insist enough on the fact that the pharmaco-pornographic regime of sexuality cannot function without the circulation of an enormous quantity of semiotechnical flow: the flow of hormones, the flow of silicone, and the flow of digital, textual, and representational content . . . In other words, it cannot function without the constant trafficking of gender biocodes. Gender in the twenty-first century functions as an abstract mechanism for technical subjectification; it is spliced, cut, moved, cited, imitated, swallowed, injected, transplanted, digitized, copied, conceived of as design, bought, sold, modified, mortgaged, transferred, downloaded, enforced, translated, falsified, fabricated, swapped, dosed, administered, extracted, contracted, concealed, negated, renounced, betrayed . . . It transmutes.

In terms of political agency, subjection, or empowerment do not depend on the rejection of technologies in the name of nature, but rather on the differential use and reappropriation of the very techniques of the production of subjectivity. No political power exists without control over production and distribution of gender biocodes. Pharmacopornographic emancipation of subaltern bodies can be measured only according to these essential criteria: involvement in and access to the production, circulation, and interpretation of somato-politic biocodes.

7. BECOMING T

Victor, the lover I left for VD, has been working for six months for a phone sex chat line. He goes out every day at 7:00 p.m. and comes home at one in the morning. We get up around eleven, eat breakfast while reading the paper with MTV playing in the background, then take Justine for a walk in the park; when we get back home, we have sex until five in the afternoon. We've taken to being two guys as far as we can. Two gay guys, except for the fact that we don't have a penny, or regular jobs, or a house; we've got nothing, neither back-rooms nor dicks; but there are more dildos where we live than there are cocks in the saunas of Paris. During these three months in 2004, the issue of the structural lack of public space for lesbians, drag kings, and trans guys in Paris doesn't bother us—even if it does pose a real problem. We fuck each other all day. As soon as we have a moment free. The process of adapting to silicone can take a long time. At the beginning, I'm the one who fucks him. He has the beauty of an Arab smuggler, the elegance of a rogue who reads Artaud, and the calm of a pharaoh's dog. With black eyes and a freckled face, he's the best thing since sliced bread. His drag king vagina swallows everything. Without regard to size. No need to begin with size M; why not go directly to XL.

Victor is an impassable "bottom." He can take everything I find. He smiles when he comes and never tires out.
Every day, at 5:30 p.m., bus 69 takes him to his work as a
linguistic masturbator. When he leaves the house, his skin
is hyperoxygenated, but his legs are trembling. He dozes on
the bus before arriving at the job, then spends six hours on
the phone doing his whore routine. This has been working
particularly well since he began to specialize in sadomas-
ochistic clients. His arrangements with me in private end
up serving to soothe the sexual deprivation of a gang of
masturbators who spend the day stuck on the telephone.
It's what the Negrists of the radical Left call "biopolitical
work," or, in other words, jerking off the planetary cock.
It consists of the transformation of our sexual resources
into work, of our sensitivity into an object of commerce,
of our erotic memory into text paid by character count,
of our sexual arrangements into anonymous scenarios
performed repetitively by indifferent actors. During the
seven hours in which Victor "works biopolitically," I write.
Paid by the French state just enough to eat and take care
of bills, I've accumulated nearly a thousand pages on the
impact of feminism on contemporary aesthetic and political discourse. The philosopher's minimum wage. Ensconced
at my work table like a pilot in his cockpit, with Enrique
Morente playing in the background, I read Foucault, Sloterdijk, or Buckminster Fuller, or write an unpaid article about
sexual segregation in public space. It calms me when sex
and philosophy approach each other. These are precious
hours, enveloped in translucent silence, the peace of isolation. A balance composed of two equally drifting masses

that achieve equilibrium in my brain; reading flows toward writing, and the other way around. Without anxiety. I'm on the point of finishing *Anus Public: An Interview with Nobody*, a conversation in which no one asks me the questions that I answer about the reasons that led to my giving up queer politics. I have no intention of publishing this text. I think it's still inadequate, too tender for the brutality of the century, too obviously selfish in the face of the impending collective suffering and the gradual disappearance of the living. Television helps me get away from the island of reading-writing. News from the heterosexual world: i-Télé. P in a leopard shirt and black sunglasses, and BB, looking like a pop Jesuit, discussing the life of Janis Joplin. Obviously, she was a lesbian. At this moment, I don't know that Mr. Leopard Shirt is the person who broke the heart of my future lover. That is what allows me to continue to lead a normal life, in an automatic way, without concern. When Victor comes home, I get ready for dinner. Sometimes there's enough energy left for us to fuck for thirty or forty minutes. Or else we fuck only with our mouths, endless fucks, emitting electric signals received everywhere else in the body. Sometimes we fall asleep immediately after having dined with Justine. These months form a long tunnel of sex, drag king days, tantric rituals, soft-packing, days of incest and vampiric sleep that I go through in a semiconscious state, with the certainty that something or someone will end up taking me out of this infernal paradise. I would have never imagined that VD, your death, and testosterone would be waiting at the end of the tunnel. In this case—and who knows if it was only this one, or more generally the case—complete ignorance of the future was the condition that provided the possibility of continuing to live in the present. Just as it is necessary to forget to keep living, it is necessary not to know the future to wait naively for time to pass. At the height of his career, the architect Adolf Loos burned all his drawings, letters, diaries, fetish objects. He burned everything. With fire, he built an archive made of smoke, a dense mass of forgetfulness from which it would be possible to begin to live again. If there were a precise psychosomatic memory of the previous breakup, no one would fall in love again; nor would we if we knew in advance the exact circumstances of the end of the love we were about to begin having. If I'd known that your death, the love of VD, and addiction to T were at the end of the tunnel, then excitement, fear, and an irrepressible desire would have prevented me from living. It seems that not having certainty, not knowing, can be confirmed as a condition of biopolitical survival.

In the meantime, I enjoy what I have. The unique pleasure of writing in English, French, Spanish, of wandering from one language to another like being in transit between masculinity, femininity, and transsexuality. The pleasure of multiplicity. Three artificial languages, expanding as they become entangled, fight to become or not become a single language. Blend. Finding their meaning only in this blending. Production among species. I write about what matters most to me, in a language that doesn't belong to me. This is what Derrida called the monolingualism of the other;[1] none of the languages that I am speaking belong to me, and yet

---

1. Jacques Derrida, *Le Monolinguisme de l'autre, Ou la prothèse de l'origine* (Paris: Galilée, 1996).

there is no other way to speak, no other way to love. None of the sexes that I embody possess any ontological density, and yet there is no other way of being a body. Dispossessed from the start.

STATE-COUCH-BODY-MOLECULE

During the two months before your death I wake up consistently every night at four in the morning, the hour when cows give birth and the owls go hunting. The history of life is revealed before me night after night with the slowness of insomnia. It calms me to think that I was once bacteria and that someday I'll become it again. My bacterial self helps me sleep. For more than two thousand years, it rained on earth until these empty pools that had become oceans and evaporated after the explosion of a giant meteorite filled up with water again. I tell myself that if the oceans could dry up and then refill, my heart as well can purge itself of politics and be filled again. What I don't know yet is that soon my heart will be filled with your death and, almost at the same time, VD's love.

During the day, I swing between frenetic activity and total emptiness. In the periods of emptiness, I spend the majority of my time sitting on the couch. I don't search for a comfortable position, try to make it an elegant gesture; I merely flop shapelessly on the rectangular surface of the couch, and wait. During these recumbent hours, I sweat, tremble; sometimes, but rarely, I cry, and from time to time, I manage to fall asleep. I go out only to walk Justine.

Buy the paper, but don't read it. Buy something to eat, but don't eat it. The dog eats, though. This couch could be a bed in a psychiatric hospital. Yes, that's it, a home office for the medical and legal institutions of the Republic of France, a country in which I'm not even a citizen. The couch is a tentacle of the control system, an installation within inner space in the form of living room furniture. It's a political device, a public space of surveillance and deactivation that presents an advantage in comparison with other classical institutions, such as the prison or the hospital. Its purpose is to uphold the fiction that this apartment, its fifty-five square feet, which can be locked with a key, is my private territory. A slippage of paranoia from the sofa to my skin. My body could be a lifelong center of imprisonment, a mechanism that is conscious of the system of control implanted in my biological structure, an avatar of pharmacopower with my name attached to it. My body, my cells are a political appliance par excellence, a public-private space of surveillance and activation that affords an advantage compared with other classical institutions such as the school or army and that upholds the fiction of my subjectivity and its biochemical support, its cells, its supposedly impenetrable fifty-five square feet as my unique and ultimate individual possession. I stop the paranoia and kiss Justine. How can I escape form this cozy prison? What can I know? What am I supposed to do? What am I allowed to hope for?

I look for keys to survival in books. I cling to Foucault's published seminars, Guattari's *Trois ecologies*, the biography of Walter Benjamin, his writings, Butler, Violette Leduc, Genet, Haraway, Wittig again, Susan Stryker, Edmund

White. But, more than anything, there are your books. I don't think about calling you when I'm at my worst. From time to time, you leave a belligerent message on my answering machine. "When are you going to write something that's worth the trouble?" "It's you or me." "Stop attacking me." I don't answer. Ever. I don't understand what you're talking to me about. I don't know what to say to you. If you only knew what was happening to me. But you don't have the slightest idea. Your stupid messages calm me down because they allow me to dodge the question: I don't call you so that I don't have to tell you that I'm going to start taking testosterone. I should speak to you about it, inform you of it. Now that I'm going to transform myself into one of yours, we'll be able to fulfill the old dream of fucking each other. I don't know that these days are the last before your death, and I don't call you.

I spend entire days reviewing the archive of American feminism in the 1970s. Certain voices are engraved permanently in my memory. Others are disappearing for good. Faith Ringgold remains, as does her way of saying eye to eye to a journalist that the only way to survive the colonial and patriarchal enemy is to laugh in his face. She's not kidding; on the contrary, she's shouting right at him, interrupts him when he speaks, doesn't pay him the slightest attention. Laughter is a form of resistance, survival, a way of mustering forces. Shouting, too. When you belong to an oppressed group, you have to learn how to laugh in the face of the enemy, says Ringgold. The problem is that things aren't so clear anymore. You end up not knowing anymore who's the oppressor and who's the oppressed; or rather, it's difficult to see yourself as both the oppressor and the one who is oppressed. I guess that in that case you have to laugh at yourself.

Jill Johnston's voice is imprinted in me: "As long as all women aren't lesbians, there will be no political revolution." Nancy Angelo and Candace Compton: "Listen closely. You don't believe that I'm going to end my life within these four walls? No one can force me to. Listen to me. I've had it up to here with living locked inside my body. I'm sick of it." My mind is a sexual sheath in which my body is huddled, a shut case, a tomb, a trap. I'm a fascist political message that is drifting. My body is the message, my mind the bottle. Exploding. It's the only thing that makes me get hard.

Every day, I try to cut one of the wires attaching me to the cultural program of feminization in which I grew up, but femininity sticks to me like a greasy hand. Like my mother's warm hand, like the oceanic sound of Spanish in my dreams. Like Faith Wilding in her performance in the *Womanhouse* project, I keep waiting to be taken into someone's arms, waiting for life to begin, waiting to be loved, for pleasure to arrive, waiting . . . But I'm also a trans man. With or without T. To the list of feminine waiting, I must add the endless list of ways of hoping for the advent of masculinity: waiting for my beard to grow, waiting to be able to shave, waiting for a cock to grow from my loins, waiting for girls to look at me as if I were a man, waiting for men to speak to me as if I were one of them, waiting to be able to give it to all the little sweeties, waiting for power, waiting for recognition, waiting for pleasure, waiting . . . I wonder when it will be too late to undo this program of gender production. Maybe beyond a certain threshold, the process becomes irreversible. What are the temporal parameters of this production? What are the contours of its construction; what is its direction?

In her 1967 *SCUM Manifesto*, Valerie Solanas had seen things with a certain precision.[2] More than forty years have gone by, and one element seems to have changed: all the grotesque characteristics that Solanas attributes to men in capitalist society at mid-twentieth century seem to have spread to women today. Men and women are the bioproducts of a bifurcated sexual system with a paradoxical tendency for reproduction and self-destruction. "To be male is to be deficient, emotionally limited . . . egocentric, trapped inside himself, incapable of empathizing or identifying with others, of love, friendship, affection, of tenderness." Men and women are isolated units, creatures condemned to constant self-surveillance and self-control by a rigid class-sex-gender-race system. The time they devote to this brutal political arrangement of their subjectivity is comparable to the whole extent of their lives. Once all their vitality has been put to work to reduce their own somatic multiplicity, they become physically weakened beings, incapable of finding any satisfaction in life and dead politically before they have taken their last breath. I do not want the female gender that has been assigned to me at birth. Neither do I want the male gender that transsexual medicine can furnish and that the state will award me if I behave in the right way. I don't want any of it.

2. Valerie Solanas, *SCUM Manifesto* (New York: Verso, 2004).

BECOMING MOLECULAR

When I take a dose of testosterone in gel form or inject it, what I'm actually giving myself is a chain of political signifiers that have been materialized in order to acquire the form of a molecule that can be absorbed by my body. I'm taking not only the hormone, the molecule, but also the concept of hormone, a series of signs, texts, and discourses, the process through which the hormone came to be synthesized, the technical sequences that produce it in the laboratory. I inject a crystalline, oil-soluble steroid carbon chain of molecules, and with it a bit of the history of modernity. I administer myself a series of economic transactions, a collection of pharmaceutical decisions, clinical tests, focus groups, and business management techniques; I connect to a baroque network of exchange and to economic and political flow-chains for the patenting of the living. I am linked by T to electricity, to genetic research projects, to megaurbanization, to the destruction of forests of the biosphere, to the pharmaceutical exploitation of living species, to Dolly the cloned sheep, to the advance of the Ebola virus, to HIV mutation, to antipersonnel mines and the broadband transmission of information. In this way I become one of the somatic connectives through which power, desire, release, submission, capital, rubbish, and rebellion circulate.

As a body—and this is the only important thing about being a subject-body, a technoliving system—I'm the platform that makes possible the materialization of political imagination. I am my own guinea pig for an experiment on the effects of intentionally increasing the level of testosterone in the body of a cis-female. Instantly, the testosterone turns me into something radically different from a cis-female. Even when the changes generated by this molecule are socially imperceptible. The lab rat is becoming human. The human being is becoming a rodent. And as for me: neither *testo-girl* nor *techno-boy*. I am a port of insertion for $C_{19}H_{28}O_2$. I'm both the terminal of one of the apparatuses of neoliberal governmentality and the vanishing point through which escapes the system's power to control. I'm the molecule and the state, and I'm the laboratory rat and the scientific subject that conducts the research; I'm the residue of a biochemical process. I am the future common artificial ancestor for the elaboration of new species in the perpetually random processes of mutation and genetic drift. I am T.

THE DEVIL IN GEL FORM

After the fifth dose of Testogel, I began to make out variations in the range of excitation, muscular tension, the tendency for outward expressions of my body. All drugs are poisons. The only difference between a poison and a medicine lies in the dose. But what is the right dose of testosterone? The one that yields my body, or another? What would hormonal justice be? And if there is a hormonal justice, should I apply that justice to myself?

Testosterone is the devil in a colorless gel. The cutaneous administration of fifty milligrams of testosterone in gel form twice a week for three months isn't easy to detect with the naked eye in the body of a cis-female, in my body. It is changing the hormonal composition of my body substantially. *Modus molecularis*. It is a matter of a potential transformation of my own endocrinal ontology. The changes are not purely artificial. Testosterone existing externally is inserted into a molecular field of possibilities that already exist inside my body. Rather than rejection of it, there is assimilation, incorporation. *Mit-sein*. Being-with-testosterone.

Testosterone does not radically alter the perception of reality or the sense of identity. This particular dose of testosterone isn't strong enough to produce in the body of a cis-female identifiable exterior changes labeled as "virilism" by mainstream medicine (beard and mustache, noticeable increase in muscle mass, changing of the voice . . .). It does not change the way others decipher my gender. I've always had an androgynous body, and the microdoses of testosterone that I'm giving myself don't alter that situation. However, they produce subtle but decisive changes in my affect, in my inner perception, in my sexual excitation, in the odor of my body, and in resistance to fatigue.

Testosterone isn't masculinity. Nothing allows us to conclude that the effects produced by testosterone are masculine. The only thing that we can say is that, until now, they have as a whole been the exclusive property of cis-males. Masculinity is only one of the possible political (and nonbiological) by-products of the administration of testosterone. It is neither the only one nor, over the long term, the one that will dominate socially.

The consumption of testosterone, like that of estrogen and progesterone in the case of the Pill, do not depend on any ideal cultural constructions of gender that would come to influence the way we act and think. We are confronted directly by the production of the *materiality* of gender. Everything is a matter of doses, of melting and crystallization points, of the rotary power of the molecule, of regularity, of milligrams, of form and mode of administration, of habit, of praxis. What is happening to me could be described in terms of a "molecular revolution." In detailing this concept in order to refer to the revolt of May 1968, Félix Guattari certainly was not thinking of cis-females who self-administer testosterone. On the other hand, he was attentive to structural modifications generated by micropolitical changes such as the consumption of drugs, changes in perception, in sexual conduct, in the invention of new languages.[3] It is a question of becomings, of multiplicities. In such a context, *molecular revolution* could be pointing to a kind of political homeopathy of gender. It's not a matter of going from woman to man, from man to woman, but of contaminating the molecular bases of the production of sexual difference, with the understanding that these two states of being, male and female, exist only as "political fictions," as somatic effects of the technical process of normalization. It's a matter of intervening intentionally in this process of production in order to end up with viable forms of incorporated gender, to produce a

---

3. Félix Guattari, *La Révolution moléculaire* (Paris, Recherches: 1988). See also Félix Guattari, "Plan sur la planete. Capitalisme mondial intégré et révolutions moléculaires," in *Minorités dans la pensée*, eds. Jean-Pierre Faye, Marc Rombaut, Jean-Pierre Verheggen (Paris: Payot, 1979); Gilles Deleuze and Félix Guattari, *A Thousand Plateaus: Capitalism and Schizophrenia*, trans. Brian Massumi (Minneapolis: University of Minnesota Press, 1987), 232–309.

new sexual and affective platform that is neither male nor female in the pharmacopornographic sense of the term, which would make possible the transformation of the species. T is only a threshold, a molecular door, a becoming between multiplicities.

For a body accustomed to regulating its hormonal metabolism in terms of the production of estrogen, the intentional increasing of the level of testosterone in the blood constitutes an endocrinal reprogramming. The slightest hormonal change affects all the functions of the body: the desire to eat and to fuck, circulation and the absorption of minerals, the biological rhythms regulating sleep, the capacity for physical exertion, muscular tone, metabolism, the sense of smell and taste—in fact, the entire biochemical physiology of the organism. None of these modifications can be qualified as masculine. But of all the mental and physical effects caused by self-intoxication based on testosterone in gel form, the feeling of transgressing limits of gender that have been socially imposed on me was without a doubt the most intense. The new metabolism of testosterone in my body wouldn't be effective in terms of masculinization without the previous existence of a political agenda that interprets these changes as an integral part of a desire—controlled by the pharmacopornographic order—for sex change. Without this desire, without the project of being in transit from one fiction of sex to another, taking testosterone would never be anything but a molecular becoming.

8. PHARMACOPOWER*

Pharmacia (*Pharmakeia*) is also a common noun signifying the administration of the *pharmakon*, the drug: the medicine and/or poison. . . . Socrates compares the written text Phaedrus has brought along to a drug (*pharmakon*). The pharmakon, this "medicine," this philter, which acts as both remedy and poison, already introduces itself into the body of the discourse with all its ambivalence. . . . The *pharmakon* would be a substance—with all that that word can connote in terms of matter with occult virtues, cryptic depths, refusing to submit their ambivalence to analysis, already paving the way for alchemy—if we didn't have eventually to come to recognize it as antisubstance itself: that which resists any philosopheme, indefinitely exceeding its bounds as nonidentity, nonessence, nonsubstance; granting philosophy by that very fact the inexhaustible adversity of what funds it and the infinite absence of what founds it. . . . The *pharmakon* properly consists in a certain inconsistency, a certain impropriety, this nonidentity-with-itself always allowing it to be turned against itself. What is at stake at this overturning is no less than science and death. Which are consigned to a single type in the structure of the pharmakon, the one and the only name for that potion that must be awaited. And even, in Socrates's case, deserved.[1]

* This chapter has been modified and developed for this English-language edition by the author.

1. Jacques Derrida, "La pharmacie de Platon," in *La Dissémination* (Paris: Editions du Seuil, 1972), 86, 87 and 148. See also Derrida, *Dissemination*, trans. Barbara Johnson (Chicago: University of Chicago Press, 1983), 70 and 119.

NARCOSEXUAL WITCHCRAFT

Pharmacopornographic hegemony, which wouldn't become explicit until the end of the twentieth century, has its roots in the origins of modern capitalism, transformations of medieval systems of production at the end of the fifteenth century that would open the way to industrial and colonial economies, to the biopolitical fiction of the nation-state and to regimes of scientific and technical knowledge. In order to understand how new relationships of body-power, pleasure-knowledge, and *pharmakon*-subjectivities were established in the West, we must first make an indispensable detour through the relationship between capitalism and the destruction of our entheogenic[2] traditions.

To gain access to the question of the *pharmakon*, we have to go the way of witches. Farmers, harvesters, and preparers of medicinal plants were condemned during the Inquisition. Witches, alchemists, and midwives were declared to be heretics and satanic deviants. At the same time, Europe colonized the Americas. "Witch-hunt[s] occurred simultaneously with the colonization and extermination of the populations of the New World, the English enclosures, [or] the beginning of the slave trade."[3] Feminist historian Silvia Federici has shown that the witch hunt was a double

2. Denis Richard, Jean-Louis Senon and Marc Valleur, *Dictionnaire des drogues et des dépendances* (Paris: Larousse, 2004), 267. Entheogenic comes from the Greek *entheos*, meaning trance, possession. A neologism suggested in 1979 by the Hellenist Carl Ruck, the ethno-botanist Gordon Wasson and the philosopher Jonathan Ott, pertaining to psychoactive substances capable of inducing states of ecstatic trance or shamanic possession. This term does not cover the same territory as the word psychedelic, which is related to 60s Western culture.

3. Silvia Federici, *Caliban and the Witch: Women, the Body and Primitive Accumulation* (New York: Autonomedia, 2004), 164.

attempt to appropriate women's bodies as reproductive force and to end the use of natural resources as "commons" (meadows, forests, rivers, lakes, wild pastures). The process of enclosing land, expropriating folk wisdom, criminalizing practices of "voluntary intoxication," and privatizing plant germ plasm was only beginning. It reached its apex in the modern period with the colonial expropriation of plants, animals, human bodies, and knowledges; the persecution of the producers, consumers, and traffickers of "drugs"; the gradual transformation of natural resources into pharmaceutical patents; and the confiscation by juridical-medical institutions of all experiments that involved self-administration.[4]

Most medieval preparations with hallucinogenic properties were topically absorbed, dissolved in an oil-based ointment and smeared on the neck, armpits, or stomach. The way these salves were applied closely resembles transgender people's use of testosterone in gel form today. Contemporary historians of medieval pharmacological traditions and the Inquisition hypothesize that most of the visions and acts of magic condemned as satanic by the tribunals of the Inquisition were the result of the accidental or intentional ingestion of psychoactive substances. By consulting the records of the inquisitors of the period and the ancient treatises of herbalists, today's researchers have been able to identify the different hallucinogenic and narcotic substances extracted from vegetable and animal matter that were then in use.

4. Richard Stallman, "Biopirates ou biocorsaires?," *Multitudes* 1 (mars 2000): 114–17.

A number of these recipes for ointments and concoctions mention psychoactive solanaceous ingredients, substances such as henbane (of the nightshade family), stramonium (thorn apple), belladonna, and mandrake. All of them included extracts of such plants as the poppy (source of opium, heroin, and morphine) and hemp (marijuana, hashish); toads, whose skin, we now know, contains a strong psychotropic substance; and a certain kind of "flour of damp cereals," probably having to do with the ergot fungus that attacks rye and from which LSD would be extracted. Hallucinogenic visions worthy of the rhetoric of Deleuze and Guattari (becoming animal, becoming a plant, having sexual relations with animals, talking with trees, astral projection, etc.) could have been caused by the psychotropic effects on the organism after the ingestion or cutaneous application of these plants with hallucinogenic or aphrodisiac powers. In the 1960s, Walter Pahnke scrupulously followed the formula for an ointment appearing in a fifteenth-century book and then experimented, along with other colleagues, by smearing it on the area of the neck and armpits. All the researchers reported having been plunged into "a twenty-four-hour sleep during which they dreamed of daredevil flights, frenetic dancing and other strange adventures similar to those that took place during medieval orgies."[5]

During periods of drought and severe food shortages, to increase the production of bread, substitute grains like rye were used, and these might have contained mycotox-

---

5. Antonio Escohotado, *Historia General de las Drogas* (Madrid: Espasa-Calpe, 2008), 169.

ins, which were metabolites produced by the bread molds, the effects of which were poisonous to mammals, causing hallucinations and vomiting. Today we know that the victims of Ignis Sacer (Saint Anthony's fire) were suffering from the effects of the hallucinogen lysergic acid diethylamide (abbreviated after 1938 as LSD)—a mycotoxin that appeared during the baking of bread contaminated with ergot—as well as from other mycotoxins, such as belladonna alkaloids, extracted from the fruit of the mandrake root. Several more centuries were necessary before some of these mycotoxins would appear again, in the manufacture of antibiotics.[6]

The transcript of the sentencing of a woman accused of witchcraft during the Inquisition in Carcassonne, from 1330 to 1340 (the period in which the term *witch's Sabbath* first came into use), records, "She encountered and greeted a gigantic goat to which she gave herself. In exchange, the goat taught her about venomous plants cooked in a caldron over an evil fire, and poisonous plants. . . . Since that time, she has devoted herself to the preparation of certain noxious ingredients and potions."[7] The 1580 treatise *De la démonomanie des sorciers* by Bodino established a criminal relationship between herbcraft and witchcraft.[8]

That was how herbalists, bonesetters, bards, and druids and priests and priestesses of other faiths, including all those who dared practice herbcraft (for therapeutic, ritu-

6. Ibid., 164–69. See the English short version Antonio Escohotado, *A Brief History of Drugs from the Stone Age to the Stoned Age*, trans. Kent Symington (Rochester, VT: Park Street Press, 1999). See also Dale Pendel, *Pharmako/Dynamis: Stimulating Plants, Potions & Herbcraft* (San Francisco: Mercury House, 2002).

7. Escohotado, *History of Drugs*, 277.

8. Ibid., 358.

alistic, or simply recreational purposes) came to be listed under the category of the "unspeakable" and were persecuted, without any further distinction, for "sorcery." The Inquisition would function as an authority of control and repression as much for the pharmacological knowledge of women belonging to the lower class as for the *potentia gaudendi* generated by the body's metabolism of the chemical composition of these plants, as well as by the discourse and shared knowledge attached to social rituals.

The feminist activist and pagan witch Starhawk argues that the persecution of witches in Europe (and eventually in the American colonies) from 1430 to 1740 was part of a larger process of eradicating knowledge and lower-class power while simultaneously working to reinforce the hegemonic knowledge of the expert, something indispensable to the gradual insertion of capitalism on a global scale.[9]

The *Malleus Maleficarum*, a handbook for the Inquisition and its techniques for extracting knowledge, condemns female sexuality, nonproductive sexuality (anal practices and masturbation), and all experimentation with psychoactive substances.[10] As Starhawk points out, the Inquisition punished aggressiveness and pleasure in women and imposed passivity, submission, and silence on them in the domain of sexual practices.[11] All of it was connected: the emergence of proto-industrial capitalism and its scientific forms of production and transmission of knowledge; the extermination of a part of the population that had

9. Starhawk, *Dreaming the Dark: Magic, Sex, and Politics* (Boston: Beacon Press, 1997), 200–4.

10. Arthur Evans, *Witchcraft and the Gay Counter-Culture* (Boston: Fag Rag Books, 1981).

11. Starhawk, *Dreaming*, 215.

been endowed with pharmacological awareness; the use of racial discourses as religious and biological arguments for enslavement and oppression; the appearance of new methods of segmenting, demarcating, and enclosing land; the raising of livestock that would sustain the future textile industry; colonial expansion in America, Africa, the Indies, and the Far East; and the invention in Europe of servile and pro-slavery models of labor.

Contrary to the generally accepted idea, women did not wait until the twentieth century to become part of the labor market. Their practice of fields of knowledge and their production of wealth were carefully ousted from the circuits of medieval economy so that such exclusion would strengthen early capitalism. Angela Davis has taught us that the "white woman" as mother and housewife is an invention of modern capitalism: the creation of bourgeois concepts of wife and reproductive mother are accompanied by the economic devaluation of the household and the exclusion of housework from the productive sphere.[12]

Starhawk finds a correlation between this economic analysis and the criminalization of witchcraft:

> The Witch persecutions were tied to another of the far-reaching changes in consciousness that occurred during the sixteenth and seventeenth centuries. The rise of professionalism in many arenas of life meant that activities and services that people had always performed for themselves or for their neighbors and families were taken over by a body of paid experts, who were licensed or otherwise recognized as being the guardians of an officially approved and restricted body of knowledge.

12. Angela Y. Davis, *Women, Race, & Class* (New York: Vintage, 1983), 8–12.

The Catholic Church had for centuries served as a model for an approved body that dispensed approved grace. Many of the charges against Witches and heretics can be seen as charges of giving or receiving "Brand X" grace, one that lacked the official seal of approval; of transmitting knowledge without approval. Witches' powers, whether used for harming or for healing, were branded as evil because they came from an unapproved source.[13]

During the medieval period, women were in charge of caring for and healing the body by employing traditional forms of knowledge that were based on the use of herbs in the context of ritualistic practice. Female caregivers, whether scholars or midwives, represented a threat to the professional orders, at the center of which were the new information experts, who would soon be legitimized as scientific, and who included those in the field of medicine. Such members of these orders would organize to form guilds at the beginning of the sixteenth century. Licenses to regulate the exercise of the medical profession were created. These excluded white women and nonwhite people of all genders who were learned in pharmacology.

At the end of the Middle Ages, the drainage of lakes and swamps, the cutting of forests, the fencing of land, the institution of private property for farming and cattle raising worked simultaneously to crush the pagan community, where the mythical forces of the popular imagination and the ecosystem were located, and in which grew those plants and substances used in the "art of witchcraft." From this

13. Starhawk, *Dreaming*, 199.

perspective, the persecution of witches can be interpreted as a war between expert knowledge and the non-professional knowledge of the multitude, a war between white patriarchal power and narcosexual knowledge as it was traditionally practiced by women, colonized peoples, and nonauthorized sorcerers. It became a matter of exterminating or confiscating a certain ecology of body and soul, hallucinogenic treatments, and forms of pleasure or excitation. Modern colonial capitalist knowledge came to pathologize those technologies of subjectification produced by the collective and physical experience of rituals, the process of the transmission of symbols, and the absorption of any hallucinogenic or sexually arousing substances. Using the accusation of heresy and apostasy (denial of God), witch hunts did nothing more than conceal the criminalization of practices of "voluntary intoxication" and sexual and hallucinogenic self-experimentation. It was on this forced oversight that electrical and hormonal modernity would be erected.

SOMATIC FICTIONS: THE INVENTION OF SEX HORMONES

> *The sweet ferment of subjectivity eating away at itself.*
> —PETER SLOTERDIJK[14]

Everything we are today, our way of comprehending ourselves as free, individual, and desiring bodies, begins with printing, the Industrial Revolution, magnetism and its transformation into electricity, rapid transport, long-

---

14. Peter Sloterdijk, *Sphères*, trans. Olivier Mannoni, *Ecumes*, vol. 3 (Paris: Hachette Littératures, 2003), 26.

distance communication, and the organization of the modern city and its territorial grid. It also begins with the displacement of millions of non-white human bodies from Africa to Europe and America as labor and as a reproductive force for capitalism, but also as bodies used to produce pleasure and wealth. It also includes the commercialization of white male bodies as prostheses of wage-earning industrial work; the transformation of the white female body into a reproductive, domestic being; and the changing of the surface of the planet into a single, endless railway . . . In this context dominated by communication, travel, trade, connection, and distribution, it isn't surprising that a growing interest in the circulation of fluids and transmission of information inside the body came to the fore, to create conditions for the invention of hormones as communicating secretions.

From the beginning of the twentieth century to the current day, the processes of the imagining and conceptualizing of hormones, as well as their production techniques, have been carried out using animals and then human guinea pigs, usually coming from the disciplinary institutions to which they had been sent (army, jail, psychiatric hospital, school . . .) or from colonized territories regulated by a new articulation of sovereign (necropolitical) and biopolitical techniques.[15] Bodies of rats, rabbits, chickens, bulls, pigs; the "infrahuman" bodies of "niggers," "nuts," "fairies," "criminals" . . . Our models for gender—which are not only conceptual categories but also embodied somato-political

15. For more about the articulation of sovereign and biopolitical regimes, see Roberto Esposito, *Bios: Biopolitics and Philosophy*, trans. Timothy Campbell (Minneapolis: University of Minnesota Press, 2008), 33–34.

fictions—were manufactured at the crossroads at which human, the supposedly nonhuman, and animal meet. Such a process obviously suggests a complex feedback relationship: human and animal are, as Donna J. Haraway has argued, the technobiocultural results of these practices of discursive materialization, which unite and separate them with the same movement.Once again, this traffic begins in the biological laboratories.

In 1767, the surgeon John Hunter, brother of the famous anatomist William Hunter, performed the autograft tissue transplantation of gonads onto castrated rats, and experimented with the heterograft transplantation of cocks' testicles into the abdominal cavity of hens, which led to his establishing for the first time a relationship between testicles and masculinity.[16] A century later, Arnold Adolf Berthold, a physiologist at the University of Göttingen, engaged in a series of experiments on roosters, removing their testicles and transplanting them onto another place on the body. His treatise, which was published during a period when the notions of "heterosexuality" and "homosexuality" were being invented as clinical concepts, would be one of the first to resort to the heterosexual rhetoric of male superiority and the complementary nature of the sexes, as an explanation for variations in internal secretions.[17] What interests me about this—aside from the heteroscientific caricature created by Berthold's seeing the

16. Jan Bondeson, *A Cabinet of Medical Curiosities* (London: I.B. Tauris, London, 1997), 187.

17. This treatise on anatomy and physiology by Berthold has been abundantly analyzed by such contemporary female readers as Nelly Oudshoorn and Anne Fausto-Sterling, who have underlined the use of gender metaphors within biological narratives. Numerous accounts and critiques of the cultural history of scientific technical practices that led to the invention of hormones as pharmacological artifacts are also available. See Anne Fausto-

roosters given testicles "as warriors sent out in pursuit of the hens" and castrated capons as "languid and peaceloving"—is the way in which an internal secretion is interpreted for the first time as distributed information. His treatise concludes with the necessary condition of a chemical, rather than neuronal, transmission of the information contained in the testicles, since these secretions seem to circulate through the entire body by means of the bloodstream and are not dependent on the location at which the testicles were reimplanted.

Toward the end of the nineteenth century, it seemed probable that the "internal secretions" of certain organs were the origins of physiological processes in different parts of the body.[18] Charles-Edouard Brown-Séquard, the founder of "organotherapy," focused on the sex glands and decided to employ "animal organ extracts" to therapeutic ends. Extracts from testicles, thought Brown-Séquard, could guarantee eternal youthfulness and vigor for men. Similarly, potions containing extracts of guinea pigs' ovaries were used to treat various forms of uterine disease, as well as cases of hysteria.[19] However, the unusual thing about Brown-Séquard, which would place him at the edge of the scientific conventions of the time, is his penchant for self-experimentation and public claims regarding such processes, the way in which he becomes fascinated by the

Sterling, *Sexing the Body: Gender Politics and the Construction of Sexuality* (New York: Basic Books, 2000); Nelly Oudshoorn, *Beyond the Natural Body: an Archeology of Sex Hormones* (New York: Routledge, 1994). See also Chandak Sengoopta, *The Most Secret Quintessence of Life, Sex, Glands and Hormones 1850–1950* (Chicago: University of Chicago Press, 2006), 33–36.

18. Nelly Oudshoorn, "Hormones, technique et corps: L'archéologie des hormones sexuelles 1923–1940," *Annales HSS* 53, no. 4–5 (julliet–octobre 1998): 775–93.

19. Ibid., 779.

increases promised by these extracts and uses his own body as a field for clinical experimentation.

The science historian Chandak Sengoopta reports that in 1889 Brown-Séquard "nearly ruined his hard-won reputation by declaring before an assembly of august scientists in Paris that he had 'rejuvenated' himself by injections of testicular extracts of dogs and guinea pigs."[20] The results, he proclaimed, were "spectacular": a marked gain in vigor and mental lucidity. In addition, he maintained that the female patients to whom he had administered preparations of ground guinea pig ovaries had also experienced physical and mental improvements. Although several doctors reacted to these affirmations with skepticism, organotherapy would become enormously popular. "Within a decade, however, the new treatments fell into disrepute. Brown-Séquard admitted that the effects of his testicular injections were short-lived, probably the result of the power of suggestion."[21]

Brown-Séquard's failed experiment would, however, contribute to the elaboration of a theory on the long-distance transmission of bio-information, in which secretions would for the first time be understood as resembling "chemical messages."[22] A few years later, Edward Schäfer, a professor of physiology at London University College, measured the effects of injecting adrenal, thyroid, pancreas, and liver extracts into the bloodstream. Schäfer recorded, "Every part of the body does, in fact, take up materials from the

---

20. Sengoopta, 36–37. See also, Anne Fausto-Sterling, *Sexing the Body*, 182.
21. Fausto-Sterling, *Sexing the Body*, 149.
22. Ibid., 150.

blood, and does transform these into other materials. Having thus transformed them, they are ultimately returned into the circulating fluids and in that sense every tissue and organ of the body furnishes an internal secretion."[23]

The year is 1905. Freud writes his *Three Essays on the Theory of Sexuality*, and Dr. Ernest Henry Starling and William Bayliss invent the concept of the hormone. While Freud is imagining an invisible geography that he calls "the unconscious"—a virtual space that is both deep within and parallel to the body and in which desire, the affects, and the sexual identity of the subject are at play—science, emerging biotechnology, and disciplinary institutions are taking on subjectivity and sexuality and transforming them into biochemical nodes of technical management. While Freud is inventing sexuality as an entity independent of anatomical sex, Starling and Bayliss are studying human reactions as if they were the effects of substances released from different parts of the body. Their breakthrough was the identification of what they called "secretin," a substance produced by the duodenum that stimulated pancreatic secretion.[24] Secretin will become the paradigm for a new kind of physical functioning that they name *hormone*, from the Greek *horman*, which means to excite, or activate, and which worked, independently from the nervous system, as a *chemical messenger*. As a historian of medicine has noted, "The middle of the nineteenth century finds an awareness of glands that had no ducts, glands that communicated

23. E.A. Schäfer, "On Internal Secretions," *Lancet* (August 10, 1895): 321–24.

24. Icon Group International, *Hormones: Western Timeline History, 1656–1972* (San Diego: ICON Group International, 2009), 6.

only with blood vessels."[25] The paradigm of wireless sex had been established.

Within a European colonial and industrial capitalist context defined by the practices of telecommunication, travel, traffic, and exchange, Starling and Bayliss are conceptualizing hormones according to an early form of information theory: "These chemical messages, or hormones, as they could be called, have to be carried from the organ where they are produced to the organ which they affect by means of the bloodstream and the continually physiological needs of the organism must determine their repeated production and circulation throughout the body."[26] The invention of the notion of "hormone" represents an epistemological break, not only in relation to the modern model of the mechanical body, but also in relation to the emerging psychological model of the sexual unconscious. Whereas Freud is conceptualizing the subject as an archeological terrain of invisible signs, the hidden strata of which have to be revealed by patient linguistic excavation, Starling and Bayliss are sketching a diagram of the modern individual as a silent biochemical communication network, a complex interlacing of densely connected circuits that emit, receive, and decode biochemical information. In opposition both to Descartes's and La Mettrie's mechanical body, and to the Freudian archeology of the ego, appears a new hormonal, electrochemical, media-related, and ultraconnected sub-

25. John Henderson, "Ernest Starling and 'Hormones': an historical commentary," *Journal of Endocrinology* 184 (January 2005): 5–10, doi: 10.1677/joe.1.06000.

26. Ernest Starling, "The Croonian Lectures on the Chemical Correlations of the Functions of the Body" (lecture, the Royal College of Physicians of London; June 20, 22, 27, and 29, 1905), 6.

ject. The modern biopolitical body, as Foucault suggested, is no longer a one-dimensional surface where power, law, and punishment come to be inscribed, but rather a *thick interiority* where life, but also political control, take place in the form of exchange, traffic, and communication.[27] If biopower has to go into and through the body (*passer à l'intérieur du corps*), the space of the body must be extended, inflated, opened up, and magnified to become a communication system. In 1904, Maurice Adolphe Limon gave the name *endocrinology* to the science of internal secretions, defining *interiority* (*endo* means "inside" or "within" in Greek) as a space of intense, yet invisible, chemical traffic.

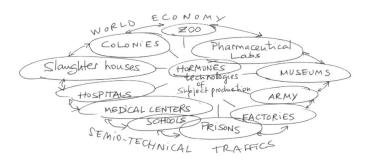

Between 1860 and 1910, the fifty-year period during which the concept of hormone is being elaborated, James Clerk Maxwell announces the existence of radio waves and Heinrich Rudolph Hertz demonstrates that rapid variations of electric currents can be projected into space in the form of waves that resemble those of light or heat, and

27. Michel Foucault, *"Les rapports de pouvoir passent à l'intérieur du corps,"* [1977] in *Dits et Ecrits II* (Paris: Gallimard, 1994), 228–36.

these discoveries permit the invention of the telegraph and the radio. The press and mail delivery are now available to the masses. Hormonal theory represents another form of mass communication—an attempt to conceptualize the body as a system of biocommunication. Endocrinology can be read as the biologization of a theory of broadcasting, distribution, and treatment of information—in a world gradually undergoing globalization. For Starling and Bayliss, hormones are characterized by their capacity for invisible action from a distance: "a substance which has to be turned out into the blood at repeated intervals to produce in some distant organ or organs a physiological response proportional to the dose."[28] Starling described hormones as "carriers" of "chemical messages transported by blood from the organ where they are produced to the organ where they must act."[29] The hormone, then, operates according to a logic of tele-action: the capacity to modify an organ by the emission of biocoded information from some distance away. Conceptualized as a tele-transmitter, the hormone implies transport, distribution, exportation, availability for extradomestic use, outflow, escape, flight, exodus, and exchange; but also reading, decodification, and translation. Similar to the process of writing in Derrida's deconstruction, Starling's and Bayliss's hormone is a biological postcard, a chemical telephone message, a long-distance biocall.[30] It confronts us with a new way of understanding

28. John Henderson, "Ernest Starling and 'Hormones'," 9.
29. Ernst Starling, "The Croonian Lectures on the Chemical Correlations of the Functions of the Body," 6.
30. For a deconstructive theory of the telephone that could respond to this genealogy of hormones see Avital Ronell, *The Telephone Book, Technology, Schizophrenia, Electric Speech* (Lincoln, NE: University of Nebraska Press, 1991).

the production of power and subject, distinct from that suggested by Foucault in his description of the orthopedic and architectonic disciplinary mechanisms of the prison or the panopticon. The tele-cinematic hormonal theory is a biomedia theory, a theory about a form of communication in which the body is no longer just a means of transmission, distribution, and collection of information, but the *material effect* of these semiotechnical exchanges. We have come face to face with a new understanding of space and the body, but also of the production of power and of the subject (both subjugation and subjectification) that, I shall argue, demands a new theory of biopolitics going beyond the one developed by Foucault in *Discipline and Punish* and the *History of Sexuality*. What are the specific practices through which power is spatialized according to endocrinological knowledge and techniques? How do these practices differ from the institutional disciplinary architectures of the hospital and the prison that defined, according to Foucault, nineteenth-century biopolitics?

The apparatus (*dispositif*) of subjectification that we can reconstruct starting with hormonal theory at the beginning of the twentieth century is a collection of institutional and technical networks in which living artifacts are produced, and are given political recognition within a predetermined cultural context.[31] The pharmacopornographic subject will emerge from a techno-scientific-pop apparatus that con-

---

31. In the pharmacopornographic regime, the difference between "apparatus" and human being, as described by Giorgio Agamben, is put into question. On the contrary, the techno-living emerges like an apparatus from a process of techno-political construction; cf. Giorgio Agamben, *"What Is an Apparatus?" and Other Essays*, trans. David Kishik and Stefan Pedatella (Stanford, CA: Stanford University Press, 2009).

nects elements as heterogeneous as slave ships, whale testicles, impotent soldiers, penal institutions, pregnant slaves, biochemical texts, and currency. As Nelly Oudshoorn has emphasized, the emergence of sex endocrinology was characterized by a shift from descriptive, morphological approaches to experimental approaches, which created the need for obtaining new research materials.[32] Claiming that sex hormones were produced and stored in the gonads, endocrinologists and pharmaceutical industries fought to obtain large quantities of ovaries and testicles, both animal and human.

Looking for a solution to the shortage of glandular extracts, Alan Parkes, an English physiologist, obtained blue whale ovaries with the help of the British Museum.[33]

Because whales do not habitually swim near laboratories in the western world, this source was not a structural solution to the problem of scarcity. To gain access to the enormous quantities of required material, scientists had to create new infrastructural arrangements to secure a steady supply of organic matter. The previous arrangements in the laboratory and the clinic were no longer sufficient. To find access to research materials, laboratory scientists and gynecologists had to leave their laboratories and clinics. The most likely places where large quantities of ovaries and testes could be obtained were the slaughterhouses.[34]

32. Nelly Oudshoorn, *Beyond*, 67–68.
33. Ibid., 68.
34. Ibid.

A similar process of glandular expropiation and industrialization was taking place with human animals. Laboratories waited for the execution of men who had received the death penalty in order to collect their testicles.[35]

These new scientific and commercial practices established the first regular trafficking networks of biological materials among gynecologists, laboratory researchers, pharmaceutical industries, prisons, and slaughterhouses. Sex hormones are the result of such traffic. They *are* this traffic. Each time I give myself a dose of testosterone, I agree to this pact. I kill the blue whale; I cut the throat of the bull at the slaughterhouse; I take the testicles of the prisoner condemned to death. I become the blue whale, the bull, the prisoner. I draft a contract whereby my desire is fed by—and retroactively feeds—global channels that transform living cells into capital.

In 1926, this dense trafficking of body fluids, tissues, and organs used in attempts to detect the raw materials that would allow the "manufacture" of hormones led two German gynecologists to suggest that the highest hormonal concentration was found in human urine.[36] This waving of a magic wand debunked the idea of the gonads as the organic medium of hormones and achieved a radical modification of those institutional spaces that had until then held power over sex hormone research. The pharmaceutical firms,

35. On the trafficking of animal and human organs and glands, see David Hamilton, *The Monkey Gland Affair* (London: Chatto & Windus, 1986), and David Hamilton, *A History of Organ Transplantation*, (Pittsburgh: University of Pittsburgh Press, 2012).

36. Hans O. Haterius, "The Female Sex Hormones," *The Ohio Journal of Science* 37, no. 6 (November 1937): 394–407.

which had contracts with the slaughterhouses to obtain testicles or ovaries from animals sacrificed for this purpose, lost their dominant position. The discovery of urine as a reserve of hormones changed power relationships between production groups. Henceforth, gynecological clinics would be first in line for experimental production because it is easy to obtain urine from the bodies of pregnant women. For male urine, the pharmaceutical laboratories turned to nonmedical institutions, places where large concentrations of bioproducer bodies were available: the army, schools, factories, prisons, police stations . . . "In 1931, the German chemist Adolf Butenandt collected 25,000 liters of urine on the premises of the Berlin police stations. From this method, he was able to isolate 50 mg of a crystalline substance that he called 'androsterone,' thinking that it was the male hormone par excellence. This was the first time such a term had been used."[37] The concentration camp (a hybrid of the animal slaughterhouse and the colonial laboratory) would reduce human bodies to biomaterial for research, revealing the inner links between the biopolitical apparatus and necropolitical techniques.[38]

The process of isolating hormones allows us to establish a cartography of sexopolitical disciplinary spaces and locate within them the different institutions where fluids and organs were collected and treated as technical enclaves

---

37. Adolf Butenandt received the Nobel Prize for chemistry in 1939. See Jie Jack Li, *Laughing Gas, Viagra, and Lipitor: The Human Stories behind the Drugs We Use* (New York: Oxford University Press, 2006), 114.

38. See Robert Jay Lifton, *The Nazi Doctors: Medical Killing and the Psychology of Genocide* (New York: Basic Books, 2000).

of gender production. The trafficking of human fluids developed among the different disciplinary institutions of reclusion, which came to share a common system of production of body-capital: the gynecology clinic, hospital, factory, prison, laboratory, pharmaceutical industry, concentration camps . . .

A network of power, knowledge, and capital would determine where and how different fluids, tissues, organs, and bodies circulate, creating differences along gender, sex, race, disability, and class lines. Fluids from women's bodies would also have to move from a disciplinary space that was difficult to reach (the space of domesticity) to spaces to which the mechanisms of public management are strongly attached (the hospital, the gynecology center) only to return later to the supposedly private space of the home where hormones were distributed on a massive scale in the form of the Pill. Racialized bodies on the paths of slavery or extermination and bodies stigmatized as "handicapped" or sexually abnormal would be rapidly inserted into this industrial system of capitalization of the living. A large part of the clinical tests for hormones would therefore be carried out in colonial (for example, the Pill would be mostly tested on Puerto Rico's non-white population) and psychiatric (homosexuals and transsexuals would be declared mentally ill and subjected to violent surgical and hormonal protocols whereas "disabled" bodies would be sterilized[39]) enclaves, as well as among the pregnant populations of penitentia-

---

39. On disability and sterilization see Marsha Saxton, "Disability Rights and Selective Abortion," in Lennard J. Davis, ed. *The Disability Studies Reader*, (New York: Routledge, 2006), 105–16.

ries and other correctional settings, until hormonal technologies could be assimilated by the anonymous masses in domestic spaces and schools.

The epistemological model for the study and production of hormones is built on animal "sex change," even if the actual notion of "transsexuality" does not appear until later, with the works of Magnus Hirschfeld, D. O. Caudwell, and Harry Benjamin: "At the turn of the twentieth century scientists began to search actively for chemical substances in the sex glands using techniques of castration and transplantation. In this surgical approach, scientists removed ovaries and testes from animals like rabbits and guinea-pigs, cut them into fragments, and reimplanted them."[40] The psychological concept of transsexuality popularized by Benjamin in the 1960s ensues—paradoxically—from this game of cut-and-paste on the bodies of non-human animals, even though the notion of "psychological sex" conflicts with the scientific idea of "animality."

After the 1930s, hormonal classification becomes more complex; for the first time, it seems clear that no hormones are specific to one or the other sex, but that all bodies produce both estrogen and testosterone, the difference lying in the variable quantities of this production. Nevertheless, the terminology and technical use of male and female hormones remains the same: sex hormones are defined as *chemical agents* of masculinity and femininity, working as "the missing link between the genetic and the physiological models of sex determination."[41]

40. Oudshoorn, *Beyond*, 19.
41. Ibid., 21.

Hormones, beginning with estrogen and progesterone and followed by testosterone, go from having the status of a molecule to having that of *pharmakon*, from silent chains of carbon to biopolitical entities that can be legally inserted in a human body in a manner that is intentional and deliberate. Hormones are bio-artifacts made of carbon chains, language, images, capital, and collective desires. This is how they will reach me.

POP CONTROL: MODES OF PHARMACOPORNOGRAPHIC SUBJECTIFICATION

Following the gradual change in their consumption since their invention at the end of the 1940s, estrogen and progesterone, the molecular basis for the production of the contraceptive pill, are today the most manufactured synthetic substances in all the pharmaceutical industries of the world; they are also the most employed molecules in the entire history of medicine. The surprising thing is not this massive industrial production of hormones placed under the category of *sexual*, but the fact that these molecules were used primarily, and almost exclusively, on women's bodies, at least until the beginning of the twenty-first century. [42] The fiction of biofemininity, as it is "produced" in the West today, doesn't exist without a whole array of media and biomolecular technologies: "Diagnostic pro-

---

42. On the pharmaceutical management of women's bodies, see Anita Harden, Janita Janssen and Ivan Wolffers, *Marketing Fertility. Women, Menstruation and the Pharmaceutical Industry* (Amsterdam: WEMOS, 1989).

cedures and therapies such as in vitro fertilization (IVF), hormone replacement therapy (HRT), screening programs for breast and cervical cancer, the contraceptive pill, and a wide variety of other contraceptives for women have accentuated the distinct reproductive role of women and thus designated the female body as a natural object of intervention."[43] Cis-females, like hormones, are modern industrial artifacts, techno-organisms from the capitalist-colonial laboratory. This pharmacological imbalance in the production of gender changes after 1998 with the discovery of the side effects on the penis of the molecule sildenafil.[44] In 1969, when French feminist activist Françoise d'Eaubonne invented the term *phallocracy* to refer to the symbolic and political domination of the penis in Western culture, she couldn't have imagined that this same penis would become the object of intense surveillance and that it would quickly find itself at the center of a rise in pharmacopornographic normalization. Between the middle of the twentieth century, when David O. Caudwell, Harry Benjamin, and John Money experimented with the effects of sex hormones on genital response to excitation, and the beginning of the twenty-first, when the laboratories Pfizer, Bayer, and Lilly, using the names Viagra, Levitra, or Cialis, quarreled over the commercialization of a vasodilator molecule that can prompt a lasting erection, masculinity ceased to be an exclusive preserve of natural privilege and became a domain of capitalization and biopolitical engineering. At

43. Nelly Oudshoorn, *The Male Pill: A Biography of a Technology in the Making* (Durham, NC: Duke University Press, 2003), 4.

44. On the pharmacological use of sildenafil, see Meika Loe, *The Rise of Viagra: How the Little Blue Pill Changed Sex in America* (New York: New York University Press, 2006).

the same time, male impotence went from being a shameful private affair to being a health condition. As a pharmaceutical product, the sildenafil molecule has enjoyed the fastest takeoff ever recorded for a new drug.[45] The social anxiety and economic speculation that have sprung up around the penis during the first decade of the new millennium are without precedent. Today, instead of using the term *phallocracy*, it makes more sense to speak of *phallocontrol*—referring to that collection of pharmacopornographic mechanisms struggling to design the frontiers of the new technomasculinity. The time of female monopoly over victimization is drawing to a close; we are entering an era in which the technomolecular control of sex, gender, and sexuality will extend to everything and everyone. The twenty-first century will be the century of the production and pharmacopornographic control of masculinity. Viagra and testosterone are currencies of that new molecular production.

Hormonal research has been characterized historically by a second biopolitical imbalance: pharmacological interest in testicles and male hormone supported the normative representation of men's bodies, associating testosterone from the start with youth, strength, sexual desire, vigor, and vital energy; conversely, research projects on hormones considered to be female were aiming only to control women's sexuality and their capacity for reproduction. Masculinity is still produced according to a model of sovereign patriarchal power, whereas femininity is regulated according to a set of biopolitical techniques intended to control

45. B. Handy, "The Viagra Craze," *Time* 151 (May 4, 1998): 39.

the reproduction of the nation's population in hygienic and eugenic terms, enforcing the reduction of "deviancy" understood in terms of class, race, sexuality, sickness, and disability.[46]

In both cases, the objective is the normalization and capitalization of the living. On one side, Viagra works as a normative molecular prosthesis that comes to repair the nonerectile male body considered as sperm producer. On the other side, women's bodies are still constructed by the pharmacopornographic regime as a public reproductive system (womb, reproductive cells, vagina, placenta . . . understood as "public goods" and research materials) at the service of the national interest.

There is no universal human body, but a multiplicity of gendered, racialized, and sexualized living beings and organic tissues. Within modern capitalism, male and female hormones and organs don't have the same biopolitical value. As Nelly Oudshoorn observes:

> With the introduction of the concept of sex hormones, scientists explicitly linked women's reproductive functions with laboratory practice. The study of women as the Other was thus extended from the clinic to the laboratory and thereby firmly rooted in the heart of life sciences. . . . This asymmetry in the institutionalization of female and male reproductive bodies in medicine prevailed until well into the second half of the twentieth century. It was only in the late 1970s that the scientists and clinicians

46. For a critical reading of biopolitical regulations, see Lennard J. Davis, "Constructing Normalcy: The Bell Curve, the Novel, and the Invention of the Disabled Body in the Nineteenth Century," in *The Disability Studies Reader*, ed. Lennard J. Davis (New York: Routledge, 1997), 9–28.

established andrology as a medical specialty devoted to the study and medical treatment of male reproductive bodies.[47]

A brief genealogy of surgical practices reveals this biopolitical asymmetry. Beginning in 1870, the ablation of ovaries became a standard operation for curing certain "menstrual disturbances and various mental illnesses ascribed to the ovaries."[48] On the other hand, the ablation of testicles was a technique reserved for penal castrations (practiced, for example, in the United States on black subjects accused of having raped white women),[49] used for the eugenic treatment (both surgical and chemical) of "maniacs" and the "mentally retarded" and for therapy for "sexual psychopaths." The biopolitical techniques of castration remained at a distance from the white, male, middle-class heterosexual body; its masculinity, as well as its organic enclaves—testicles and penis—were the embodiment of sovereign power and could not be simply uprooted.[50]

At the beginning of the twentieth century, the pharmaceutical industry became interested for the first time in the production of preparations from ovarian extracts for the treatment of hysteria and infertility in cis-females, as well as testicular extracts of animal origin for the treatment of

47. Oudshoorn, *Male Pill*, 6.

48. Harold Speert, *Obstetrics and Gynecology: A History and Iconography* (New York: Informa Healthcare, 2004), 407.

49. The foundations of penal castration for sex crimes are linked as much to the production of race as to that of gender; see Davis, "Rape, Racism, and the Myth of the Black Rapist," chap. 11 in *Women, Race & Class*.

50. See Piotr O. Scholz, *Eunuchs and Castrati: A Cultural History* (Princeton, NJ: Marcus Weiner Publishers, 2001); Gary Taylor, *Castration: An Abbreviated History of Western Manhood* (New York: Routledge, 2002).

impotence or sexual fatigue. During World War I, German laboratories were pioneers in experiments on dogs using derivatives of animal testosterone, but also on human bodies. In the 1930s, the laboratory Schering AG carried out the harvesting and conversion of urine; and after the 1960s, this laboratory would become the leader in the production and marketing of the contraceptive pill Yasmin.

After World War II, infectious diseases in wealthy countries fell behind illnesses related to aging, the management of sexuality, the modification of affect and mind control, and the regulation of reproduction and the body's immune system in highly toxic environments. This is the point at which the production and commercialization of synthetic hormones unveil their true pharmacopornographic function.

Testosterone bursts onto the sports scene after 1950. John Ziegler's laboratories in Germany produce Dianabol (an oral variant of anabolic steroids that is not very effective because stomach enzymes can destroy testosterone molecules) and Methandrosterolone (the injectable, more effective variant) to supplement the American weightlifting team for the Olympic Games. After the 1960s, anabolic steroids enter the pharmaceutical market, along with growth hormone, and become the molecular hardware of such well-known users as Arnold Schwarzenegger and Sergio Oliva. From then on, all steroids, testosterone, anabolics, and so on, will be sold on the medical pharmaceutical market as well as on other markets, open or black. Contemporary men live in technotesto times.

THE EDIBLE PANOPTICON

During the period when the notion of gender, the H-bomb, silicone breast implants, electric prostheses, the computer, and Formica furnishings begin circulating in Western societies, a pioneering domestic, portable, and consumable nanotechnology of hormonal modification is produced. In 1951, a mistake made by Gregory Pincus at G. D. Searle and Company laboratories leads to the invention of the first contraceptive pill in the form of the molecule norethindrone, a synthetic variant of the active molecule progesterone that can be administered orally. The production of a portable and edible contraceptive pill enables the entrance of synthetic hormones (and therefore endocrinological and governmental birth control techniques) into the domestic space, which becomes a consumption/production knot within the pharmacological network. This is part of a larger biopolitical process of the medicalization and pharmacological regulation of domesticity that was already at work earlier in the twentieth century.

At the farthest boundary of the same traffic, moving from the domestic to the colony, endocrinological programs for controlling natality and gender production were targeting the racialized body, circulating first within the slavery trade and later within urban segregated spaces, as well as the "disabled," or the "sexually deviant." As we will see, most clinical trials with sexual hormones are done in colonial settings, in psychiatric institutions (where homosexual, intersexual, and transsexual bodies, regarded as physical or mentally ill, are submitted to endocrinological and surgical procedures), and in penitentiaries and correctional institutions until hormones, produced and designed as consumption goods, end up being absorbed into the everyday American heterosexual domestic space.

There is a Pill geography where bodies, fluids, molecules, and capital are produced and distributed. An examination of the economic and technical networks that resulted in the production of the Pill reveals that, while originating with Pincus's project, the Pill was perfected by John Rock within the unexpected framework of experimental research on aiding procreation for sterile white Catholic families.[51] Pincus's and Rock's research projects, although conflicting in relation to their vision of the function of white women in society, shared an understanding of nonwhite and deviant subjects as bodies whose reproductive power should be restricted by the state in order to "reduce hunger, poverty, and disease while fostering economic stability."[52] The antibaby molecule was intended to be made into a "simple, cheap, safe contraceptive to be used in poverty-stricken slums, jungles, and among the most ignorant people."[53] In the context of an emerging politicization of racial, ethnic, and sexual minorities in the United States, the contraceptive molecule was thought of as an urban eugenic device and as a method of controlling nonwhite population growth, as

---

51. For the invention of the Pill, see Marks, *Sexual Chemistry*, 89–137. See also Tone, *Devices*, 203–85.
52. Tone, *Devices*, 207.
53. Margaret Sanger's declarations quoted by Tone, *Devices*, 207.

well as the population growth of nations that had not yet entered postwar liberal capitalist economies.

Protocols of research and evaluation of the Pill's technical effectiveness reveal its disciplinary and colonial roots. After the success of the preliminary Boston trials for the Pill in 1954 and 1955, John Rock and Gregory Pincus needed a large-scale human group to test the new molecule in order to receive approval from the US Food and Drug Administration, or FDA, to bring the drug to market. The first large clinical contraceptive pill trials were performed by Searle on several groups of female psychiatric patients at Worcester State Hospital and on male prison inmates in the state of Oregon in 1956–57. The tests were intended to measure the effectiveness of using synthetic oral hormones as a method of birth control in women, and also the effectiveness of these substances in controlling and decreasing "homosexual tendencies" in men.[54] In fact, the relationship between hormonal research and the Worcester State Hospital was crucial for the development of the Pill. Founder and feminist activist Katherine McCormick had decided to invest in research on the Pill in order to fight the hereditary transmission of mental illness.[55] Her husband was diagnosed with schizophrenia, and since at that time the illness was considered hereditary, she tried to locate a safe way of preventing pregnancy in people suffering from the condition who were potential parents. In 1944, the McCormicks helped Dr. Hudson Hoagland found the Worcester Foun-

54. Tone, *Devices*, 220.

55 See Armond Fields, *Katharine Dexter McCormick: Pioneer for Women's Rights* (Westport, CT: Praeger, 2003), 115.

dation for Experimental Biology, dedicated to the study of the influence of hormones on mental conditions, and this transformed the Worcester Hospital into a major pharmacological laboratory.

Constructed in 1833 following the Thomas S. Kirkbride plan, also known as the "building as cure" theory, according to which architecture itself was meant to have a therapeutic effect, the Worcester State Hospital in Massachusetts was one of the most prestigious institutions of its time, well known for having been visited by Freud in 1909 when he traveled to the United States. The Worcester State Hospital was the American version of the modern *machine à guérir* (cure machine), to use the expression coined by Jacques-René Tenon in his *Mémoires sur les hôpitaux de Paris* (1788), which Michel Foucault used as the key document in his study of the emergence of a new set of techniques of "public hygiene" that came to spatialize the sick body within the modern city.[56] As Foucault argued, after the end of the eighteenth century, the modern hospital and the prison became the paradigmatic architectures of a pervasive medicalization of social and political space. A visual and spatial machinery to produce knowledge about madness and reason, the Worcester Hospital combined prison architecture with large collective rooms and numerous workshops for experimental treatment, such as saunas and rotating chairs

56. René Tenon, *Mémoires sur les hôpitaux de Paris* (Paris: Doin, 1998). This text was originally published in Paris in 1788. A similar plan was also at work in the projects by Bernard Poyet and C.P. Coquéau. For a discussion of these hospital projects, see Colin Jones and Michael Sonenscher, "The Social Functions of the Hospital in Eighteenth-Century France: The Case of the Hôtel-Dieu of Nîmes," *French Historical Studies* 13, no. 2 (Autumn 1983).

intended to cure patients. Whereas the architecture and the treatment were still derived from the nineteenth-century disciplinary biopolitical model for understanding madness and therapy, the hospital also introduced within its walls new "soft" and molecular techniques invented during the Cold War period. But mental and prison institutions where not ideal settings for testing the Pill.

The Worcester and Oregon trials were not enough to obtain approval from the FDA to commercialize the Pill or to test the ability of ordinary women to take the Pill regularly outside medical institutions. Since strong anti–birth control laws in Massachusetts and in many other states made it impossible for Searle to conduct the large study of humans required by the FDA, it turned to Puerto Rico, which already had a long history of governmental birth control programs. The pseudocolonial island of Puerto Rico became the most important clinical site for testing the Pill outside the national disciplinary institutions of the asylum and the prison and functioned as a parallel, life-sized biopolitical pharmacological laboratory and factory during the late 1950s and early 1960s. During the Cold War period, Puerto Rico would become the United States' biggest pharmacological backyard. The island was the invisible factory behind the Playboy mansion and the white liberated middle-class American housewife.

In 1955, American physician Edris Rice-Wray, the medical director of the Puerto Rican Family Planning Association, already working with Searle, offered Pincus the possibility of conducting the Pill trials at Rio Piedras, a suburb of San Juan where a new housing project had been set up as part of a slum clearance campaign. In the summer of 1955, Pincus visited Puerto Rico and immediately decided that the Rio Piedras housing was the perfect location for a large-population, long-term Pill trial.

The general features of legally enforced pharmacological experimentation in an environment of imposed isolation spread from Europe and North America to colonial and postcolonial regions, transforming the design models of their penal and medical institutions.[57] Puerto Rico was a paradigmatic case of transition from the colonial regime to postcolonial economic and political control. At the end of the nineteenth century, the Spanish colonial regime left the island overpopulated and in extreme poverty. After the end of the anticolonial war of 1898, the island became a US territory. Already in 1917, the Puerto Rican ruling classes and the American government, inspired by neo-Malthusianism ideas, had drawn up the first population control plan for the island. In 1925, in the overpopulated slums of Ponce, Dr. José A. Lanause Rolón founded the Birth Control League, built on an educational program.[58] These early birth control programs understood sterilization as a safe means of reduc-

57. About disciplinary techniques in colonial settings, see Satadru Sen, *Disciplining Punishment: Colonialism and Convict Society in the Andaman Islands* (New York: Oxford University Press, 2000); Ian Duffield, "From Slave Colonies to Penal Colonies: The West Indians Transported to Australia," *Slavery and Abolition* 7, no. 1 (1986): 24–45. Imperial authorities also imposed racial quarantines between colonial settlers and indigenous people. See Barbara Bush, *Imperialism, Race, and Resistance: Africa and Britain, 1919–1945* (New York: Routledge, 1999); D.T. Goldberg, *Racist Culture: Philosophy and the Politics of Meaning* (Oxford, UK: Basil Blackwell, 1993), 3; Sheldon Watts, *Epidemics and History: Disease, Power, and Imperialism* (New Haven, CT: Yale University Press, 1997).

58. About Puerto Rico as experimental colonial site for contraception techniques, see Annette B. Ramirez de Arellano and Conrad Seipp, *Colonialism, Catholicism, and Contraception: A History of Birth Control in Puerto Rico* (Chapel Hill, NC: University of North Carolina Press, 1983).

ing natality and "cleansing" the slums, where reduction of population was to be a first step followed by urban modernization and the development of employment, to transform agrarian Puerto Rico into an industrial economy. In fact, Puerto Rico was not a stranger to forced sterilizations. As early as 1907, the United States had instituted public policy that gave the state the right "to sterilize unwilling and unwitting people." By 1936, there were more than one hundred birth control clinics operating on the island under federal law. As Katherine Krase has argued, in order to "catalyze economic growth" and respond to "depression-era unemployment," in 1937 the "Eugenics Board" passed Law 136, an event that signified the institutionalization of these population control programs and the legalization of sterilization techniques. "Both U.S. government funds and contributions from private individuals supported the initiative."[59] Laws similar to Law 136 were passed in thirty states. These policies identified the "insane," the "feeble-minded," the "dependent," and the "diseased" as incapable of regulating their own reproductive abilities, thereby justifying government-imposed sterilizations. Legitimizing sterilization for certain groups led to further exploitation, as group divisions were made along race, class, and disability lines.[60]

From the beginning of the experimental trials with hormones, the challenge was how to switch from animals

59. Katherine Krase, "Birth Control—Sterilization Abuse," *Our Bodies Ourselves*, accessed December 3, 2011, http://www.ourbodiesourselves.org/book/companion. asp?id=18&compID=55. Originally published in *Newsletter of the National Women's Health Network* (January/February 1996).

60. Ibid.

to human subjects confined to institutions and finally to the general population. As McCormick infamously said, in stressing the connection between imprisonment and scientific control, the key issue was to find a "cage of ovulating females": "Human females are not easy to investigate as are rabbits in cages. The latter can be intensively *controlled all the time*, whereas the human females leave town at unexpected times so cannot be examined at a certain period; and they also forget to take the medicine sometimes—in which case the whole experiment has to begin over again, —for scientific accuracy must be maintained or the resulting data are worthless." (emphasis in text)[61] For Pincus, the island of Puerto Rico offered the most accessible and most easily monitored population pool that McCormick could ever want: the island itself was already a hermetic cage. Puerto Rican women were considered to be not only as docile as laboratory animals, but also as poor and uneducated and therefore an exemplary group: if they could follow the regimen involved in taking the Pill, any white American woman could do the same. The island of Puerto Rico itself was treated as an extended, nonwhite, female body to which the Pill was administered in terms of what Foucault called "urban therapeutics."[62]

As historians of medicine Jordan Goodman, Anthony

61. Katherine McCormick, quoted in Lara Mark "A 'Cage of Ovulating Females.' The History of the Early Oral Contraceptive Pill Clinical Trials, 1950–1959," in *Molecularizing Biology and Medicine: New Practices and Alliances, 1910s–1970s*, eds. Soraya de Chadarevian and Harmke Kamminga (Amsterdam: Harwood Academic Publishers, 1998), 208.

62. Michel Foucault, "Le pouvoir psychiatrique (1974)," in *Dits et Écrits* (Paris: Gallimard, 2001), 1, 1543–54. Here Foucault studies the spatialization of the psychiatric power outside of the hospital.

McElligot, and Lara Marks have shown, Puerto Rico's trials are not an exception but rather belong to a larger history of colonial and hygienist scientific experimentation
involving humans that occurred during the twentieth century: "Doctors and biohygenists became the determinators
of a bioracially constituted state; they saw themselves as
its gatekeepers and guardians, programmed with the mission to secure a utopian healthy society."[63] However, after
World War II, with the scandals of Nazi medicine and the
Nuremberg Code,[64] the role of the state in pharmacological and medical experimentation became less clearly visible,
as this experimentation moved from state institutions to
industrial pharmacological companies. As part of a larger
mutation from a disciplinary to a pharmacopornographic
regime, "research became 'de-centered' as it became more
commercialized, and moved beyond the immediate sphere
of the state or state-related agencies and transcended
national borders, borne on the wings of multinational corporations."[65] The birth control programs tested in Puerto
Rico clearly show the complicity between national eugenic
programs and private pharmacological interests before the
war and the transition from the colonial and state model
to the postcolonial and neoliberal multinational model of
drug production and population control after the 1940s.

63. Jordan Goodman, Anthony McElligot and Lara Marks, eds., *Useful Bodies: Humans in the Service of Medical Science in the Twentieth Century* (Baltimore: John Hopkins University Press, 2003), 5.

64. See George J. Annas and Michael A. Grodin, eds., *The Nazi Doctors and the Nuremberg Code: Human Rights in Human Experimentation* (New York: Oxford University Press, 1992).

65. Goodman, McElligot, and Marks, eds., *Useful Bodies*, 13.

From the Colonial Brothel to the Pharmacopornographic Lab

In the past few years, several historical essays have developed a postcolonial reading of the relationship between space, prostitution, gender, and race on the island of Puerto Rico. Radost Rangelova has argued that in Puerto Rico, the relationship between gender and space has been historically and socially contingent on colonial domination, the legacy of slavery, and racial purification of the nation.[66] We can conclude from studies by Eileen Suárez Findlay, Vázquez Lazo, and Laura Briggs on the history of prostitution in Puerto Rico before World War II that, beginning with the early years of colonization, the island functioned as a pornotopic colonial site and later became a post- and neocolonial site of pharmacological development.[67] Although colonially promoted from the time of Carlos I, prostitution entered the realm of legal, medical, and media discourse during the nineteenth century as female slavery turned into domestic and sex labor.[68] Conforming to the ideas of such European theorists as William Acton and Parent Duchâtelet, the management of spaces of prostitution within the island became a medical as well as colonial task that "enjoined a sharp geographic separation between *gente*

66. See Radost A. Rangelova, "House, Factory, Beauty Salon, Brothel: Space, Gender and Sexuality in Puerto Rican Literature and Film," (PhD dissertation, the University of Michigan, 2009).

67. Laura Briggs, "Familiar Territory: Prostitution, Empires, and the Question of U.S. Imperialism in Puerto Rico, 1849–1916," in *Families of a New World: Gender, Politics, and State Development in a Global Context*, eds. Lynne Haney and Lisa Pollard (New York: Routledge, 2003), 40–63; Eileen Suárez Findlay, *Imposing Decency: The Politics of Sexuality and Race in Puerto Rico, 1870–1920* (Durham, NC: Duke University Press, 2000); Nieve de los Ángeles Vázquez Lazo, *Meretrices: La prostitución en Puerto Rico de 1876 a 1917* (Hato Rey, Puerto Rico: Publicaciones Puertorriqueñas, 2008).

68. Briggs, "Familiar Territory," 58.

decente and prostitutes,"[69] implementing a double process of inclusionary exclusion and spatialization of difference as techniques of urban formation.

For Rangelova, the traditional European and North American segregation of spaces according to gender (private/public, domestic/nondomestic) and sexuality (places for family and places for prostitution) was reorganized in Puerto Rico according to a colonial logic that separated reproductive spaces from prostitutional spaces in terms of race. Black and poor working-class women were often represented as prostitutes, being excluded from the nineteenth-century autonomist narrative of the *"gran familia* of Puerto Rico."[70] Kept separate from the "white" and the "mother" figure, poor nonwhite women were not understood as bodies for the reproduction of the nation, but rather as "deviants" (*elementos divergentes*) to be medically and legally monitored. Poor nonwhite women were first redefined and managed as potential sex workers. The same bodies would later be the object of contraception management and experimentation, enabling an unexpected transformation from colonial brothel to pharmacopornographic laboratory.

As was the case for the early theories of Restif de la Bretonne and Parent Duchâtelet regarding the construction of the utopian state-brothel in Europe, Puerto Rico's policies associated disease, delinquency, and the presence

---

69. Ibid., 59.
70. Findlay, *Imposing Decency*, 12.

of female sexuality within public spaces. But in Puerto Rico, the biopolitical configuration of urban space in the island's principle cities, Ponce and San Juan, was determined by the complex crossing of gender and class categories with colonial constructions of race. Thus, nonwhite marginal women were the object of a network of disciplinary institutions; hospitals (where gynecological exams took place twice a week), prisons, and brothels (within "zones of tolerance") created a penal closed-circuit network of control intended to remove the black sexual female body from the public space, as well as to regulate the nonwhite female's reproductive system. According to Rangelova, "Space was the main axis along which women's bodies and the practice of prostitution were regulated, restricted and controlled."[71] Vázquez Lazo provides numerous examples of this spatial control developed by the 1890 Reglamento de Higiene Pública, which divided prostitutes into three main topopolitical categories, depending on the type of house in which they practiced prostitution.[72] Segregation was simultaneously meant to be a preventive, protective, and therapeutic technique. According to this segmentation of space, the residence of prostitutes was not considered "domestic," since it was not to be a site for the reproduction of family and nation, but rather a "brothel," meaning a space that the government could inspect, control, and govern. This regulation of sexual spaces dismantled the traditional public and private divisions of the domestic space and reconstructed the nonwhite working class and impoverished domestic space

71. Rangelova, "House, Factory, Beauty Salon," 255.
72. Ibid.

as a site that would be ready for absorption by liberal and pharmacological companies after World War II. In Puerto Rico, the colonial and national state brothel was mutating into a pharmacopornographic heterotopia. The racial and sexual zoning of spaces that had occurred previously would provide the ideal site for the testing of contraceptives.

The Pharmacological Industrialization of the Domestic

In the 1930s, the process of excluding and monitoring nonwhite female sexuality and reproduction in Puerto Rico went from techniques of control used in medical and prison settings into several active eugenics programs, such as Law 136, which for the first time authorized sterilization for other than medical reasons. Between 1933 and 1939, a large network of maternity hospitals and sterilization and birth control clinics were established on the island. A liberal eugenics law, the network of birth control clinics, and the possibility of combining clinical trials with housing development and inexpensive labor for American companies and pharmacological industries made Puerto Rico the ideal setting for the Pill trials, which were the largest series of clinical tests ever performed.

In 1948, the US government, with the support of the local government under Luis Muñoz Marín, began "Operation Bootstrap," which aimed to encourage rapid industrialization on the island.[73] Puerto Rico offered tax exemptions,

73. For more about gender production, space, and labor transformation in Puerto Rico, see Alice Colón Warren, "The Feminization of Poverty among Women in Puerto Rico and Puerto Rican Women in the Middle Atlantic Region of the United States" *Brown Journal of World Affairs* 5, no. 2 (1998): 262–82; Luz del Alba Acevedo, "*Género, trabajo asalariado y desarrollo industrial en Puerto Rico: la división sexual del trabajo en la manufactura*," in *Género*

low-cost labor, and differential rental rates to encourage US industrial facilities to settle there. As a result, in a few years the island's economy shifted from colonial labor-intense agrarian industries, such as those of tobacco and sugar, to pharmaceutical, chemical, and electronics production. In a period of twenty years, Puerto Rico became the biggest bio-chemical and pharmaceutical laboratory in North America.

Access to contraceptive techniques was, in fact, designed as a component of a larger project involving hous-ing, urban modernization, and industrialization on the island. Control of reproduction and modern housing were, according to the American government, the two major forces that could guarantee the improved standard of living in Puerto Rico. The main location for the first contracep-tive trial, begun in 1955, was a G. D. Searle and Company clinic located in El Fanguito (often shown in US documents as El Fangitto, "the little mud hole"), the "worst slum" on the island, located just outside San Juan. Soon it would be razed in order to build a mass-produced planned commu-nity with "functionalist, seven-story residential buildings with running water and sunny balconies." Mass-produced single-family houses also were built by federal programs in Delano and in other villages: they were low-priced versions of white middle-class American suburban houses, closer to military housing units and the spaces and living conditions of the residential ghettos of the Chicago Black Belt than to

y trabajo: La industria de la aguja en Puerto Rico y el Caribe Hispánico, ed. María del Carmen Baerga (San Juan, Puerto Rico: Editorial de la Universidad de Puerto Rico, 1993), 161–212.

the Levittown model. Nevertheless, as Lara Marks argues, "Many of these families highly prized their new accommodation and were therefore unlikely to move away during the course of the trial. This would make them easy to monitor."[74] The Pill trials were a biopolitical program of "modernizing" life that extended to the transformation of the family house, but also to sexuality and reproduction. With its strict spatial partitioning, the "modern" home became the site in which to reproduce the "American way of life," but also a site of reproductive surveillance. The El Fanguito housing program was the "cage of ovulating females" that McCormick dreamed of and that Searle needed to transform its molecule into a commercial drug. As part of the same urban development, several American pharmacological companies built factories on the island, transforming the same women who at night were testing the oral contraceptives at home into factory workers during the day.

In 1956, when the trials were initiated, the pill selected for use was Enovid, Searle's brand name for a synthetic oral progesterone—a white pill that came in an ordinary glass bottle and that women had to take on a regular basis according to a strict timetable:

> When taking the medication, the women were expected to swallow tablets every day (about one every six or eight hours) between the fifth and twenty-fifth day of their cycle. A number of women also had to inject themselves with the compound or insert it as a vaginal suppository.

74. Lara Marks, "Parenting the Pill: Early Testing of the Contraceptive Pill," in *Bodies of Technology*, eds. Ann Rudinow Saetnan, Nelly Oudshoorn and Marta Kirejezyk (Columbus, OH: Ohio State University, 2000), 157.

Each woman had to take her own basal temperature readings and vaginal smears on a daily basis. All this data had
to be marked on a chart. The women also had to collect
urine over a forty-eight-hour period on the seventh and
eighth postovulatory days for hormone analysis. Often
the only way to collect urine over such a period would
have confined women to their homes where they were
near a toilet.[75]

Given the high rates of illiteracy among women in Rio Piedras, compliance with the instructions and data collecting
had to be ensured by regular visits from social workers, who
moved daily from house to house collecting fluids, recording information, and encouraging women's cooperation
with the pharmacological regimen—a practice that forced
women to stay at home (when not at the factory) so they
could be easily contacted by the social workers.

The most important difference between the Pill trials conducted at Rio Piedras by Searle and previous clinical pharmacological trials lay not in the substance but in
the space where they were performed: the Pill trials were
the first clinical tests to be externalized outside medical
and pharmacological institutions and to take place in the
domestic environment. It was Edris Rice-Wray, medical
director of the trials, together with Rock and Pincus, who
decided to use the housing program of El Fanguito as a
home setting for the trial. Having the women take the Pill
at home not only reduced the institutional cost of the trials
but also placed the subjects within the domestic context of

75. Ibid., 161.

ordinary life, thus extending the scope of the trial outside medical institutions: every private home could potentially become an experimental site. The El Fanguito housing complex became an externalized and extended domestic pharmaceutical laboratory.

The high doses of progesterone determined by Searle, to ensure that no pregnancies occurred during the trial, rapidly proved that the hormonal oral contraceptive was extremely reliable. By 1958, because a large part of the population participated in the trial, the birth rate in Puerto Rico had begun to decline. In the early 1960s, other pharmacological companies, such as Synthex (and its ten-milligram pill Orthonovum) and Wyeth Pharmaceutical (Norgestrel and Mestranol) came to the island and extended the trials.[76] Meanwhile, the Pill trials had also moved to other pseudocolonial locations, such as Haiti, where Dr. Rice-Wray had initiated a new Searle trial as early as 1957, and Mexico, where Syntex launched a new trial for the Norlutin pill. In most cases the strategy was the same: using housing modernization as a way of installing a micropharmaceutical laboratory within the domestic environment.

A transversal analysis of geopolitical and institutional spaces, as well as of the racial, sexual, and gender implications of the uses of the first molecules of estrogen and progesterone, extend our definition of the Pill beyond that of being a simple method for managing births to include, also and most important, a new *pharmacodomestic tech-*

76. As Puerto Rican physician and advocate against eugenics Helen Rodríguez-Trias has shown, a strong social and political reaction against the Pill trials had started on the island as early in 1964. Apart from the trials, and as a result of the application of Law 136, by 1969, 35 percent of Puerto Rican women had been sterilized.

nique for (re-)producing race, a form of neocolonial bio-technological eugenics for controlling the reproduction of the species.[77] From this perspective, the Pill functions as a semiotic-material element (in its incarnations as both molecule and discourse, machine and organic substance) in the hegemonic racial and sexual grammar of Western culture, obsessed, as Donna J. Haraway has argued, by the contamination of lineage, the purity of race, the separation of the sexes, and the control of gender.[78]

From the time of the Worcester Hospital and the Puerto Rico trials, the Pill has functioned as a technique not only for controlling reproduction but also for producing and controlling gender and race. Although the Pill was an effective form of birth control, the FDA rejected the first version invented by Pincus and Rock in 1951 and tested at Puerto Rico from 1956 on, because the agency's scientific committee felt it threw doubt on the femininity of American women by suppressing their periods altogether. FDA standards led to Searle's production of a second pill, commercialized in 1959, that was equally effective but could, unlike the first, technologically reproduce the rhythms of a natural menstrual cycle, inducing bleeding that created the illusion of a natural cycle's taking place and somehow "mimicking the normal physiological cycle."[79] The Pill forces us to extend

---

77. For more on the Pill and racial purification, see Dorothy Roberts, *Killing the Black Body: Race, Reproduction, and the Meaning of Liberty* (New York: Vintage, 1998).

78. For more on "purity" as the target of technobiopower, see Haraway, *Modest_Witness*, 78–82.

79. Anna Glasier, "Contraception, Past and Future," *Nature Cell Biology* 4 (October 2002): s4, doi: 10.1038/ncb-nm-fertilityS3.

Judith Butler's concept of gender performativity from theatrical imitation and linguistic "performative force" to *living mimicry*, the technical imitation of the very materiality of the living being, the pharmacopornographic production of somatic fictions of femininity and masculinity. I will call this process *biodrag*, in reference to the culture and practices of drag, drag queens, and drag kings, and define it as the pharmacopornographic production of somatic fictions of femininity and masculinity. What is being represented and imitated technically by the Pill is already no longer a sartorial code or a physical style, but a biological process: the menstrual cycle.

The process of feminization as it is linked to the production, distribution, and consumption of the Pill reveals that hormones are sexopolitical fictions, technoliving metaphors that have the capacity to be swallowed and digested, absorbed and incorporated. They are pharmacopornographic artifacts that can create physical formations that become integrated with vaster political organisms such as our medico-legal institutions, the nation-states, or global networks through which capital circulates.

PACKAGING DISCIPLINARY ARCHITECTURE: DIALPAK AND THE INVENTION OF THE EDIBLE PANOPTICON

Following the Puerto Rico trials, in 1957 the FDA approved the use of Searle's Enovid for the treatment of menstrual irregularities and—two years later—for birth control. Nevertheless, Puerto Rican women's resistance to following instructions caused Searle to suspect that commercialization for American women could be difficult without pharmacological control. Although highly efficient, the routine of taking hormonal pills seemed almost impossible to control outside the pharmacological housing programs: never before had a pharmacological product depended so much on disciplining the patient in a domestic setting. As we shall see, the invention of a domestic, portable dispenser for the Pill in the early 1960s would answer this need for self-surveillance and discipline.

Originally, Enovid was commercialized in two doses, ten milligrams and five milligrams, and like all prescriptions for the Pill at the time, it was filled in a small bottle. Oral contraceptive hormones entered the American middle-class domestic environment in a brown glass container, but without the pedagogical regime of the Rio Piedras pharmacological-housing complex, any mistake in the intake timetable could cause what Enovid was trying to prevent. Instructions for taking the Pill seemed straightforward: the user was supposed to take the first tablet on the fifth day of menstruation, continue with one tablet every day for twenty days, and then stop; she would begin menstruating in two to three days, and on the fifth day of menstruation she was to start another twenty-day cycle of tablets. But the brown bottle in no way aided memorizing or controlling the intake routine.

In 1962, Illinois engineer David P. Wagner (whose background was in developing new fasteners for Illinois Tool Works) created an early prototype dispenser for the Pill, three round plastic plates held together by a snap fastener, to divide his wife's monthly pill supply into daily doses.[80] Wagner explained the process of producing the dispenser: "With just a ¼" electric drill, a fly cutter to be used in the drill, paper, a saw, a staple, pencil, double-faced transparent tape, several drill bits, a snap fastener that I took off a child's toy, and several flat, clear sheets of either acrylic or polycarbonate plastic, I fashioned the first Pill box for packaging birth control Pills."[81] The bottom plate had the day-of-the-week pattern. The middle plate held twenty wooden "pills" and rotated to match the day pill taking would begin. A single hole in the top plate moved over the Pill to dispense it, revealing the day of the week as a reminder of when the pill was taken.[82]

Wagner sent the prototype to Searle and to Ortho Pharmaceutical. Searle rejected Wagner's project and in 1963 Ortho Pharmaceutical launched the first DialPak "memory-aid" dispenser, designed according to Wagner's model.[83] Reaching the market a few months later, Searle's Enovid E Con-pac and one-milligram Ovulen pill dispensers were also closely inspired by Wagner's distributor. To distinguish itself from Searle's Con-pac, a 1964 Ortho-Novum advertisement showed the DialPak 21 dispenser for the oral contraceptive for the first time, highlighting a watchstrap calendar "to keep key days always at hand."

80. In 1994, David P. Wagner donated his collection of prototypes of drug and pill packaging to the Division of Science, Medicine, and Society at the Simithsonian Museum of National History, enabling historian Patricia Peck Gossel to develop a first study of the design process.

81. Patricia Peck Gossel, "Packaging the Pill," in *Manifesting Medicine: Bodies and Machines*, ed. Robert Bud (London: Taylor & Francis, 1999), 107.

82. Ibid., 106.

83. Neither Searle nor Ortho bought Wagner's patent. Ortho was later legally forced to pay $10,000 to Wagner to compensate for using his prototype.

According to historian of medicine Emilia Sanabria, the material aspects of packaging and pharmaceutical transformation are often overlooked when the history of medical techniques is described:

> In the manipulation which occurs in the pharmaceutical process, liquid, semi-solid and solid pharmaceutical substances are manufactured—or temporarily stabilized—into pharmaceutical "objects." The possibility of effecting this handcrafting is understood to define the effects that these pharmaceutical objects can have, physiologically-speaking, on their "patients." Pharmaceuticals have increasingly been analyzed as objects. This carves out a particular place for pharmaceuticals in the analysis of material things, and of material things in the analysis of pharmaceuticals. Whilst material culture analyses provide elements to theorize drugs as "things," it produces problems when these things are drugs. I argue that the consumable and changeable aspects of these "things" are left un-theorized. This problem stems from a common assumption in anthropological analyses of material culture, which tends to take the object for granted. That is to say, the process of object-making is often eclipsed by the object itself.[84]

Insisting on the need to pay attention to the medical and social repercussions of pharmacological marketing, historian Patricia Peck Gossel has studied the packaging techniques that were used for the commercialization of the DialPak, the first compliance package of the Pill, pro-

---

84. Emilia Sanabria, "The Medicine, an Evanescent Object: Test on the Manufacture and the Consumption of the Pharmaceutical Substances," *Techniques & Culture* 52–53, no. 2–3 (2009): 168–89.

duced in 1963.[85] According to Gossel, the Pill was not only a political and gender revolution but also a revolution in drug packaging. The Pill is the first pharmaceutical molecule to be produced as a design object.

Gossel understands Wagner's design of the Pill packaging as a couple's "problem solving" process, in which the husband (and designer) aided his wife in managing a complex intake time schedule, reinterpreting the bond between husband and wife as a model of the designer-user relationship.[86] For Gossel, the DialPak appears to be the first "compliance package" for a prescription drug—one that intended to help the patient to comply with the doctor's orders.[87]

For Gossel, the invention of the dispenser for the Pill indicates the emergence of a new model of pharmaceutical design, one that does not rely on the aims of advertising companies aims, but rather on the designer-user relationship. Following Gossel's design history, we could argue that the Pill (taking into account the difficulties of the intake schedule) is not only a chemical product (the molecule isolated and marketed as edible capsule) but also an individual portable pharmacomechanism, able to discipline the tablets' intake. The 1960s Pill, as a social domestic practice and individual hormonal prosthesis, cannot exist without the

85. Gossel, "Packaging the Pill," 105–21. For more about the history of packaging, see also Stanley Sacharow, *The Package as a Marketing Tool* (Radnor, PA: Chilton, 1982); Thomas Hine, *The Total Package: The Evolution and Secret Meaning of Boxes, Bottles, Cans, and Tubes* (Boston: Back Bay Books, 1995); Steven Lubar and W. David Kingery, eds., *History from Things: Essays on Material Culture* (Washington, DC: Smithsonian Institution Press, 1993).

86. Gossel explains, as if she needed to justify the Wagners' decision for birth control: "Doris Wagner began taking the Pill after the fourth child, Jane, was born on November 14, 1961, and the Wagners decided that their family was complete," Gossel, "Packaging the Pill," 105.

87. Gossel, "Packaging the Pill,"105.

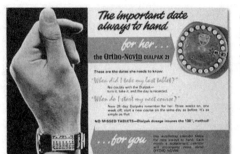

Ortho-Novum DialPak
became the second
oral contraceptive on
the American market in
February 1963.

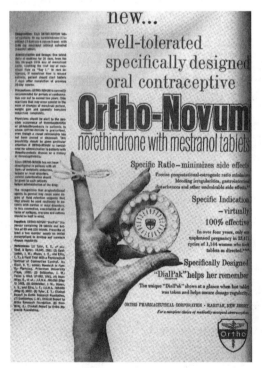

Advertising
campaign,
1964, National
Museum of
American History,
Behring Center,
Smithsonian
Institution.

dispenser. Whereas a single tablet of an oral contraceptive, if separated from the container, would be recognized only by a pharmacist, the distinctive package of the Pill made it the most readily recognizable prescription drug on the market during the 1960s. Reversing the traditional relationship between content and container, the packaging *is* the Pill.

Wagner's DialPak design resulted from two operations: spatialization of time and camouflage. First, the dispenser spatialized time by making the administration dates visible within the circular box. Like the rotary-dial telephone, the most popular domestic communication appliance of the Cold War years, the circular box established abstract relationships between three systems—holes, numbers, and network stations for the phone, and holes, Pills, and the dates of the menstrual cycle for the DialPak. The dispenser divided duration into successive segments, each of which indicates a specific time. The spatialization of time produces what Foucault called an "anatomic-chronological scheme of action" that combines architecture, design, and body movement, transforming the user into an efficient (non-) reproducing machine.[88] According to Wagner, and later to the Searle and the Ortho Pharmaceutical advertising campaigns, the dispenser's main aim was to reduce "forgetfulness," with the dispenser being presented as a prosthesis to women's lack of memory and responsibility. In this respect, the DialPak was a technique for packaging not only pills but

---

88. Michel Foucault, "Docile Bodies," in *Discipline and Punish: The Birth of the Prison*, trans. Alan Sheridan, 2nd ed. (New York: Vintage, 1995), 156–66.

89. According to the same logic, the IUD contraceptive device was described by *TIME* magazine as "memory in plastic." See "Contraception: Freedom from Fear," *TIME*, April 7, 1967, *http://www.time.com/time/magazine/article/0,9171,843551,00.html.*

also memory and time, responsibility and trust.[89]

The monthly package of pills, with its imperative of daily administration but also the risk of forgetfulness or incorrect management, with its time-based ritual and pop design, evokes a chemical calendar in which each day is indicated by the indispensable presence of a pill. Its presentation in circular form invites the user to follow the movement of time on a dial, as if on a clock, where the alarm announces the time of ingestion.[90] It functions as a device for the domestic self-surveillance of female sexuality, like a molecular, endocrinological, high-tech mandala, a book of hours, or the daily examination of conscience in Ignatius's *Spiritual Exercises*. It is a hormonal domestic microprosthesis that regulates ovulation, but it also produces the "mind" and living body of the heterosexual woman as modern sexual reproductive subject.

On the other hand, Wagner intended to camouflage a birth control technique as a "female" ordinary-use object: he designed the dispenser to be the size and form of a makeup compact, so women could carry it discreetly in their purses—a way of employing in public space a technique that was originally meant for only the domestic space. Although soon used by millions of American women, the dispenser was meant to be totally "private," the perfect box in which to keep a female secret.[91] This domestic and undisclosed character of a birth control technique may

90. The first packages of pills, designed in the sixties, were equipped with an integrated alarm.

91. Gossel, "Packaging the Pill," 115. Gossel thoughtfully notices that by the 1980s, the cosmetic compact design was displaced by the "wallet" or the "credit card" look.

QUICK! QUICK! QUICK!

Creme Puff – that's enough!

No other make-up brings you such complexion loveliness in seconds

MAX FACTOR

Creme Puff

Left: Max Factor Creme Puff Compack design, 1959. Below: First advertising campaign for Enovid-E Compack pill dispenser, Searle and Company, 1964.

Your **Enovid-E** *Compack*

This modern dispensing package...with push-button ease... was specifically designed for you... to make birth control with "the Pill" easy and pleasant as well as reliable. You will be pleased with the distinct advantages it offers. Your Compack contains no moving parts. It is easy to understand and to use. Each pill is sealed for maximum protection. A completely automatic record is kept of your cycle and of your pill days.

HOW TO USE YOUR COMPACK

1. With your pills facing you, position the Compack Refill so that the arrow points to the day your period starts.

   Snap the Refill into locked position by pressing down around the button catch. The Refill should be flat in the Compack. To remove it, lift up at any day and pull off.

2. Your first pill is to be taken five days after your period starts. It is marked with a circle around it.

3. To remove a pill, push the pill down through the bottom opening of the Compack. The pill pops out.

OUTER ROW — MIDDLE ROW — INNER ROW

4. The pills should be taken consecutively: The pills in the outer row one each day of the first 7 days, the middle row the second 7 days, and the inner row the last 6 days.

explain why most of the package inserts suggested keeping the dispenser at home, putting it, for example, on the kitchen counter or on the night table in the bedroom or in the bathroom medicine cabinet. As historian Patricia Peck Gossel recalls: "A Philadelphia women's health clinic recommended that women take their Pill when they heard the theme music for the 11 o'clock news, at bedtime,"[92] something that amounts to trying to transform a national broadcasting media into a technique to regulate intake. In some cases, "the package of birth control Pills was presented in a box with a toothbrush, a small bar of soap, a 'Remember Me' sticker for the bathroom mirror and the slogan 'Brush your teeth, wash your face, take your Pill . . . once a day, every day, at the same time.'"[93]

In 1965, Mead Johnson invented the twenty-eight-day regime, adding placebos that enabled the user to take a pill every day. C-Queens sequential pill by Eli Lilly contained two different formulations to be taken in sequence. The package resembled a calendar, with four rows of five tablets. The twenty-eight-day regime made the DialPak calendar format obsolete; the key now was that the pills be taken in the proper sequence, leaving behind the importance of when the cycle started. But with time, the Pill became a female life-regulator: the Parke and Davis placebo twenty-eight-day regime included one milligram of Norlestrin Fe to "compensate for mineral loss during menstrual bleeding,"

---

92. Gossel, "Packaging the Pill," 115. The Starter Kit for Forgetful Women by Organon, Inc., distributed in 1993, included helpful suggestions for forgetful pill-takers of their Desogen oral contraceptive.

93. Organon, Inc., cited in Gossel, "Packaging the Pill,"116.

and some other designs incorporated a dial to remind the user to examine her breast for tumors at the optimum time of her cycle.

The process of camouflage, miniaturization, and privatization reached a higher level in 1964 when the Population Council's Center for Biomedical Research demonstrated that hormones could be released from a silicone rubber capsule implanted in the body. The first clinical trials of a six-capsule Silastic (silicone and plastic) drug delivery system, implanted under the skin of the upper arm, were conducted in 1975, and this system was first approved for use as Norplant in Finland in 1983. "In this case," as Patricia Peck Gossel noted, "dosage form and the container have, in a sense, merged."[94] The implant remained within the body, invisible, as long as the drug was released, for five years, after which it was surgically removed. The Norplant prosthetic implant would be later followed by infusion pumps, transdermal patches, and osmotic systems.

Bringing Emilia Sanabria's and Gossel's conclusions about pharmaceutical packaging further into a general history of biopolitics, I shall argue that the transformation of the oral contraceptive pill into "the Pill" through packaging can be understood not only as a cultural process that implies social and medical effects but also as the translation of an architectonic model, a disciplinary system of power and knowledge relationships derived from Enlightenment architectures of the hospital and prison, into a domestic

94. Gossel, "Packaging the Pill,"116.

and portable (and later bodily and prosthetic) technique. The art historian Aby Warburg has given us an iconographic method for thinking about the transmission and survival of forms through different cultural mutations. In his *Der Bilderatlas Mnemosyne* (The Mnemosyne Atlas, 1924–29), Warburg lays out a possible visual history of Europe, made of two thousand images, among which can be found Roman sculptures, maps from different periods, Darwinian diagrams of animal evolution, Renaissance frescos, Christian oil paintings, and photographs from the beginning of the twentieth century. Inspired by this method of visual traceability, one can recognize, and not without terror, a vestige of Jeremy Bentham's model in the original design for the package of contraceptive pills that was marketed after the 1960s. In their internal divergence, Bentham's architectural motifs reclaim their place at another scale: the contraceptive pill is an edible panopticon. Social orthopedics is mutating into pharmacopornographic microprosthetics. DialPak transformed the panopticon into a domestic, portable female hormonal compact.

The panopticon, prefigured by the hospital plans of Bernard Poyet and C. P. Coquéau and by Louis Le Vau's project for a menagerie at Versailles, first emerged as a model of industrial (but not yet penal) architecture, developed in 1786 by the philosopher Jeremy Bentham, brother of the naval engineer Samuel Bentham (in fact, it was Samuel who conceived the basic architecture of the building), in response to a commission from the Russian prince Grigory Potemkin.

Originally, the panopticon was an industrial "inspection house" designed to optimize surveillance, control, and worker production in a factory complex. Bentham's architectural structure was based on two concentric rings, with an observation tower at the center of the entire structure and a series of cells radiating out from it. Each of these cells had two windows, an external one to let in light, and an internal one facing the surveillance tower. The occupants of the cells were isolated from each other by walls and subjected to the collective and individual (audiovisual) scrutiny of a guard in the tower, which, as Foucault speculates, could have been empty or occupied by the abstract eye of God, which would remain hidden. As pointed out by Christian Laval:

> The panoptic is not only the eye of power, a kind of imaginary figure suspended over a splintered and isolated people, but also, in the reverse sense, the eye of the people that must remain constantly focused on the ruling class so that the latter won't betray the interests of the greatest number. This double meaning of surveillance is based on the principle of the goal of generalized transparency. The model of the panoptic has the advantage of combining what is usually thought to be distinct and separate: the most intrusive social control, the free market and the most advanced democracy.[95]

This original design became the model for internment and disciplinary centers built in the nineteenth and twentieth centuries, centers such as Rahway Prison in New Jer-

---

95. Christian Laval, "De l'utilité du panoptique," afterward to *Panoptique: Mémoire sur un nouveau principe pour construire des maisons d'inspection, et nommément des maisons de force*, by Jérémie Bentham, trans. Christian Laval (Paris: Éditions Mille et Une Nuits, 2002), 64.

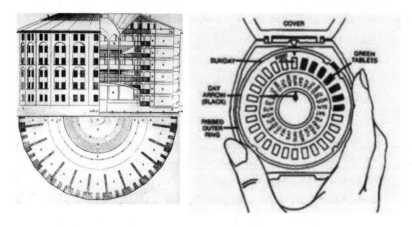

Left: Elevation, section, and plan of Jeremy Bentham's Panopticon, drawn by architect Willey Reveley in 1791. Right: First dispenser for the Pill, 1963.

sey; national prisons in Dublin, Bogotá, and Cuba's Isle of Pines; and the jail in Mataró, Spain, designed by Elies Rogent. For Foucault, the panopticon isn't just a simple disciplinary device. It's the *material model* of disciplinary knowledge-power as a form of "social orthopedics":[96] power and its specific modes of knowledge and surveillance materialized in the form of physical architecture (whether of a prison, school, hospital, barracks, or factory) that automates movement, controls the gaze, programs action, and ritualizes everyday bodily practices. In all such cases, disciplinary power is, according to Foucault "exercised through its invisibility . . . and the examination is the technique by which power, instead of emitting the signs of its potency,

96. Michel Foucault, *Power: Essential Works of Foucault 1954–1984*, ed. James D. Faubion, trans. Robert Hurley (New York: The New York Press, 2000), 57.

instead of imposing its mark on its subjects, holds them in a mechanism of objectification."[97] The purpose of these forms of architecture is not simply to provide *habitat* or represent the individual—instead, like true *performative* devices, they tend to produce the subject they claim to shelter. The convict, the student, the patient, the soldier, and the worker are the political precipitate of these architectural *technologies of subjectification.*

We can think of the Pill as a lightweight, portable, individualized, chemical panopticon with the potential to change behavior, program action, regulate sexual activity, control population growth and racial purity, and redesign the sexual appearance (by refeminizing it synthetically) of the bodies that self-administer it. The surveillance tower has been replaced by the eyes of the (not always) docile user of the Pill who regulates her own administration without the need for external supervision, following the spatial calendar marked on the circular or rectangular package. The whip has been replaced by a convenient system of oral administration. Henceforth, the prison cell has become the body of the consumer, which sees itself chemically modified without being able to determine the exact effects or where they come from, once the hormonal compound has been ingested. Punishments and edifying sermons have been replaced by rewards and promises of freedom and sexual emancipation for women. The Pill is a miniaturized pharmacopornographic laboratory distributed within the domestic environment and destined to be placed inside

97. Foucault, *Discipline and Punish*, 187.

the body of each consumer, thus fulfilling the demolition of imprisonment institutions predicted by Deleuze and Guattari in their epilogue to *A Thousand Plateaus*.[98] The Pill works according to what Maurizio Lazzarato, following Deleuze and Guattari, calls the logic of "machinic enslavement." "Machinic enslavement," explains Lazzarato:

> consists in mobilizing and modulating the pre-individual, pre-cognitive and pre-verbal components of subjectivity, causing affects, perceptions and sensations as yet un-individuated or unassigned to a subject, to function like the cogs and components in a machine. While subjection concerns social selves or global persons, those highly manipulable, molar, subjective representations, 'machinic enslavement connects infrapersonal, infrasocial elements thanks to a molecular economy of desire which is far more difficult to maintain within stratified social relationships,' and these are the elements that mobilize individuated subjects. Machinic enslavement is therefore not the same thing as social subjection. If the latter appeals to the molar, individuated dimension of a subjectivity, the former activates its molecular, pre-individual, pre-verbal, pre-social dimension.[99]

It is no longer necessary to shut up individuals within state institutions in order to subject them to biochemical, pedagogic, or penal tests, because experiments on the living human being can now be carried out at home, in the valuable enclave of the individual body, under the watchful, intimate supervision of the individual herself. And all of it

98. Gilles Deleuze and Félix Guattari, *A Thousand Plateaus: Capitalism and Schizophrenia*, trans. Brian Massumi (Minneapolis: University of Minnesota Press, 1987).

99. Maurizio Lazzarato, "The Machine," epilogue to *Tausend Maschinen: Eine kleine Philosophie der Maschine als sozialer Bewegung*, by Gerald Raunig (Vienna: Verlag Turia + Kant, 2008).

happens *freely*, by virtue of the sexual *emancipation* of the controlled body. The biopolitical promise of governing *free* bodies that Foucault identified is here fully accomplished.

Still, the differences between the panopticon and the Pill are significant. Within the length of hardly a century, they underline the transition from a disciplinary regime into a pharmacopornographic regime. In the first case, we're faced with an external political architecture that defines the position of the body in a space that is collectively regulated, creating specific positions of power (monitor/monitored, doctor/patient, professor/student . . .) and allowing the generation of a form of knowing (visual, statistical, demographic) concerning those individuals being controlled. In the second case, we're faced with a mechanism that—without any change in its effectiveness—has reduced its scale to that of a biomolecular technology that may be consumed individually and introduced by bodily orifices. In the pharmacopornographic era, the body swallows power. It is a form of control that is both democratic and private, edible, drinkable, inhalable, and easy to administer, whose spread throughout the social body has never been so rapid or so undetectable. In the pharmacopornographic age, biopower dwells at home, sleeps with us, inhabits within. The dominant manifestations of the pharmacopornographic era (pills, prostheses, food, images, fellatio, and double penetration) share the same relationship between the body and power: a desire for infiltration, absorption, total occupation. We could give in to the temptation of representing this relationship according to a dialectical model of domination/oppression, as if it were a unidirectional movement in which miniaturized, liquid power from the outside infiltrates the obedient body of individuals. But no. It is not power infiltrating from the outside, it is the body desiring power, seeking to swallow it, eat it, administer it, wolf it down, more, always more, through every hole, by every possible route of application. Turning oneself into power. *Baise-Moi*, fuck me (Despentes), says the body, all the while seeking forms of autocontrol and autoextermination: "Why do people always desire their own slavery?" (Spinoza). Biopower doesn't infiltrate from the outside. It already dwells *inside*.

But machinic enslavement also determines new possibilities for subversion. The Pill—defined by the need for an individual decision to take it and by the time-based calculations of the user—immediately induces accident. It takes accident into account, programs it, sees accident as a sine qua non possibility of female sexuality. The heteronormative logic of the Cold War period that dominates the Pill seems to respond to this double, contradictory requirement: every woman must simultaneously be fertile (and be so through heterosexual insemination) and able to reduce the possibility of her own fertility at all times to levels asymptotically close to zero, but without reducing it altogether, so that accidental conception remains possible. But the accident is also the possibility of subversion and resignification: the fact that the Pill must be managed at home, by the individual user in an autonomous way, also introduces the possibility of political agency.

The massive, high-dose administration of estrogens and progesterone to the bodies of Western cis-females after

World War II permitted the production and reproduction of femininity as a standardized and ready-made biocode. This new microprosthetic femininity is a patented pharmacopornographic technology, which can be commercialized—or transferred to and implanted in—any living body at all. Gradually, it will be revealed that the estrogens and progesterone administered in high doses during this period are toxic and carcinogenic and to blame for various cardiovascular changes, but such findings do nothing to lower consumption of the Pill (in fact, its consumption increased exponentially beginning in the 1970s); nor do they change recommendations coming from the World Health Organization (WHO).

The amount of estrogen and progesterone intended for a month of treatment has changed from 150 micrograms of estrogen and 200 milligrams of progesterone in the 1970s to 10 micrograms of estrogen and 15 milligrams of different variants of progesterone in today's contraceptive treatments. As a measure to improve security, the current micropill (which is the most prescribed drug for periods of breast-feeding) administers a weaker dose during a greater number of days, reducing the number of days in which a placebo pill is taken, during which what we could call the *technoperiod* is produced—in other words, a technologically induced bleeding that produces the illusion of a natural cycle. These are technological methods of biodrag whose objective is the "mimicking of the normal physiological cycle." From Pincus's second pill to today's micropill, these technologies of hormonal invention have been functioning according to a principle of biocamouflage: first, interrupting the natural hormonal cycle, and then, technologically provoking an artificial cycle that re-creates the illusion of nature. The first of these actions is contraceptive, the second is the consequence of an intended pharmacoporno-graphic production of gender—seeing to it that the bodies of twentieth-century technofemales perpetuate the illusion of being the outcome of natural, unchanging, transhistoric, and transcultural laws.

A recent study carried out at Boston University reveals the relationship between consumption of the contraceptive pill, the decline in the levels of bioavailability of testosterone (a reduction from 40 percent to 60 percent), and the drop in women's libido. The study warns that taking synthetic estrogen can modify hormonal production on a global scale and recommends administering testosterone gel in microdoses to increase "the sexual functioning of female consumers of the pill."[100] But today, administering testosterone to women still remains a hormonal taboo with political implications. The production of femininity in the pharmacopornographic regime functions according to a paradoxical logic: on the one hand, the Pill is being administered to cis-females in a generalized manner, and on the other, a pharmacological way of overcoming depression and frigidity is the goal.[101] The cis-female of the twenty-

100. Katrina Woznicki, "Birth Control Pills May Produce Protracted Effects on Testosterone Levels," *MedPage Today*, January 3, 2006, http://www.medpagetoday.com/ OBGYN/HRT/2423; C. Panzer, S. Wise, G. Fantini, D. Kang, R. Munarriz, A. Guay, and I. Goldstein, "Impact of Oral Contraceptives on Sex Hormone-Binding Globulin and Androgen Levels: A Retrospective Study in Women with Sexual Dysfunction," *The Journal of Sexual Medicine* 3 (January 2006): 104–13.

101. This logic is comparable to the relationship between the repression of masturbation and the production of fits of hysteria using mechanical means in the sex-discipline agenda of the nineteenth century. See an analysis of this paradoxical production in Beatriz Preciado, *Manifeste contra-sexuel* (Paris: Balland, 2000), 73–88.

first century is the result of this somato-political short-circuiting; her subjectivity grows within the narrow margin of freedom created by these fields of divergent force.

The formation of the pharmacopornographic society was characterized by the two new vectors of production of sexual subjectivity at the middle of the twentieth century. On the one hand, as we have seen, there is the introduction of the notion of "gender" as a technical, visual, and performative device for sexing the body, the reorganization of the medico-judicial, educational, and medical system that until that time had been articulating the notions of "normalcy" and "perversion" in the context of the binomial concept of heterosexuality/homosexuality and will now begin considering the possibility of technically modifying the body of the individual to "invent" a masculine or feminine "mind." On the other hand, we are witnessing techniques of social control that are suitable for the disciplinary system gradually filtering into the individual body. What is at issue is no longer only the punishment of the sexual offenses of individuals or the surveillance and correction of their aberrations by means of a code of external laws or interiorized disciplines, but the modification of their bodies in their capacity as living platforms. We are treated as producers and consumers of organs, flux, neurotransmitters, as supports and effects of a biopolitical program. We are certainly still confronting a form of social control, but this time it's a matter of *control lite*, a bubbly type of control, full of colors and wearing Mickey Mouse ears and the Brigitte Bardot low-cut look, as opposed to the cold, disciplinary architecture of the panoptic illustrated by Foucault.

After the 1950s, the construction of biofemininity becomes a process of somato-political construction (bio-drag). It consists of a progression of molecular overcodification—a transformation of the structure of life, and not a simple disguise or mask, as postmodern theories of gender like to claim.[102] The breasts, for example: their weight, form, and consistency have acquired a plastic pertinence (in the medical sense of the term), transforming them gradually into a techno-somatic signifier of the production of gender.[103] They have materialized as a place for new pathologies, such as hypomastia (small-breast symptom) or breast cancer, which appeared at the same time as the techniques of mastectomy and breast reconstruction using synthetic implants, the incidences of which increased exponentially beginning in the 1960s.[104] The H-bomb, the birth control pill, silicone implants, breast cancer . . . From ablation to reconstruction to augmentation, the twentieth-century breast functions above all as prosthesis. In other words, every biobreast exists in relation to its own cultural prosthesis. Accordingly, it's just as suitable to speak of techno-breasts when referring to cis-females as it is when referring to transsexual bodies, rather than making a distinction between the natural female breast and the prosthetic.

102. For example, an extreme example of a postmodern theory of gender would be that developed by Jean Baudrillard in *Simulacres et simulation* (Paris: Editions Galilée, 1981); this shouldn't be confused with the performative definition of gender developed by Judith Butler or Sue Ellen Case.

103. Sander L. Gilman, *Making the Body Beautiful: A Cultural History of Aesthetic Surgery* (Princeton, NJ: Princeton University Press, 2001).

104. Elizabeth Haiken, *Venus Envy: A History of Cosmetic Surgery* (Baltimore: The John Hopkins University Press, 1999).

Since the beginning of the twentieth century, new synthetic materials, architectural structures, the techniques of artistic collage and of film editing have moved toward the domain of corporal transformation.[105] For example, paraffin was one of the first substances used in the construction of "island flaps," the envelopes for breast implants but also for testicular implants (typically used for soldiers who had lost one or two testicles during war), as well as for the reconstruction of the "syphilitic nose." In the 1920s, paraffin was abandoned in favor of gum arabic, rubber, cellulose, ivory, and various metals. In 1949, Ivalon, a derivative of polyvinyl alcohol, would be used to produce the first breast implant by subcutaneous injection. The first recipient of these rudimentary implants were Japanese female sex workers, immediately following the war, whose bodies would need to undergo a process of standardization that conformed to the heterosexual requirements of American army consumption.[106] Body transformations have reached a global scale; just as bodies were affected by radiation from the plutonium used in the H-bomb, they will henceforth be affected by polymerized silicone. After 1953, pure silicone becomes the preferred material for the manufacturing of prosthetic implants. Shortly after that, Dow Corning markets the first tube of silicone gel for clinical use. Although highly toxic, its use will continue until the beginning of the 1990s.

105. See Mark Nelson and Sarah Hudson Bayliss, *Exquisite Corpse: Surrealism and the Black Dahlia Murder* (New York: Bulfinch, 2006), which notes the unusual study about the relationship between the surrealist aesthetic and the murder of the Black Dahlia, whose name will become the title of a novel by James Ellroy.

106. Marilyn Yalom, *A History of Breast* (New York: Ballantine Books, 1998), 236–38.

Contrary to what one might think, the biodrag dimension of the pharmacopornographic production of the body (*somatic camp*) doesn't depend exclusively on the use of synthetic materials in its reconstruction of a corporal normality deemed natural. One of the first techniques of breast reconstruction will make its appearance at the end of the nineteenth century when Dr. Vincent Czerny collects a large lipoma growing on the back of his patient to use as material to compensate for a breast that was removed, thereby performing an autograft.[107] Years later, the same principle will be used in the development of autoimplants of body fat for face lifts and the reshaping of the body.

The difference between *bio-* and *techno-* is not a difference between organic and inorganic. In this text, I am not evaluating a passage from the biological to the synthetic but identifying the appearance of a new type of corporality. Recent technologies for the production of the body are not faithful to a classical taxonomy according to which each organ and each tissue corresponds to a single function and location. Far from respecting the formal or material totality of the body, biotechnology and prosthetic technologies combine modes of representation related to film and architecture, like modeling and editing in 3-D. The new surgical technology, which has made possible the application of pharmacopornographic ideas of sexuality (the technical management of masculinity and femininity, the medicalization of the orgasm and sexual desire, telecontrol of

107. Gilman, *Making the Body*, 249.

the fantasy functions of sexuality, etc.) is authorizing processes of the tectonic construction of the body, according to which its organs, tissues, fluids, and, ultimately, molecules, are transformed into the raw materials from which a new incarnation of nature is manufactured.

Microprosthetic Control

Placing research on producing a male birth control pill on the back burner, the pharmaceutical industries have turned toward the development of new methods for administering hormones to women, designed to reduce the scope of management that individual use of the Pill permitted. Most current clinical tests serve the goal of producing a technique of hormonal administering that avoids the oral and intentional route. According to the claims of the pharmaceutical companies, this promotes the following advantages: reduced assimilation of steroids by the liver, reduced risk of short-term memory loss, and improved absorption by effusion of a constant level of doses of hormones into the blood. The first injectable combinations of estrogen and progesterone at a frequency of once a month appeared in the 1990s (like Depo-Provera). The following decade witnessed a gradual program of marketing implants with a base of progestogen, from a six-capsule subdermal implant of silicone progesterone for the skin of the arm (Norplant) to two capsules (Norplant 2, Jadelle) or a single capsule (Implanon). These implants, which currently can release their hormonal compound for between one to five years, become invisible and undetectable once they are placed under the skin (from which they sometimes cannot be removed).[108] Again, here it's possible to identify the liquid and microprosthetic future of technologies for controlling sexuality, which used to be a rigid, exterior, visible, and weighty affair.

Implanon isn't very different from the classical intra-uterine system (the IUD), especially the model that releases progesterone into the uterine cavity. The difference lies in the place of insertion on the body. Implanon is placed under the skin of the arm, which gives the illusion that it intervenes less in the regulation of sexuality, because the mechanism doesn't directly touch the organs cultur-ally considered to be sexual. Other mechanisms that have recently been marketed are the vaginal ring (inserted into the vagina and left there for twenty-one days, then removed for five days to simulate the natural rhythms of menstrua-tion), and especially, the transdermal contraceptive patch, which is becoming more and more popular. Both devices contain ethinylestradiol combined with progesterone.

At the other extreme of the gender equation, a growth in the administration of synthetic testosterone as a substi-tution therapy for cis-males has established new perspec-tives for hormonal research and marketing.[109] The German laboratory Schering, a world leader in contraception with its Yasmin pill, has faced a situation of increasingly intense

108. For more about injectable contraceptives and implants, see Robert A. Hatcher, James Trussell and Anita L. Nelson, eds., *Contraceptive Technology*, 19th ed. (New York: PDR Network, 2008), 145–70.

109. For more about testosterone deficiency and testosterone replacement therapy for cis-males, see Nelson Vergel, *Testosterone: A Man's Guide*, 2nd ed. (Houston: Milestones Publishing, 2011).

commercial competition for some time now. Hoping to remain in the vanguard in this expanding market, in 2004 Schering began the first clinical trials evaluating the effectiveness of various contraceptive implants or injections for men, all aiming to decrease sperm levels. Such male contraception is founded on principles similar to those behind the female pill. Its effectiveness is based on a formulation of a base of progestogen that acts to suppress the production of spermatozoids; its use would be combined with a substitution therapy derived from a base of testosterone in order to maintain levels of libido and erection. In the twentieth century, no new contraceptive methods have been developed for cis-males. Rubber condoms and sterilization today remain the only low-tech techniques for directly controlling the social circulation of male reproductive cells. It is interesting to note that, although the male pill has not been marketed yet, China and India have tried to develop biopolitical programs of reproductive control that include the management of the male body.[110] The pharmacopornographic challenge of the twenty-first century will be the marketing of a panoply of hormonal compounds (often supplemented with testosterone) for cis-males without calling into question the natural makeup of masculinity.

At the same time, as a way of compensating for the established scientific relationship between hormones and cancer, the new contraceptive pills for cis-females are presented as instruments of beauty and feminization—

110. See Oudshoorn, *Male Pill*, 7.

a molecular supplement for somatic refeminization.[111] Today's pharmaceutical companies announce their desire to produce a contraceptive pill based on "selective estrogen receptor modulators" (SERMs) that will lower the risk of breast cancer—similar to butter that lowers cholesterol levels or methadone as a substitution drug that reduces heroin addiction.

The Pill, a key performative prosthesis of the pharmacopornographic regime, is evolving from a simple technique of birth control to a genuine program for the cosmetic pro-

111. The gynecologists whom I've visited over the last fifteen years, disinterested in my announcement of my trans-queer sexuality, which is exclusively dildoic or anal, suggested with astonishing frequency that I use the Pill as a contraceptive measure. They praise its virtues as a "regulator of the menstrual cycle" and as a way of "alleviating menstrual pains," without mentioning its side effects, except for the carcinogenic risks of its interaction with tobacco. In reality, this is a means of administering cis-females the necessary pharmacopornographic dose of estrogen and progesterone to transform cis-females into a normalized heterosexual female body, with a depressive but stable temperament and a passive or frigid sexuality.

duction of femininity; it is appearing more and more frequently as a therapy for the treatment of acne or hirsutism (body and facial hair on cis-females) or to increase the volume and improve the form of the breasts. Accordingly, new pills with a base of progesterone are being manufactured, among them Drospirenone, which is marketed in Germany and, thanks to its anti-mineral-corticoid properties, promises weight loss and reduced water retention. Today, hormonal therapies also appeal to women in a consumer public who are looking to reduce the frequency and intensity of their periods. Use of these therapies as contraception is decreasing as they become more common in managing menstrual cycles (for example, the new implants allow total elimination of the period for five years). As we have seen, such potential is not new; it was, on the contrary, one of the side effects of the first contraceptive pill developed in the 1950s. During that decade, which saw the gradual displacement of the disciplinary sexopolitical mechanism toward new pharmacopornographic techniques, these effects seemed incompatible with the metaphysics of sex that established an inexorable equation between femininity, fertility, and maternity.

At the same time, we are witnessing a growing spate of marketing campaigns in which the Pill is referred to as an "emergency postcoital contraceptive," as in the "morning-after pill," and the abortion pill Mifepristone, also known as RU-486. China was the first country to approve the use of Mifepristone, which was commercialized by the French pharmaceutical company Roussel Uclaf in 1988; China began its own domestic production in 1992. Although current bioethical debates tend to establish a difference between the Western use of contraceptives and the use of abortive methods within totalitarian regimes, political agency does not depend only on the molecules but rather on their use and critical reappropriation.

In the context of a fast-expanding pharmacoporno-graphic sexopolitical model in which a multitude of potential consumers have increasing access to the molecular production of their gender and sexuality, modulated by the fluctuations of the pharmaceutical market, implants and micropills are heralding a new type of high-tech heterosexuality (which differs radically from nineteenth-century Victorian heterosexuality): the techno-Barbie, remaining eternally young and supersexualized, almost entirely infertile and nonmenstruating but always ready for artificial insemination and accompanied by a sterile supermacho whose erections are technically produced by a combination of Viagra and audiovisual pornographic codes emitted through computerized digital channels. Finally, pharmacopornographic heterosexual fertilization is happening in vitro.

With the creation in the 1970s of postmenopausal hormonal substitution therapies using a base of estrogen and progesterone (in the form of gels, very similar to the Testogel that I administer, but also in the form of patches or nasal spray), and their expansion beginning in the 1990s, the cis-female of the twenty-first century is becoming a potential consumer of synthetic hormones who will be taking them for almost fifty years of her life. Now we must add ten or fifteen years of postmenopausal treatment to forty years of contraceptive treatment. In the near future, we will have mastered other methods that today are experimental: the contraceptive vaccine, also known as immuno-contraception, which "immunizes" the organism against the development of an embryo or prevents the ovum from accepting a spermatozoid. One could press on much further with the inventory of such microtechnologies for the management of sexual subjectivity, but in any case, one thing is clear: when it comes to the allocation of funds for financing clinical research, such methods of contraception are in competition with the urgent need to develop methods of prevention of, or a vaccine against, the HIV virus.

The Enemy Hormone: Testosterone and Gender Terrorism

The twentieth century began with the first attempt to market a patch for testosterone for cis-females. In 2004, after several years of clinical tests, the US Food and Drug Administration refused Procter and Gamble authorization to market Intrinsa, the first patch, which administers three hundred micrograms of testosterone a day to cis-females as a remedy for "hypoactive sexual desire disorder" (HSDD), or lack of sexual desire.[112] The product was intended, according to Procter and Gamble, for "women who have had their ovaries removed," but the company was hoping to indirectly reach a much larger public: all the consumers of the Pill who were suffering from lowered testosterone levels. The evaluation of hormonal risks, carried out by the

112. While I was finishing the corrections for this book, Intrinsa had just received a license for pharmaceutical exploitation, beginning March 2007, in the United Kingdom and the rest of Europe.

FDA, obviously did not use the same criteria as those used in the evaluation of progesterone as treatment for ovary ablation or for menopause. Numerous articles, including one published in the overly scrupulous *New York Times* denounced the "political character" of this medical decision and pointed out the pressure that could be exerted on the many "conservative members" of the relevant committee of the FDA. It was the opinion of this committee that "despite the promising results of this substance in improving the sex lives of patients, its use does not seem to be justified." Even more surprising is the fact that the committee characterized testosterone for women as a "lifestyle drug"—something like Ecstasy or poppers, but for menopausal women. In place of the "strengthened orgasm" promised by Intrinsa (formulated with testosterone), the FDA proposed a range of legal drugs (whose effectiveness is doubtful) to stimulate the sexual function for cis-females: vaginal creams with vasodilator properties (Orexia, Provesta, Vigorelle, Estravil . . .).[113]

Nevertheless, the potential market for Intrinsa is enormous. A study of the market recently conducted in the US by a pharmaceutical company focusing on sexual stimulants for cis-females delivered the following results: 46 percent of women say they have never had an orgasm, and 64 percent of married heterosexual women think their sex life is unsatisfying. Another sign of biopolitical displacement: whereas the disciplinary regime of the eighteenth

113. See Kathy Hill, "FDA Panel Rejects Intrinsia," *About.com*, December 2004: *http:// uspolitics.about.com/od/healthcare/a/Intrinsa_d03.htm.*

and nineteenth centuries pathologized and medicalized the sexual desire of women as a cause of hysteria, masturbation, nymphomania, perversion, or homosexuality, the new pharmacopornographic regime for the first time sanctions the lack of sexual pleasure and desire in women and plans its technical production. And here is the name of that new illness (or somato-political fiction): FSD, female sexual dysfunction. According to these estimates, ten million women in the United States could be candidates for a therapy to promote sexual desire and sexual functioning, in addition to thirty million menopausal women who could gradually attain the status of potential consumers of the product. What could be the FDA's reasons for turning down such a growth market? Pharmacopornographic capitalism clashes with the boundaries of the gender binary epistemology, which continue to function according to models of femininity and masculinity inherited from the nineteenth-century sexopolitical regime that established a strict continuity between sex, sexuality, and reproduction. The gender barriers will not fall easily. Instead, the pharmacological and medical industries prefer to look for new molecules to offset the side effects of testosterone in women ("virilism," "hirsutism"), which are considered undesirable in a heterosexual system. The pharmacopornographic regime does not simply displace the disciplinary biopolitical regime of the nineteenth century, but rather establishes unexpected and strategic alliances with it, creating new somato-political fictions as strange as the Viagra-user-sperm-donor or the sexually-dysfunctional-female-consumer-of-the-Pill.

The T Uber-male of the Future

Although the administration of microdoses of testosterone to cis-females is still rare, testosterone has been recommended for more than thirty years in hormonal substitution therapies for cis-males. The most common method of administration is through AndroGel, distributed in the form of a testosterone gel comparable to the Testogel that I'm taking and produced by Unimed Pharmaceuticals in the state of Illinois.

Anabolic steroids, derivatives that are more or less similar to testosterone, have been used for thirty years to treat hypogonadism, a physiological condition in which the testicles don't produce "enough" testosterone. For the medical establishment, testosterone functions as a substance for the manufacture of masculinity. But it isn't defined as a molecule used to make up for a lack. The role of synthetic testosterone consists in producing the masculine subject that it pretends to supplement; however, the possibility of it being incorporated in a variety of bodies, and its transfer from skin to skin, also opens the way for postidentity drift.

The Nazi government, followed by the American government, were the first to experiment with administering doses of testosterone to animals, as well as to their own soldiers, the civilian population in concentration camps, and prisoners of war. Technologies of gender and technologies of war—the same business. Necropolitics meets biopolitics under the skin. By the 1980s, the pharmaceutical use of testosterone became widespread. In 2006 in the United States, there were four million cis-males undergoing hormonal substitution therapy formulated with testosterone.

According to the medical establishment, thirteen million Americans over the age of forty-five suffer from what is now known as "low-T syndrome," a condition characterized by an insufficiency of testosterone. The symptoms: a decrease in libido, erectile dysfunction, fatigue, depression, and so on—eventually, the ordinary life of any average cis-male.[114] Clinically, there is not enough testosterone being produced in United States.

As seen in contemporary scientific discourse, it has become evident that estrogen, progesterone, and testosterone are transverse substances produced by all bodies, independently of their gender (biopolitically assigned at birth), and that, like the molecules secreted by the pancreas and hypothalamus and by the parathyroid, thyroid, thymus, and pineal glands, function in a systemic and decentralized manner. Cis-females also produce testosterone in the ovaries and in the adrenal glands. Moreover, today we know that in cis-females, testosterone may be responsible for muscular development, the growth of bones, and sexual desire.

The singularity of all hormonal systems (and not the difference between just two systems) resides in the microquantities of hormones occurring in each body, in the number of hormonal receptors, and in systemic interactions with the other hormones and receptors. An examination of several clinical endocrinology manuals reveals that the question of the "normal" quantity of testosterone produced by cis-males and cis-females is closely related to the cultural and biopolitical definition of gender difference. For exam-

114. Vergel, *Testosterone*, 2.

ple, the average levels of testosterone in the blood of bodies politically considered to be normally male range from 437 to 707 nanograms per deciliter. But certain bodies produce no more than 125 nanograms per deciliter, and their sexual assignment is still male. According to another manual, also of clinical endocrinology, the "normal" quantity of testosterone production in adult cis-males varies from 260 to 1,000 nanograms per deciliter of blood. It can rise as high as 2,000 nanograms during adolescence. In cis-females, it is 15 to 70 nanograms per deciliter of blood. To such epistemological chaos we must add several absurd pieces of data coming from scientific research: testosterone increases the desire to smoke, but the consumption of cigarettes lowers the production of testosterone; testosterone increases aggressiveness and libido, whereas sex and aggressive reactions increase testosterone levels. Stress inhibits the production of testosterone . . . In the end, we are brought face to face with a vast domain of nonknowledge and potential technopolitical intervention.

Given such complexity, an implacable biopolitical rhetoric about gender, sexual, and racial differences, similar to that elaborated by Arnold Berthold at the beginning of the twentieth century, always dominates hormonal classification and its technical management. Although the experimental programs that determine the production of marketable doses of testosterone, estrogen, or progesterone rely on an ultraconstructivist theory of sex and sexuality, the criteria for the commercialization and public distribution of these molecules continues to respond to a naturalistic metaphysics of sexual difference that claims the biologically and historically unchangeable existence of two sexes (man and woman), two sexualities (heterosexual and homosexual), and, more recently, two genders (male and female), from which springs the field of deviance and pathology.

For the moment, no Western nation has accepted the legalization of testosterone for women and allowed it to be freely administered to them, understanding that such a situation would risk a semiotechnical virilization of the female population on its both social and political levels. Two slight somato-political problems that would modify the visual and auditory deciphering of gender are facial pilosity and voice change. It is astounding that in the West, at the beginning of the twenty-first century, in a society that has extremely high-tech methods for the management of reproduction, the deciphering of gender is reduced to degree of facial hair and timbre of the voice. We can therefore say that the beard and the voice, and not the penis and the vagina or X and Y chromosomes, are the dominant cultural public signifiers of gender in our society. Let us cease to speak about men and women and simply say, hairy or smooth body, body with a high voice or with a low voice. These are not details but crucial sexopolitical signifiers with the ability to put into question the idea of virility as the natural prerogative of cis-males. The ultimate problem resides in revealing the politically constructed character of the genders, as well as of heterosexuality and homosexuality.

While I am following my testosterone protocol, several European governments, including the French government and the generality of Catalonia, are studying the use of "chemical castration" technologies as a penal measure (rather than a therapeutic one) for sex offenders (and especially for pedophiles). The French right-wing president Nicolas Sarkozy's intention, made public on August 21, 2007, to create a law mandating the use of chemical castration therapies for sex offenders, is one more step in the escalation of the use of biopolitical power to produce and control male sexuality. What processes of bodily transformation are really entailed by such chemical castration? When, how, and on which bodies have similar means of the pharmacological management of identity been already used? What are the underlying political fictions of masculinity and femininity connected to this legal project, and what type of subject are we trying to produce collectively?

Let us examine our pharmacopornopolitical archives: chemical castration consists in administering a cocktail more or less full of antiandrogens (cyproterone acetate, progestogen, or gonadotropin regulators), in other words, molecules that inhibit the production of testosterone. Although one of the effects of antiandrogens can be the diminishment of sexual desire (thought of in this case as excitation and erectile response), it is often not mentioned that the side effects of these drugs are a reduction in the size of the penis, the development of breasts, modification of muscle mass, and accumulation of fat in the hips. In other words, it is a process of "hormonal feminization." We ought not be surprised to discover that substances with similar antiandrogen effects are used (voluntarily) by transsexuals who are beginning a process of feminization and are changing their gender.

Despite its renaturalizing power, the pharmacoporno regime continually reveals its ultraconstructivist foundations. If we explore the political history of the chemical castration technology, we will learn that it was used in the 1950s in the repressive treatment of male homosexuality; it was, for example, the type of therapy prescribed by English law for Alan Turing, one of the originators of modern computer science. Accused of homosexuality, grave indecency, and sexual perversion, he was compelled to submit to a program of hormonal therapy.[115] One sign of a certain scientific confusion is the fact that the same drug is part of current research on a "gay bomb," a hormonal compound that the American army intends to use to transform its enemies into homosexuals.[116] While the United States needs testosterone, its enemies need hormonal feminization.

What the facts show is that chemical castration is a pharmacopornopolitical mechanism aiming less to reduce sexual aggression than to modify the gender of the supposed aggressor. It's important to draw attention to these therapies as existing exclusively to manage the male "sexual predator." And the means of punishing and controlling male sexuality is to transform it symbolically and somatically into femininity.

The double-edged effect of these pharmacopornographic policies connects with traditional modes of producing sex-

115. Alan Turing finally committed suicide in 1954. See Andrew Hodges and Douglas Hofstadter, *Alan Turing: The Enigma* (New York: Walker & Company, 2000).

116. For more about the homophobic fantasy of American war discourse, see Judith Butler, "Contingent Foundations: Feminism and the Question of 'Postmodernism,'" *Praxis International* 11, no. 2 (July 1991): 150–65. An excerpt from this article was also published with another title: "The Imperialist Subject," *Journal of Urban and Cultural Studies* 2, no. 2 (1991): 73–78.

ual difference in the disciplinary regime: political criminalization of male sexuality and victimization of female sexuality. Chemical regulation always portrays the erection, and as a corollary, masculinity, as a phenomenon that can be produced or heightened by vasodilators or controlled and repressed by chemical castration,[117] thereby placing it in the category of an involuntary impulse that is suitable for political management. Meanwhile, feminine sexuality is constructed as a passive territory on which the violence of male sexuality is exerted. There is no biological destiny beyond pharmacopornopolitical programs.

Democratizing the consumption of hormones, which continue to be viewed as sexual, would require a radical change of our gender and sexual topographies. Freely circulating and collectively used testosterone is dynamite for the heterosexual regime. It's no longer only a question of asserting the existence of four or five sexes, as several scientists and theorists of sexuality desire,[118] but of accepting the completely technoconstructed, undeniably multiple, malleable, and mutable nature of bodies and pleasures.

The Pill and State Feminism

The masterstroke of the pharmacopornographic regime is its having exploited the revolutionary and emancipatory rhetoric of the feminist movement of the 1960s to pass off the chemical and contraceptive management of the female body as a step toward sexual liberation. In the same way,

117. Let's not forget that François Evrard, the catalyst who launched this legal polemic in France, had a pack of Viagra in his pocket at the time of the rape.

118. cf. Anne Fausto-Sterling, "The Five Sexes: Why Male and Female Are Not Enough," *The Sciences* (March/April 1993): 20–24.

abolitionist feminism entrusted the management of the production and representation of pornography and the sex industry to the state, by demanding the abolition of prostitution and the penalization of pornography.[119] In the case of pornography, the result of these measures was the reduction of the sex industry to an underground economy and the marginalization and impoverishment of its workers. When it comes to the "politics of family planning," the result is administration on a vast scale of estrogen and progesterone for every cis-female in the fertile years. We can assert, and not without a certain rage, that white liberal abolitionist feminism was able to function as one of the paragovernmental ideological devices of the pharmacopornographic regime. It becomes necessary to oppose state feminism with a molecular and postpornographic transfeminism. The grammar and techniques that liberal feminism has plundered from us must be reappropriated to trigger a new counter-pharmacopornographic revolution.

As a contraceptive method, feminism could have made masturbation obligatory, promulgated a sexual strike among heterosexual and fertile women, and advocated lesbianism en masse; made it obligatory to tie the Fallopian tubes at adolescence; and legalized abortion and made it free—if not permitting infanticide when necessary. And there is a political-fiction scenario that could have been even more promising: it was possible, from a biotechnological point of view, to require all women who are of child-

119. The case most representative of using feminism as a state technique of control of prostitution and pornography occurred in the nineties in Canada, where the state solicited feminist rhetoric to establish its abolitionist politics.

bearing age to take a monthly microdose of testosterone, as both a contraceptive measure and a political method of regulating gender. Such a measure would have ended once and for all sexual differentiation and the hegemony of heterosexuality. This doesn't mean that cis-females (on testosterone) would stop having sex with cis-males, but the act would not continue to be interpreted as purely heterosexual. It would have no reproductive goal; in addition, it would no longer be a question of an encounter between two people of opposite sexual orientations, but rather, between two people of gay orientation with the added possibility of vaginal penetration. Postwar feminism could have concerned itself with the management of the cis-male body and declared it to be of national interest: castration, male homosexuality, the obligatory use of condoms, the sealing of the seminal channel, mass administration of Androcur (to lower the production of testosterone in cis-males), and so on. Yes, there were other possibilities, but liberal feminism made a pact with the pharmacopornographic regime.

Testo-trafficking

As a drug, testosterone is relatively easy to buy and sell. A large quantity of it moves through the black market in the field of athletics and cycling. It can be administered through subcutaneous injection, gel, patch, implant, nasal inhaler, or aerosol. In 2006, the sports media called testosterone "the real winner of the Tour de France" and had no qualms about claiming that "testosterone is the drug of champions." Many high-level athletes have tested positive for the presence of synthetic testosterone in their blood. It makes me chuckle a little when I read interviews in which they declare, "This testosterone is my own, it's natural." Poor idiots. It's like Pamela Anderson trying to pass her size 45E silicone prostheses off as natural just because she's a cis-female. It's not at all difficult to go to a bodybuilder's website to order ten doses of 250-milligram testosterone for seventy-five dollars, postage included. This is the paradox inherent in the strict legal controls that govern the pharmacopornographic regime: gender is for sale.

Applied to a woman's body, testosterone distorts that body's relationship to the course of time as well as its value on the heterosexual market. The temporal logic of the genders is asymmetric. Femininity loses value three times faster than does masculinity. In other words, a woman (whether cis- or trans-) is out of the heterosexual market at forty-five, whereas a man can reach sixty-five before becoming obsolete. To calculate the true age of a woman in the heterocapitalist economy, it's necessary to add fifteen years to make her equal to her male equivalent; then two years can be subtracted for each beauty advantage (breast size, thinness, length and thickness of the hair, etc.), and two years must be added for each social handicap (divorce, number of children—each counting two years more—unemployment, etc.). Let's take an example: Julie is thirty-two; she's a divorced cis-female with a child to take care of and keeps in shape, does yoga, is pretty but doesn't have a perfect body; she is slender and works in an insurance company: 32 + 15 + 2 + 2 + 2 + 2 = 45. That's the hard reality. She will have to stop thinking of herself as a youthful creature of thirty-two, because her real age in the heterocapitalist economy is forty-five. Bye-bye, Julie. Another possibility would be to go over to the equivalent dyke market, where one's true age diminishes prodigiously. A woman who has reached forty-five in the heterocapitalist economy can arrive at the lesbian economy with a status close to adolescence. Bingo.

Let us consider for a moment the possibility of a molecular revolution of the genders. What would happen if a large proportion of cis-females began collectively self-administering enough doses of testosterone to be socially identified as males? What value would natural masculinity possess? Such a politicohormonal fiction experiment becomes even more pertinent if one thinks that these future technomales, this new species of mutant cis-females identifiable as male bodies, would be capable of breeding and giving birth, corresponding to what Julia Kristeva calls the "female genius."[120] After using testosterone for six months, at a rate of four hundred milligrams a month, facial pilosity and a changed voice become irreversible. On the other hand, interrupting the administration of testosterone for a few months is enough for menstruation to return, and with it, the potential for fertilization, pregnancy, and childbirth (although the beard and the voice change remain). Fertilization would be just as possible by sexual exchange of reproductive fluids as it would by medically controlled insemination. Sex and in vitro are just two culturally assisted reproduction technologies. Let's take the example of two male bodies, a technomale that still has a vagina and uterus and a cis-male inseminating him by vagi-

120. Julia Kristeva, "Female Genius: General Introduction," in *Hannah Arendt*, trans. Ross Guberman (New York: Columbia University Press, 2001), ix.

nal penetration using a biopenis possessing fertile sperma-tozoids (something that seems rarer and rarer in today's highly toxic ecology). Seen from the outside, this scene resembles the gay pornographic aesthetic of the twentieth century; but in reality, it goes beyond gay sex and hetero-sexual sex and points to a technosex future. Obviously, as a technomale, it would be equally possible to be inseminated with donor sperm. At any rate, we would be confronting a new species of technomale postsexual reproducer. And this is the beginning of new perspectives regarding struggles and pharmacopornographic resignifications.

Since I've been taking testosterone, I look at the men and women going by me each day in the subway, supermar-ket, museum, as bodies whose political decoding has been abusively and brutally determined by the amount of tes-tosterone they produce or administer to themselves. In line with VD to see *King Kong* at the movies,[121] I amuse myself by taking each of the human forms passing into my field of vision and mentally increasing or decreasing its testos-terone level. The cis-males simply resemble women with more or less testosterone to which a biopolitical plus-value has been added, and who have been told since childhood, "You're worth more than girls; the world belongs to you; they belong to you; your cock rules over everything that exists." Cis-females are just surgically and endocrinologi-cally modified "men": sophisticated and not so sophisti-cated interlacings of synthetic collagen, silicone implants, and active estrogen, but still lacking biopolitical legitimacy.

121. Virginie Despentes, *King Kong Theory*, trans. Stéphanie Benson (New York: Feminist Press, 2010).

9. TESTO-MANIA

A week ago, during a night of work on Testogel, the barriers give way and I finally manage to understand in detail the stages in the formation of gender—all the way to the condition of sexuality itself. Each element finds its proper place, and the mechanisms link together:

$$\text{Male x Homo x Sado x Testosterone x Estrogen}$$
$$= \text{Trans} = (\mu\,)$$
$$\text{Female x Hetero x Maso x Estrogen x Testosterone}$$

Sniffing cocaine. Ingesting codeine. Injecting morphine. Smoking nicotine. Taking Prozac. Swallowing amphetamines. Taking Heptamyl. Drinking alcohol. Putting yourself on Suboxone. Going back on Special K. Shooting heroin. Getting high on laughing gas. Relapsing with crack. Smoking cannabis. Popping some E. Taking an aspirin. Snorting crystal meth. Taking Lexomil. Applying Testogel: artistocratic pharmacomania.

Why bother changing your mental state when you can change your sexopolitical status? Why change your mood when you can change identities? Behold the sexopolitical superiority of steroids.

We must know whether we want to change the world to experience it with the same sensorial system as the one we already possess, or whether we'd rather modify our body, the somatic filter through which it passes. Which is preferable: changing my personality and keeping my body, or changing my body and keeping my current manner of experiencing reality? A fake dilemma. Our personalities arise from this very gap between body and reality.

Power girls—orgasms—adrenaline—extravagance—social recognition—success—glucose—family acceptance—inclusion—strength—tension—camaraderie—financial ascent. In the space of six months, these are the political surplus values obtained by a cis-female who ingests testosterone.

Testosterone is immediate gratification, an abstract platform for the production of power, but without the abrupt comedown of coke, without the hole in your stomach that comes after the effects of crystal have worn off, without the grotesque self-satisfaction triggered by Prozac. There is only one drug like testosterone: heroin. The two drugs are politically dangerous and can lead to exclusion, marginalization, desocialization—and in the case of testosterone, cancer (as is the case for almost all industrial products) as well as hair loss (a lesser disadvantage that you can compensate for with a prosthesis).

I think about taking another dose, the last one—yet again, the last one. Am I going to become a testo-maniac?

Starting with my own experience, with my practice of voluntary hormonal intoxication, I develop a theory (a completely absurd one) about heterosexual attraction. It has always seemed inexplicable to me, since I was a child. Understanding heterosexuality as a technology of "hormonal enrichment," because my essays are leading me toward such a theory, hardly fascinates me. It is a preposterous hypothesis that reveals something that I find disquieting. What if cis-females known as "heterosexual" were trying to rub shoulders with (cis- or trans-) men to obtain their dose of testosterone from the sweat of their partner? Something as simple as that. Cis-chicks sleeping with (cis- or trans-) guys in order to collect their dose of T, through friction with their skin. That would also explain the progressive masculinization of female sex workers, who develop more facial fuzz than wage-earning cis-females, such as those who work as cashiers at convenience stores. As a result of repeated contact with the testosterone-infused sweat of their clients, the percentage of testosterone in their blood begins to increase. I'm not being serious. This idea is most probably the effect on my brain of too much reading about endocrinology; or, maybe, it's an accurate explanation of the functioning of one of the hormonal channels of our political makeup. There are two possibilities, then: either I'm losing my mind or I'm possessed by your spirit.

YOUR SPERM AND MY OVA

I can feel you next to me, as if you were alive. I remember: you come to pick me up at my house on rue Jean-Pierre Timbaud. You don't come upstairs. You don't want to see the sociologist; you can't stand her. According to you, she's like a teacher from the sticks who always wants to know if you've done your homework. You wait for me at the café next to the Center for Wobbly Knee Rehabilitation. We order two coffees. We aren't drinking alcohol. We're saving ourselves for the possibility of there being a little coke, crystal, or E at the bar where we're going tonight. You're not in a good mood. Unshaven, wearing the same white T-shirt, the same light-blue cotton sweater, and the same jeans you were wearing two days ago. *Je te trouve sexe.* You're exhaling testosterone. You say you haven't fucked anybody for a long time. That you're becoming a lesbian. I myself can think only about sex. Even so, I'm not fucking anybody right now. You order two double espressos, one right after the other. I get one espresso with a drop of milk, a noisette. When you speak to me, you don't look me in the eye. You look at my hands, roll pieces of the paper tablecloth into pellets, then flick them at me. I ask you to stop bugging me. I punch you in the shoulder, not hard, just a sharp tap, as if to say, get it together. We discuss mixing your sperm with my ova. I don't know how we get into that conversation. No one asked anyone for anything. You're reading Sloterdijk's "Rules for the Human Theme-Park." If the explosion of the first two atomic bombs over Hiroshima and Nagasaki in 1945 mark the beginning of a geopolitical apocalypse, then the appearance of the first cloned sheep known as Dolly marks the beginning of a biological apocalypse. Humanity does not exist under the sign of the divine, you say, but of the monstrous. Human stands for Human©. You think you're more important than Heidegger,

Habermas, and Sloterdijk—and you are. I'm the only one who's on your level. You and I, who are looking ahead to the future monster. We talk about synthetic reproduction. You say that it shouldn't be called *reproduction* but *synthetic production*—the fabrication of an entirely new species. A species made up of post-Jews and post-Catholics, a species that will come after the current bifurcated sexuality of either being homo or hetero, guy or girl. We're realistic. We'll have to begin by filtering the HIV out of your sperm. You say that all those procedures cost too much and that we can't afford the analyses, filtration, freezing, insemination. We could ask for a grant from the Centre national du livre, explaining that we're planning to write a political memoir on the process of genetic recombination of your infected sperm and my dyke-trans ova. Considering the number of liters of sperm you've ejaculated up to this day, we could, conceivably, inseminate half the planet. If you'd sold your sperm before becoming HIV positive, you'd have had enough money now to pay for filtration and insemination. Or we could buy back an uncontaminated sample of your sperm. But before you got HIV, spreading your genes probably wouldn't have been of interest to you. We talk about filtering your sperm to separate the spermatozoids that are carrying the HIV virus from the others. Separating the weak cells from the strong ones. The bad from the good. I know you hate me for considering the possibility of filtration, even if you're the one who's insisting that we do it like that. You hate me because I'm incapable of wanting that sick sperm as it is, incapable of jerking you off right away and putting your contaminated sperm into my vagina; you hate me because, like you, I'm afraid of dying. What would happen if it was one of your spermatozoids infected with AIDS that contained the gene of the future savior of the planet? We ask ourselves if desire, need, obsession, shame at filtering your semen are eugenist, if a possibility for life should be eliminated because it carries a deadly virus. Yes, such a desire is eugenist—it is—and deep down, neither you nor I can bear the idea of reproduction. Not from your lineage, or from mine. Fatherhood and motherhood are always a compromise between a form of Nazi eugenics and a compulsion for repetition. But which is the most eugenicist? Producing something good technologically, or letting life fight bareknuckled with death until one of them wins? In the last analysis, if one of your spermatozoids that carried the virus succeeded in fertilizing one of my ova, if our chromosomes ended up recombining and the cell that was formed in that way managed to divide and form a blastomere that could be implanted in my testosterone-infused uterus, then we would be obliged to think of these two gametes as having passed the test of life. The body that will come to save the planet really could arise from such a monstrous and absurd act, from the opportunity for your seropositive spermatozoids to swim to the life hidden in my mutant body. From Canguilhem, whose words strike deeper than Sloterdijk's: "Successes are delayed failures; failures are aborted successes. What decides the value of a form is what becomes of it. All living forms are, to use Louis Roule's expression in *Les poissons*, 'normalized monsters.'"[1]

1. George Canguilhem, *Knowledge of Life (Forms of Living)*, trans. by Stefanos Geroulanos and Daniela Ginsburg (New York: Fordham University Press, 2008), 126.

LAST SCUFFLES

Nam idem velle atque idem nolle,
ea demum firma amicitia est.
               —SALLUST

Twelve days have passed since you died. I see you coming out of a butcher shop in Belleville. The same mustache; the same raised scar on the upper lip. I spot you again walking Justine in the parc des Buttes-Chaumont: behind a bush, your form, the same way of wearing jeans, the same tuft of thick black hair poking over the neck of your white T-shirt. Your ghost rummages through my memory and digs out what it finds: you're calling me. I see the letters of your name appearing in bright blue on the black screen of my telephone. I don't answer it. I wait for you to leave a message. It's your voice. Your voice, that's the strongest. And it says, "Hey, hellooo, Preciado, why aren't you taking my call? You're pissing me off, OK? But forget it, I wanted to know whether you've got a book for the series, but it's up to you. That's it, just that. I'm calling you. I'm going to pick you up on rue Saint-André-des-Arts. We'll eat at the café on the corner of rue Suger."

I couldn't decide what I should wear to see you. I spent an hour in the bathroom. I shaved my head completely. Put on the black V-necked sweater and sneakers I was wearing the night we went out together and I saw a hairy gorilla fucking you in the ass as you got your kicks like some little fifteen-year-old chick. I've corrected several pages that I wrote during the last few days. I bring you two projects.

You don't even look at them. You say to me, "Why don't you come out with a book on that story about zoophilia and pedophilia we were talking about the other day?" You say that smilingly, slightly raising your upper lip, and your harelip scar holds back half your lip near the gum, pulls your nose downward when you speak. You couldn't care less about me. I don't know how to answer.

"You really are a son of a bitch. A real asshole." I say to you, "Yeah, and next you'll be the one who brings me paper and pencils in prison so I can keep writing radical books." Son of a bitch.

You want to get this over with. You lay it on thick. "Don't think you're so important. What's going on here is that you don't have the balls to write."

I answer that what I want to write about is the history of the transvestite movement in the 1970s, the history of radical feminist lesbians, of the revolutionary Gay Liberation Front, the "red dykes" and "*commando saucisson*," the *petroleuses*, transvestites, and transsexuals around which the political sex movement in France arose. The *camionneuses* and the girls around Hocquenghem. I tell you that I've met Hervé and that he's kept a lot of the archives from that period, and that I've also run into three dyke grannies, who are beginning to lose their memories. That almost all the others are dead. That it has to be done quickly, because soon there will be nothing left.

You barely look at me while I'm talking to you; you withdraw, doodle planets in your notebook. I inform you that I'm going to need a few bucks. That it's not going to be the way it was with the other book. That four hundred euros barely pays for the ink cartridges. You say, "You're looking for trouble, you're asking for it."

You say, "I mean, shit, what could you have to say about this queer stuff?"

You say you thought I wasn't like the other chicks, and that for me it was all about fucking, but now you realize that I'm like the other lesbians, ready to become the political nurse for anyone I meet. I answer, I'm not a lesbian, I'm trans, a boy, that the fact that I don't have a shitty biocock like yours doesn't mean that I'm not a guy. I tell you, Stop treating me like cow shit just because you take me for a girl. You tell me I bother you, that you're ashamed for me, that I shouldn't count on you publishing that fag stuff, that it would be a better idea for me to call *Têtu* and write an article. You burst out laughing. I don't want to contradict you. I don't want to get mad at you, because if you don't publish my books, who will? But I hate you for speaking to me that way.

The last time I see you alive. We're dining at Tim and Philippe's place. You want to give me an old parka that belongs to you. You're laughing as you tell me that it's a good style for eighties lesbians. You're a piece of shit. You tell me, and as for you, you're finished. What does that make you, to be outshone by Marcela Iacub? You're nothing but a pathetic asshole, you're over, dead.

LOSSES

After having taken 250 milligrams a month for two months, I suddenly begin to have continual losses of blood. Little thick brown hemorrhages that stain all my shorts. Nothing hurts, but the fact of this dark, gelatinous blood between my legs bothers me. I figure it's the price that I, who am not woman, man, or transsexual, have to pay for my addiction to testosterone.

I go to see a gynecologist. Tell about the losses of blood. Add that I take between fifty and a hundred milligrams of testosterone a week. I don't specify that sometimes it's more, sometimes less.

"As a means of contraception? But you must know there are more reliable methods," she answers.

Perhaps because you and I haven't reproduced the savior of our planet, lately, since you died, I catch myself wishing for the end of the human species. Not its progress, its betterment, but merely the end, a break in our chain of being. Your death is the sign of the arrival of what certain scientists call the "sixth extinction."[2] Everything begins with bacteria, more than twenty-seven billion years ago: after the explosion of the water molecule, which produced the hydrogen needed for the formation of their cellular components, bacteria produced a large quantity of oxygen. This same oxygen, which in principal was highly toxic, corrosive, and inflammable, changed the composition of the planet's

2. Niles Eldredge, *Life in the Balance: Humanity and the Biodiversity Crisis* (Princeton, NJ: Princeton University Press, 2000), 171-76.

atmosphere and permitted animal life to appear on earth on a large scale. The first extinction, a vast glaciation that exterminated nearly all marine life, took place 435 million years ago. Bacteria survived, and with them their system of producing oxygen. A million years later, in the second extinction, a large portion of fish and marine invertebrates disappeared again. Bacteria survived again. Another million years later, most underwater and terrestrial species were wiped out during the most extreme of all the extinctions. Bacteria survived. Two hundred and ten million years ago, a good number of aquatic species succumbed once more, and the extinction of the first mammals inaugurated the dinosaur period. Sixty million years ago, the fifth extinction caused the disappearance of the dinosaurs. Once more, bacteria survived. Gradually, small mammals spread over the continental plates, which were adrift, and the fish began populating the oceans again. I'm unsure how to choose between killing myself; becoming a serial killer; devoting my life to the trans-moral development of humanity as a species and its intentional mutation; and forming a transfeminist army whose mission would be to do in everything opposed to it, without distinction. And all that on behalf of love and planetary charity. Gradually, I'm learning to appreciate your idea of universal HIV contamination as the aesthetic culmination of the punk destiny of our species. Canguilhem again: "It is well known that species near their end once they have committed themselves to irreversible and inflexible directions and have presented themselves in rigid form."[3] We are preparing for a new era of bacterial

3. Canguilhem, *Knowledge of Life*, 125.

hegemony. Meanwhile, the proliferation of the human continues in cramped coexistence with viruses: polio, AIDS, bird influenza. Politics interests me in the same way that the virus is strongly interested by the epidemic. The issue of feminism interests me in the same way that the earth is interested by bacteria. Challenging rigid constructions of gender and fossilized forms of sexuality can be accomplished only through viral proliferation, at the same time as through bacterial survival. On all fronts, in all spaces. My body: the body of the multitude.

ADDICTIVE FRUSTRATION

I would have liked to have fallen into a dependence, have the security of permanently and chemically clinging to something. Deep down, I was hoping that testosterone would be that substance. To be attached, not to a subjectivity, but to the change produced by the ingestion into my organism of a substance without will. Depending on no one for that ingestion. Confronting my wish for an object that has no wish. My desire for an object that does not desire. Knowing that the terms of the deal are between an inanimate substance and me. Knowing that in the outside world there exists a molecule capable of integrating with my emotional metabolism and freeing me from weight, sound, taste, and the color of pure reality. Until now, I haven't been able to become dependent on anything. Not tobacco, or coke, or heroin—nothing. I wonder if I could have become hooked on testosterone. What I am certain of is that, on the molecular level, the battle of addiction has already begun.

I wake up next to her. Before opening my eyes, I hear her voice. She's telling me a story about being straight. Every morning, girls give their men blowjobs to satisfy them, so they won't sleep around. Girls' blowjobs are performative: they produce masculinity for the men they are supposed to suck, I answer. She slides a leg between my two, positions her head above my pelvis and sticks her tongue into my sex.

She talks to me about the difficulty for a woman who has, until now, been heterosexual in detecting excitement in a body that lacks a biocock. She says, "How to be sure that the other desires you?" I've never thought about it. An erect cock makes it easier to decode desire. An erect cock seems to say, "You're getting me hard, I'm going to screw you, ejaculate." She tells me how frustrated she was the first time she made love with a woman. She says that now she understands men better, their fragility when encountering a kind of desire that lacks any visible anatomical signs, that in dealing with a body without an erectile biocock, it's always possible that you're wrong about thinking you detect excitement, that you're being misled by your senses. It's as if language could be dissociated from anatomy with bodies deprived of an easily visible erectile appendix. ("I'm attracted to you, you're exciting me, but no one but me is privy to that excitement, you won't know anything about it, you won't be able to detect it against my will.") In bodies without a visible erectile appendix, desire exists within a poetic space of indeterminacy, a sexual jurisdiction that expresses itself as internalized knowledge before becoming visible. Strangely, heterophilosophy's patriarchs, Nietzsche[4] and Otto Weininger,[5] deemed this territory belonging to femininity as the space where nonknowledge, pretense, and falsehood could be located. It would be more appropriate to speak of a hyperconsciousness, a form of knowledge having the power to decide whether it does or does not wish to express itself through representation. This knowledge of desire before it becomes detectable as an erection unlocks the possibility of sex as fiction, as potentiality. In lesbian sexuality, the signs of excitement are deciphered on an extensive anatomical cartography: the glance, the movement of the hands, the accuracy of touch, the mouth's degree of openness, the amount of sweat or wetness. I remember that the first time I fucked a cis-guy, his cock seemed like a secondary object endowed with involuntary motivity, its functioning was supposed to be a trustworthy indicator of desire or excitement. On the contrary. I had the impression of being in the presence of a signifying impostor, a biopolitical ancestral leftover whose presence only overshadowed the place where desire really emerges.

4. Paul Patton, ed., *Nietzsche, Feminism and Political Theory* (London: Routledge, 1993); Peter J. Burgard, ed., *Nietzsche and the Feminine* (Charlottesville, VA: Virginia University Press, 1994).

5. Otto Weininger, *Sex and Character: An Investigation on Fundamental Principles*, eds. Daniel Steuer and Laura Marcus, trans. Ladislaus Löb (Indianapolis: Indiana University Press, 2005).

TESTO-MANIA

One's relationship to testosterone changes as soon as one leaves the framework of a medical and legal protocol for changing sex. In the medical protocol, *changing sex* implies making a unique decision, a choice made once and once only. But things are more complex than that. I don't want to change my sex, and I don't want to declare myself dysphoric about whatever it may be; I don't want a doctor to decide how much testosterone a month is suitable for changing my voice and making me grow a beard; I don't want to have my ovaries and breasts removed. Even if I do not want to procreate, I don't want my reproductive cells to be hijacked by the state; I don't want my uterus to be confiscated by the medical-industrial complex. There is no predefined direction for the changes in me that are triggered by testosterone. What I do know is that, before testosterone, my voice was not a woman's voice, my beardless face not a woman's face, my clitoris, measuring less than two centimeters, not a female organ. Simply because femaleness is a biopolitical fiction, a variable within a power regime that cannot be derived from anatomical form or reproductive function, I don't need permission from the Spanish monarchy or the French Republic to do up some testosterone. I lay claim to the irreducible plurality of my living body, not to my body as "bare life," but to the very materiality of my body as political site for agency and resistance.

The problem is as follows: outside the institutional context defined by the state, testosterone is no longer part of a therapy of hormonal substitution and becomes an illegal drug, just like cocaine or heroin. The consequences—in legal and medical terms—of my rejection of the protocol must therefore be admitted: I'm addicted to testosterone.

My relationship with V could be defined in this way: Dependent on Despentes. My relationship with T could be defined in this way: T-dependent. Even when I'm with the two of them. Especially when I'm with them. *Hooked*. It becomes obvious that my relationship with V belongs to the type of codependency categorized under the sign of addiction. *Dependence*. I've found my drug, and it is, like all drugs, available and elusive at the same time. You could say that any kind of love relationship is addictive in a certain way. But I don't believe that. It wasn't like that for me the other times. I know from experience that there are forms of love that function according to the model of a satisfying form of feedback. Why am I certain that this love, this and not another, corresponds to the addiction model and not to a cybernetic mechanism of satisfaction? First of all, because there is a dissymmetrical relationship between the ingestion of, or the presence of, the object of desire and satisfaction. Second of all, because that satisfaction takes the form of withdrawal. Right where satisfaction is supposed to take place, frustration emerges. When I'm kissing her, I think I want to kiss her; when I'm talking with her, I think I have an urgent need to talk with her. When it spills out across my skin, I think I want it to spill out across my skin; and when my body absorbs it, I think I want to absorb it, more and more. The present moment, the instant of assimilation, has no importance compared with the overweening necessity for what must come immediately after. More, more, as quickly as possible. A moment later, desire will be still more intense, and on and on, more and more. Desire doesn't destroy itself. It transforms itself, changing into an unconscious state during fatigue or sleep. I desire to continue desiring, without any possibility of satiation. Few substances have led me beyond this threshold of addiction. Alcohol has never interested me. During one period, I took crystal: megapower for the brain. I spoke French fluently, in one night, thanks to an overdose of crystal. Perhaps my accent wasn't changed, but my ability to use vocabulary and my relationship with grammar were radically improved; it was like attaining a new level of consciousness in a foreign language. Efficient, but not to be used regularly. I barely use coke, or Ecstasy or speed; or rather, I use them very rarely, only for those times when I go back to Barcelona or Madrid (when you're passing through metropolitan Spain, a certain toxicological dose is absolutely necessary), and only in those cases. These are city drugs, with the appropriate molecular charge for cohabiting and communicating in a specific urban location. My metabolism has never accepted any substance meant as a compensatory substitution. My only drugs, in all their romantic or anonymous variations, are testosterone and sex, which form, in that way, a circle of mutual production. Both of them affect me inasmuch as their being likely to put me in contact with the amorphous, with the formless, or with that which imagines a form in place of formlessness, that which produces desire without any possible satisfaction. Gender identity, or pleasure are beyond the ken of the possible.

Today, without realizing it, we're sliding into one of those abysses into which we regularly fall every ten or twelve days. Between two doses of T. Such cyclical alienation could become one of our routines, a key to stability. Through these microbreakups, which are forms of preventative distancing, our symptomatically addictive relationship destroys and regenerates itself. To be more precise, it should be said that she is the one who descends, alone, into these depressions, dragging me along with the childlike hyperactive eyes of an inconsolable rocker, who's no longer sure exactly whether she has just killed someone or learned that she's going to be murdered. The sadness in her eyes is located precisely in the tension between these two possibilities. I've identified her as the driving force of such downward movement, but perhaps it's actually I who reach the bottom, leading her there with a maximum amount of enthusiasm, kindness. Such depths are by necessity liquid; she weeps, plunges into a hot bath, starts doing a wash. It's a pre-fetal, pre-sexual, premature sadness. The day this happens is the same day I have to go for a blood test. Deep down, something is flowing, circulating within a circumscribed space, but it can spread. On this stratum, feelings exist in their gelatinous state, just before the evaporation and transformations of carbon solutions into electric currents. Such is the state of blood, water, sperm, vaginal secretions, saliva, urine, rachidian and amniotic solutions, the infusion in which the brain floats; but also what one has just ingested, the gel, and exterior nourishment for the body during the process of gastric assimilation, before it's transformed into fecal matter. *To fall in love,* Derrida said, is falling into a precise topography, rising by detachment or utter dejection to a particular stratum of being, body, city, planet, evolution, species. This is where the conversion of scale occurs: love of being, carnal love, urban love, earthly love, geological love, animal love, interspecies love. It isn't the place to conceive of a Heideggerian rictus, in any way. I'm talking about an architecture. Not a revelation, an unveiling of being by some precise inspiration, or making the real emerge in spotlit clarity. That isn't what I'm talking about. I'm talking about a tactile perception, occurring in darkness, about thumping the bottom with your stomach, crawling on a viscous mass. No illumination, but feeling around in the dark. I'm talking about discovering the surface of an interiority with your skin. It's a matter of returning to cyberreptilian life, a regression, tasting the electrically viscous truth of being, with small strokes of your tongue. No more long inhalations, because you haven't arrived at the state where being is given to us in its ethereal form. We have no other solution than to lick at being. Suck it, as the sole mode of knowledge and apprehension. It is here that the secret of addiction reveals its arithmetic. There is neither light nor oxygen, no means of respiration of being, no possibility of finding any optical or pulmonary satisfaction. It's a question of diameter, texture, and fluidity. The moment we end up in one of these gelatinous lower depths, getting out is as difficult for her as it is for me. There is the same degree of anxiety, the same sadness. When it comes down to it, there are no levels, because the bottom is just that: the bottom. We're imprisoned in a monad, a single unit. Finding how to get out means, purely and simply, changing the ground, solidifying liquefied feelings to get a foothold, or evaporating them so you can breathe. It's the time for understanding that the transubstantiation of affect won't happen today, and the only recourse is to call AS. No one is faster than he is. He comes for the first time on the last day of the year 2005, to put an end to one period and inaugurate another. He responds to the call like a doctor to an emergency, in less than ten minutes. He's in charge of several musical genres: rock, heavy metal, hip-hop, Afro-Brazilian fusion. He devotes a little of his free time to subduing addictions, at home, in record time. His arrival immediately changes the muddy ground on which we're dawdling. He rings the doorbell, Justine barks, and as soon as he enters the apartment, everything slowly becomes lighter. AS likes to talk, and he's wise enough to put on a film or play some music in the background, something that serves as a grid for verbal disorientation. The doorbell rings again. PE and EN are bringing a new guitar that needs its strings changed. Then PE takes off a pair of smoke-gray glasses, asks EN for a pair of pliers, goes into a rant against Papa Roach, breaks into "Take My Money," mocking the melody, and cuts the strings one by one. The fibers snap, like old electric snakes that could tear your head off. Like a blind person, PE caresses the guitar. Brings his face close to it, passes his fingers over it, insists on a maximum of closeness between his skin and the neck of the guitar. The new strings undulate between his fingers like young cobras rearing up, seem to find the holes in the pegs by themselves. The snakes recognize the touch of rock, find their way to the music. He attaches them with precision, and without looking; it's impossible to imagine a more perfect compassion, a more sincere devotion than that existing between the strings and his fingers. AS prepares a joint made of pure pot and begins talking. I lock myself in the bathroom to apply a dose of T. V puts on a documentary about the Monterey Pop Festival; Janis Joplin's voice opens up a universal channel of musical vibration, and, suddenly, love becomes breathable.

TRANS OR JUNKIE?

This is how things appear, and it's going to be necessary to face them: if I don't accept defining myself as a transsexual, as someone with "gender dysphoria," I must admit that I'm addicted to testosterone. As soon as a body abandons the practices that society deems masculine or feminine, it drifts gradually toward pathology. My biopolitical options are as follows: either I declare myself to be a transsexual, or I declare myself to be drugged and psychotic. Given the current state of things, it seems more prudent to me to label myself a transsexual and let the medical establishment believe that it can offer a satisfying cure for my "gender identity disorder." In that case, I'll have to accept having been born in a biobody with which I don't identify (as if the body could be a material given that is there before linguistic or political action) and claim that I detest my body, my reproductive organs, and my way of getting an orgasm.

I'll have to rewrite my history, modify all the elements in it that belong under the narrative of being female. I'll have to employ a series of extremely calculated falsehoods: I've always hated Barbie dolls, I'm repulsed by my breasts and my vagina, vaginal penetration makes me sick, and the only way I can have an orgasm is with a dildo. All this could be partly true and partly nonsense. In other words, I'll have to declare myself mentally ill and conform to the criteria established by the *DMS-IV*, the *Diagnostic and Statistical Manual of Mental Disorders*, fourth edition, of the American Psychiatric Association, in which, beginning in 1980, transsexuality was designated as a mental illness, just like exhibitionism, fetishism, frotteurism, masochism, sadism, transvestism, voyeurism . . . just like almost everything that isn't straight reproductive sexuality and its binary gender system.

If I refuse to accept that medical classification, I am entering the world beyond redemption known as psychosis. Or rather, I should say that I must choose between two psychoses: in one (gender identity disorder), testosterone appears as a medicine, and in the other (addiction), testosterone becomes the substance on which I am dependent, a dependence that must be treated by other means. I have fallen into a political trap; the problem is that this trap has the same form as my subjectivity: it is my own political body. How could we have entrusted the state with the management of desire, sexual fantasy, the material sense of embodiment? Am I a body? Or should one say, Am I the body-of-the-state? If I self-administer certain doses of testosterone and run the risk of increasing my facial pilosity and the size of my clitoris, and changing my voice and the size of my vocal fold, without identifying politically and socially as a man, I become, inevitably, nuts. I won't be able to go directly to the pharmacy to get my doses of Testogel. I'll have to ask D to send me one or two boxes from London or I'll have to buy them on expressdrugstore.com, or on the sports black market, and must take what I'm given. Hopefully, it will be testosterone manufactured in Western Europe and not one of those synthetic variations from Eastern Europe for elite athletes and bodybuilders that could set off an episode of tachycardia lasting several days. I'd rather not think about it. This week I'm going to delay the dose. I won't take it before next Wednesday.

RAIN CHECK

Until she'd understood she'd be my bitch someday, she kept her distance, as if taking advantage of her last moments of conditional freedom. At two hundred milligrams of T a week, I find it hard to go three days without fucking. I think about going away to avoid being caught up in her biochemical web. I call her, and I tell her not to worry about infidelity, making a decision, loving me back. I'm going to spend two months with D in Los Angeles. I don't actually say the words *infidelity*, *decision*, *love*. I simply say that it would be easier if I left for a while; I'd give her a "rain check," and maybe it would be better like that. D is about to visit J and certainly will be able to find me an apartment to rent in West Hollywood. Over there, I won't have any trouble finding testosterone, and I'll be able to talk about it with other trans people who are or are not taking hormones. But I will come back—that's certain. At least back to Europe. I have to go to Barcelona in February, and maybe I'll stop by Paris. She is silent for a moment, then answers that Los Angeles is her favorite city. Talks about the palm trees. I can't concentrate on what she's saying. My life stretches before me like a path that forks: one branch goes to the palm trees of Los Angeles, the other to V. Two paths interspersed with doses of T. It isn't as if I were paralyzed at the crossroads. No. I'm the one who had the idea of leaving for Los Angeles, the one who invented a way that hadn't existed until then. And I made its first steps, which are, inevitably, leading me away from her. A rain check is an embryo of congealed time, a vital possibility that can be artificially reactivated within a favorable context. It's love as a déjà vu that you can control intentionally.

She calls me two days later. She wants to go to the South of France, to Vauvert, write a book about her rape, about the period when she was a prostitute, on why the twenty-first century will or won't be feminist. She wants to go toward the sun. I give in. The arrogance of testosterone has given way in the presence of pure affect. I leave with her.

BABY CARCASS

We travel together to the South. She changes bodies and faces several times a day. I change languages in order to follow the flux. She asks me to speak to her in Spanish while we're fucking. I say into her ear: *Lo que tu quieres es que te folle como una perra* or *Tu piel es tan suave*. It doesn't really matter. What gets her hot is my voice in Spanish, she says. I remember days of incredible bliss. When we're together in the car with music playing in the background, when I watch her dancing in the bedroom, when we're walking through the labyrinth of Chartres Cathedral. But everything can shift from one moment to another. Everything changes permanently when she tells me she intends to kill herself at forty. A year ago she spent Christmas with P and M. Now, she says, she is carrying a dead child on her back. She goes about with this weight like the West Indian mothers at Barbès, except that her child, from P, is dead. She walks around with a minuscule corpse attached to her shoulders. I could cave in, but I don't. I could take her tenderly in my arms, but I don't. I am not a rock star. Stress alters hormonal levels. Testosterone changes one's resistance to stress. I need a dose, except that I'm already over my weekly 250 milligrams. I close down the channels for peripheral thoughts, avoid unhealthy thinking; if she really wanted to kill herself, she wouldn't wait to turn forty for that. *Quid moraris emori*. Her suicide was born dead, like her child with P. Postponed suicide is called depression. If she has a date and a ritual, it's because life still has meaning for her. Because she is VD. If not, she'd kill herself this very day. Tonight. Right here in Vauvert, in the marshes of Camargue. And if it were me, I'd have had it up to here once and for all. I'd open the windows and let the mistral in, I'd open the faucets that fill the tub with hot water, I'd open a box of Lexomil, I'd have a last dose of T, I'd open my mouth and drink, I'd open my esophagus as I swallowed, I'd open the veins leading to my heart, I'd open my cells where the poison had to enter, I'd open the chains of carbon and sodium, the opiate receptors. For her, the channels leading the soul to the abode of the dead would be opening, and her little one, barely born, would be coming to welcome her. Quite a lovely ending for this story, but she wants to make us wait another four years. So it will be too late. *Difficile est longum subito deponere amorem.* I don't want to listen to her. I don't want to hear her rubbish about P, about the dead child, about her being incapable of love, of love for anything that's not the little corpse. I don't want to. I just want somebody to fuck her, fuck us, fuck all three of our asses to death: her, me, and the dead baby.

Sarah

The path leading from the Vauvert writers' residence to the beach at Saintes-Maries-de-la-Mer is a paradise of plants over which they've rolled a tongue of asphalt. It's a natural garden inhabited by new technoliving species: beavers, eagles, bulls, white horses, colonies of pink flamingoes, and cars. The cars that glide along that unique gray carpet are cyberpredators longing to eliminate all competition between mobile prehistoric organisms and new ultrarapid human-machine aggregates. In this cyberparadise of Vauvert, the human-automobile has become a complex organism that consumes and has its habitat, like any other animal.

The beavers swim nimbly through the river, plunging under the submerged shrubs, their fur-covered shapes rippling. And attracted by the metaphysical weight of the other shore, by the challenge of abandoning their aquatic life for dry land, compelled by the temptation of technological separation, they lift their heads above water and place their first paw on the asphalt. On dry land, their furry bodies become clumsy, their tails too heavy; their eyes, still covered by a liquid film, can barely distinguish the other shore. The cars zigzag to try to trap these viscous volumes under their tires. Sometimes they hit them head on, making them burst into blood and guts.

The locals accuse beavers of being illegal immigrants (they came from South American rivers and were introduced into Europe in the nineteenth century) that indulge in unchecked reproduction, undermining the ecosystem of Camargue. They go to great lengths to eliminate them, pitilessly. The beaver has something in common with an Arab boy from the Paris area, with the wetbacks from Tijuana, with the Africans who swim to Gibraltar. They cross over to survive. Leave their skin under the wheels. The eagles fly in circles over cars. In such a way, the eagle uses the automobile as its hunting prosthesis. After the car has gone by, the beaver, ripped open on the harsh, wintry ground, treats the native eagle to its foreign and exquisite tripe. I don't take photographs of the scene. I don't want to include a camera, the ultimate techno-eye, in this rite of cyber-ecology. The chemical traces left by the eagle and beaver on my memory will be enough.

In 1888, Van Gogh spent five days on the beach at Saintes-Maries, at the Hôtel de la poste. He painted four boats without sails or tillers, their keels cast up on a sand dune, as well as two other boats at full sail, disappearing across the water. On one of the boats, Van Gogh wrote the word *Friendship*. V and I go almost every day by car to Saintes-Maries-de-la-Mer. The church was probably built on the site of an ancient pagan temple dedicated to the Egyptian god Ra, father of the sun. The Saintes Maries de la Mer are two girls in a boat. They seem to be drifting on the gigantic, foamy waves of the Mediterranean, like Van Gogh's small crafts. Each carries between her hands a golden box. But what do they contain?

The crypt at Saintes-Maries-de-la-Mer contains Sarah, also known as Sarah the Black One, Sarah la Kali, Sarah the Nomad, the black servant of the Saint Maries, or an Egyptian goddess; Sarah, the patron saint of the gypsies. V and I go down to see her. We're carrying two empty urns. Sarah is a black porcelain head peeking out from more than fifty red, green, white, and blue gowns bordered with gold thread. Her black hair disappears beneath the gowns, and they transform the statue into an enormous article of clothing of a thousand layers on which lies a head crowned with gilded and crystalline brilliants. In her urn, V carries the child that she didn't have with P. In the form of a relic, I carry the cock that I didn't need to cut off in order to be who I am, the same one that I will have no need to graft onto me to be who I am.

There are not two sexes, but a multiplicity of genetic, hormonal, chromosomal, genital, sexual, and sensual configurations. There is no empirical truth to male or female gender beyond an assemblage of normative cultural fictions.

In the eyes of Van Gogh, the plain of Camargue leading to the Saintes-Maries resembled a Dutch landscape, but under a different light. I have the impression that it is the light of Spain shining on another plain, the same Egyptian sun that warms the backs of the immigrant beavers from the third millennium.

10. PORNPOWER

I sell frustration, not relief.

—LYDIA LUNCH

THE PORNOGRAPHIC IMPERATIVE: FUCK YOU YOURSELF

1. Pornography is a masturbatory virtual device (literary, audiovisual, cybernetic . . .). In its capacity as a cinematic industry, the goal of pornography is planetary multimedia masturbation. The pornographic image is characterized by its capacity to stimulate—independently of the spectator's will—the biochemical and muscular mechanisms that regulate the production of pleasure. Emphasizing the pornographic image's capacity to become activated in the body of the spectator, Linda Williams defined pornography as "embodied image," an image that incorporates itself as body and captures the body at the "encounter with an eroticized technological apparatus."[1]

---

1. Linda Williams, "Porn Studies: Proliferating Pornographies On/Scene: An Introduction," in *Porn Studies*, ed. Linda Williams (Durham, NC: Duke University Press, 2004), 7. See also "Body Genres," *Film Quarterly* 44 (Summer, 1991) and "Corporealized Observers: Visual Pornographies and the 'Carnal Density of Vision,'" in *Fugitive Images: From Photography to Video*, ed. Patrice Petro (Bloomington, IN: Indiana University Press, 1995), 3–41.

2. Pornography is sexuality transformed into spectacle, virtual, digital information. It is sexuality transformed into public representation, where *public* refers directly or indirectly to becoming "marketable." Given the conditions of post-Fordist capitalism, a public representation implies an ability for exchange on the global market in a digital form that can be transformed into capital. A representation acquires pornographic status when it transforms into "public" that which is supposed to remain private. Therefore, we will speak of pornography as a device for the publication of the private. Or, even better, a device that, representing part of public space, thereby defines it as private while loading it with an added masturbatory value. The word *pornographic* refers to an economic-political characterization of representation.

3. Pornography is tele-techno-masturbation. The globalization of the pharmacoporno economy by means of audiovisual digitization and its ultrafast transmission, using a host of technical media (television, computer, telephone, external data storage devices such as pods, pads, etc.), generates a *butterfly effect* in the global management of the cycles of excitation-frustration-excitation: a pussy opening in one place, a mouth sucking in another, producing hundreds of releasings of pleasure at the other end of the world as their virtual displacement emits a living flow of capital.

4. Pornography has the same characteristics as any other spectacle of the culture industry: performance, virtuosity, dramatization, spectacularization, technical reproducibil-

ity, digital transformation, and audiovisual distribution. The only difference for the moment rests in its underground status. The porn producer David Friedman remarked that contemporary pornographic exploitation, conceived as a performative practice and audiovisual consumption, is an extension of the popular circus, the freak shows at fairs, and the amusement parks of the pre-cinematic era.[2] Pornography and prostitution could be regarded as fields of the industry of the spectacle, condemned to ostracism and illegality during the nineteenth and twentieth centuries. The modification of the aberrant, perverse, or deviant (disabled, freak, homosexual, nymphomaniac, whore . . .) body from the status of carnival attraction to that of the mentally ill or criminal typical of the disciplinary biopolitical regime will accentuate this process of exclusion from public and economic domains.

5. The relationship of the pornographic industry to the industry of culture and the spectacle is equivalent to the relationship of traffic in illegal drugs to the pharmaceutical industry. It represents two of the covert engines of capitalism of the twenty-first century. Pharmacopornographic production functions on ambivalence: it is a marginal and hidden aspect of the contemporary cultural industry, but it is also a paradigm for all other types of post-Fordist production. Within *übermaterial* capitalism, all forms of production offer benefits to the extent to which they approach the model of pharmacopornographic production.

2. David Friedman, porn producer: "The pornographic exploitation business was an extension of the circus carnival—girlie shows, freak shows, gambling games, rides, ballyhoo, hullabaloo . . ." Legs McNeil, Jennifer Osborne and Peter Patvia, *The Other Hollywood: The Uncensored Oral History of the Porn Film Industry* (New York: ReganBooks, 2005), 1.

6. As an underground sector, the sex industry reveals the truth about all other aspects of the communications and entertainment industry. Literature, film, television, the Internet, comics, video games, and so on want pornography, wish to produce pleasure and pornographic surplus value without having to suffer the marginalization that comes with pornographic representations, in the same way that contemporary producers of the legal pharmaceutical industry want to produce pleasure and sexual (addiction) and toxicological surplus value without suffering the marginalization and criminalization that come with doing business in illegal drugs.

7. In pornography, sex is *performance*, which is to say that it is composed of public representations and processes of repetition that are socially and politically regulated. Let's look again at the relationship between the industry of culture and the industry of sex. Judith Butler defined gender, masculinity, and femininity in terms of performances, regulated processes of repetition, norms internalized in the form of bodily style, representation, and public dramatization.[3] In a parallel vein, in the 1980s, Annie Sprinkle introduced a new performative shift in the understanding of identity by defining not only gender, but also sexuality, in terms of performance.[4] For Sprinkle, the truth of sexuality that pornographic representation claims to capture is merely the effect of a system of representation, an array of corporal choreographies regulated by gender codes of representa-

---

3. Butler, *Gender Trouble*.
4. Annie Sprinkle and Gabrielle Cody, *Hardcore from the Heart: The Please, Profits and Politics of Sex in Performance* (London: Continuum, 2001).

tion that are comparable to those that prevail in dance, traditional cinematic action, and classical theater. It follows that, for Sprinkle, pornography has no empirical or documentary value outside of a given system of representation.

8. The distinctive feature of pornography as image has more to do with issues of scenography, dramatization, and light than with content; it's enough for a body (whether natural or artificial, "living" or "dead," human or animal) to be very well lit,[5] and as desirable as it is inaccessible, possessing a masturbatory value directly proportional to its ability to act as an abstract and dazzling fantasy.

9. The popular view of pornography as degree zero of representation is based on a sexotranscendental sovereign necro-political principle that we could call "spermatic Platonism," and for which ejaculation (and death) is the only real thing. Foucault pointed out that sovereign (masculine, theological, monarchic) power was characterized by not the power of giving life but the power of *giving death*. From that standpoint, snuff is the ontocinematic model of this type of pornographic production: filming the *real*, the ejaculation, death in real time, and even better, making ontocinematic death and ejaculation coincide. The peculiarity of the dominant form of pornography is its tendency to produce the visual illusion of irruption within the purely real. Pornographic excitation is structured according to the boomerang: pleasure-in-the-desubjectification-of-

---

5. Roland Barthes, *Sade, Loyola, Fourier* (Pairs: Editions du Seuil, 1971), 132.

the-other/pleasure-in-the-desubjectification-of-the-self: watching a subject that can't control the force of its sexual production (*potentia gaudendi*) and seeing it at the very moment it renounces that force, to the benefit of an all-powerful spectator (oneself, the person who is watching) who, in turn, and through the representation, sees him- or herself desubjectified, reduced to a masturbatory response. *The one watching is pleasured by his or her own process of desubjectification.* If we consider the fact that the goal of all pornographic visual material is to make represented ejaculation coincide with the spectator's ejaculation (understood in the abstract as a cis-male, the universal visual ejaculator), we should be able to conclude that the pleasure of the pornographic eye resides in a cruel contradiction. On one hand, the spectator receives the impression—by means of the desubjectification of the porn actors—that he's the one who possesses the *potentia gaudendi* of the actors; on the other hand, the body of the spectator is being reduced to an involuntary receiver of ejaculatory stimuli, thereby putting him in a position deprived of any power to make sexual decisions. The distinctive feature of pornographic subjectivity is the visual swallowing of its own sperm, the fact of simultaneously being both a universal erect cock and a universal receiving anus; and this is something that points us toward a pornosophic precept: *pornete ipsum.*

10. Pornography tells the *performative* truth about sexuality. It is not the degree zero of representation. Rather, it reveals that sexuality *is always performance*, the public

practice of a regulated repetition, a staging as well as an involuntary mechanism of connection to the global circuit of excitation-frustration-excitation. Today's entertainment industry, with its division of representation into categories, such as "G" (general audience—all ages admitted) or "NC-17" (no children under seventeen admitted) denies the performative value of pornography by reducing it to "hardcore sex," as if—from a theatrical point of view—there were an ontological difference between a kiss, a brawl, and anal penetration. The current hegemony of the nonpornographic cultural industry stems from this moral axiom that labels organs considered sexual (in particular, the cock, pussy, and anus) as extra-cinematic objects (literally *ob*-scene, or "outside the scene") whose value as "truth" cannot be absorbed by representation and transformed into performance. But behind this hegemony hides the cultural industry's wish to affect the techno-organic centers of the production of subjectivity (centers for the production of pleasure, affect, a feeling of omnipotence and comfort) with the same efficiency as pornography. The cultural industry is *porn envy*. Pornography isn't simply a cultural industry like others; it's the paradigm for all cultural industries.[6] Pornography— which sexualizes production and converts the body into information—and its closed circuit of excitation-capital-

6. This assertion shouldn't be confused with the often-debated Fredric Jameson maxim that "every image is pornographic." In this case, Jameson is employing a critical definition of pornography as a way of describing the "ideological" status of the image, faced with the radical truth of the historical text in the Marxist sense of the term; cf. Fredric Jameson, *Signatures of the Visible* (New York: Routledge, 1990), 1.

frustration-excitation-capital provide in a particularly clear way a key to understanding any other type of post-Fordist cultural production.

11. When it comes to critical reactions, the traps are more numerous than the points of escape. Taking sexuality out of the framework of production and work (paid or not) isn't enough to free it from contemporary biopolitical control, not any more than entrusting its regulation to the state would be. It would be impossible to go back to the romanticism of a nonpublic sexuality, or to attain a private and nonindustrialized body. And free market undertakings, whether emancipatory or abolitionist, would fail as well. From now on, in fact, it's a matter of inventing other common, shared, collective, and copyleft forms of sexuality that extend beyond the narrow framework of the dominant pornographic representation and standardized sexual consumption. In 1990, Annie Sprinkle opened the way by using the term *postpornography* to present *The Public Cervix Announcement*, a performance during which she invited the audience to explore the inside of her vagina with the help of a speculum. Such a representation of sex is a critique of the codes of visibility produced by medicine and by traditional pornography. To the "truth of pornographic sex"— to allude to Foucault's expression—Sprinkle opposes the theatrical and artistic production of multiple sex fictions. And Sprinkle's scheme has proliferated in the work of others: Shelly Mars, Fatal Video, Virginie Despentes and Coralie Trinh Thi, Del LaGrace Volcano, Maria Beatty, Bruce LaBruce, Shu Lea Cheang, Post Op, Giuseppe Campuzano,

Nadia Granados La Fulminante, Porno Porsi, and so on. The common denominator for this great variety of aesthetic and political strategies (postporn, camp, drag king, BDSM, anarchopunk, cyber, queer-indigenous, etc.) is an epistemological inversion, a radical displacement of the subject of pornographic enunciation: those who had been passive objects of the pornographic and the disciplinary gaze ("women," "porn actors and actresses," "whores," "fags and dykes," "perverts," "crips," etc.) become subjects of representation, thereby putting in question the (aesthetic and somato-political) codes that make their bodies and sexual practices visible and producing the impression of the natural stability of sexual relations and gender relationships.

Such a critique makes a breach in the history of the representation of sexuality, transforming pornographic techniques into a field of political intervention.

THE PORNIFICATION OF LABOR

I have no need to remind you—not you, who are reading this book—that the province of sex (and I mean *your* sex) is not the individual body (your body) or the private domain (your private domain) or any domestic space (your domestic space). That not the individual body, or the space called private, or domestic space escape political regulation. Sex, excitation, the demand for erection and ejaculation are at the center of pharmacopornographic political production and economy. Accordingly, the situation can be defined in the following terms: *labor sexus est*. In the cyberextended pharmacopornographic city, the material process of work depends on a collection of sexual tractions, psychosomatic instincts, hormonal escalations, the establishment of synaptic connections, and the emission of chemical excretions. Sex is work. Nevertheless, the object of work is not to satisfy, but to excite: setting in motion the somatic mechanism that regulates the excitation-frustration-excitation cycle. We are working at the porn factory: a technosomatic industry fueled by sperm, blood, urine, adrenalin, testosterone, insulin, silicone, psychostimulants, and estrogens, but also the digitized signs that can be transmitted at high speed, whether number, text, sound, or image. We call the *pornification of labor* the capture of sex and sexuality by economy, the process by which sex becomes work.

Thus, in order to understand the praxis of post-Fordist labor, it is necessary to study in detail three domains that, until now, were considered peripheral or marginal to capitalist cycles of production and consumption:

1. *The production, trafficking, and consumption of (legal or illegal) drugs.* By *drug*, in this case, I mean what Derrida calls *pharmakon*: not only every chemical substance of natural or synthetic origin that typically affects the functions of the central nervous system of the living organism, but also, in a larger sense, all biologically active legal or illegal substances that are able to modify the metabolism of the cells on which they work. Texts and visual signs are also *pharmakon*.[7]

7. Some of the principles governing the flow of psychotropes were touched upon in chapter 8 of this book, "Pharmacopower."

2. *The production, circulation, and consumption of audiovisual pornographic materials.* By *pornography*, I mean, in this case, any sexually active audiovisual technique capable of modifying the sensibility and production of desire, of activating cycles of excitation-frustration and the production of psychosomatic pleasure, in fine, of capturing the body's system of affect production.

3. *Sexual labor.* The transformation of a body's *potentia gaudendi* into a commodity by a contract (more or less formal) of service.

The power of these three platforms—drugs, pornographic audiovisual material, sexual services—for the production of capital rests in their ability to function as *prostheses of subjectivity*. What's being designed here is the logic of a *general pharmacopornographic economy* at the heart of which circulate organs, pills, financial codes, communication links, images, texts, jerk-off sessions, liters of silicone, chemical compounds, dollars, and so on.

The theorists of this new conception of labor as excitation will no longer be classical economists (Ricardo, Marx, Keynes) but the pornographers (Candida Royale, Narcis Bosch, Nacho Vidal, HPG, etc.), porn actors and actresses (Annie Sprinkle, Nina Roberts, Coralie Trinh Thi, etc.), sex workers (Michelle Tea, Norma Jane Almodovar, Claire Carthonnet, etc.), and members of drug trafficking networks, from the producers of coke and the state mafias to the impoverished workers on opium plantations, as well as herbalists adept at ancestral traditions of witchcraft, pharmaceutical laboratories, petty traffickers, and junkies. Negri with Rocco Siffredi; Judith Butler with Jenna Jameson. Freud and his hits of coke, the life and death of Escobar, Sartre's amphetamine consumption, the androgen-antidepressant cocktail now operational for the American soldiers in Iraq, Russian athletes' cancers after taking high doses of concentrated testosterone in the form of Oral-Turinabol pills, the rise and fall of Linda Lovelace from *Deep Throat*, the crystal lines snaking from fashion runways to television sound stages or to the corridors of the stock exchange, the hundreds of thousands of doses of estrogen and progesterone prescribed for the past forty years as a contraceptive for cis-females of reproductive age, biotech laboratory animals and the ones that are slaughtered by the agrifood industry, the pharaonic volume of antidepressants swallowed by menopausal cis-females, the trafficking of illegal sex workers across European borders, Armstrong's doping, the liters of sperm poured out each year during the making of porn films, the silent spread of the human immunodeficiency virus, the millions of senior citizens' stomachs lined with omeprazole, the deaths of teenagers who took part in clinical trials of growth hormone, the syringe that produced the sheep Dolly by insemination, the synthetic guilelessness of weight-lifters' muscles—these teach us more about current models of capitalist production than do all the industrial directories of the International Monetary Fund and their trivial indexes of growth or decline in unemployment. The international guide of pharmacological production of

Viagra and its underground counterfeiting market will tell us more about the production of excitation-frustration-excitation values in post-Fordist society than will all the classical economic treatises with their obsolete notions of work as mercantile production.

SEX COPYRIGHT: LEWD TECHNOSIGNIFIERS

Power experienced slippage; it shifted, throughout the previous century, from the earth to manufacturing, then toward information and life. Today, power extends to sex, gender, and race in their capacity as precise codifications of information and subjectivity. In the near future, it will function through an even more efficient mode by means of its transformation into psychotropic patents that control the production of neurological responses and synthetic hormones. However, desire, sex, and gender resemble neither the earth nor manufactured products. Desire, sex, and gender are, in reality, closer to information as an embodied technosemiotic system (Haraway). They are living codes. Like information, they defy ownership because my possession of a fragment (of information, desire, sex, gender) doesn't take it away from you. My desire, my plastic cock, my prosthetic masculinity can circulate and be shared without the pleasure becoming any less powerful. It's the opposite, in fact: *sharing* multiplies desire, sex, and gender. The problem is that, until now, desire, pleasure, sex, and gender were thought of as nontransferable essences or as private property. At first, they were conceived to be fixed substances in nature; then, as the property of God; then, as that of the state; and later, as private properties; and finally, today, as the property of pharmacopornographic multinationals.

The new global corporations produce nothing. Their only goal is the accumulation and management of patents in order to control the (re)production of bodies and pleasures. This politics of *copyright*, which oversees the sexualizing of production and the conversion of life into information, is what I've called *pharmacoporn politics*; its purpose is to transform your ass and mine, or rather, your desire and mine, into abstract profits. Your clitoris and my cock are subjected to the same fate as an ear of corn, given the way that multinationals employ genetic engineering to produce new transgenic strains whose seeds will be infertile. In the same way that the multinationals are currently controlling world production of corn thanks to the privatization of germoplasms, but are also busy—and this is primordial— transforming the entire planet into potential consumers of the new transgenic seeds (which are themselves infertile), the pharmacopornographic industry is striving for the exponential control and production of your desiring body. Along with "the computerization of agriculture,"[8] we are witnessing a process of the conversion into information of sex and gender, through which capital is seeking to produce and possess narcotic, audiovisual, molecular, and narrative models, all of which serve as regulators of desiring subjectivity. Your sex, your desire, and your gender are the new

8. Negri and Hardt, *Multitudes*, 140.

transgenic supercorn of the pharmacopornographic industry. If you want to get hard: Viagra; if you want to avoid sexual reproduction: the Pill; if you want to get pregnant: clomiphene and human chorionic gonadotropin; if you want to change the timbre of your voice or your muscle mass: androgens; if you want to have sexual fantasies: Dorcel, Hotvideo, Playboy, and so on.

PARIS HILTON IN BED WITH MAX WEBER

The Puritan erotics of power—as identified by Max Weber in *The Protestant Ethic and the Spirit of Capitalism*, with its values of emotional and moral stability, self-control, and discretion—which has dominated a large part of the Western sexual disciplinary regime since the seventeenth century, is slowly revealing its pharmacopornographic foundations. According to Weber's intuition, it wasn't materialism, but the ethics of Protestant life, that permitted the blossoming of capitalism. Until then considered punishable by God and a sign of immodest luxury, sacrificing oneself to work and to economic success became proof of one's love for God. God circulated within the body, commodities, and lands by means of capital. Accordingly, the principle regulating the production of life and the management of populations in the pharmacopornographic era is not hedonism, the satisfaction of sensual pleasures, but a post-Christian-free-market-punk ethic whose principle is the compulsive reproduction of the excitation-frustration cycle to the point of achieving the total destruction of the ecosystem.

Here is one example of a completely lifelike prosthesis heralding the porno future of Weberian free-market Protestantism: Paris Hilton.[9] A noticeable exception to the model American beyond reproach, Paris Hilton represents the zenith of the sexopolitical production of the luxury white heterosexual technobitch. The disinherited inheritor of a multimillion-dollar hotel empire and a real estate firm, Hilton rejected traditional institutions of apprenticeship and began working on television shows such as *The Simple Life* and later used her films to market her life in a pharmacopornographic way. Hilton didn't abandon Weber's Protestant ethic and the spirit capitalism. No: she incorporated it and used it to take it to the highest level of pharmacoporno media production. The vapid Hilton having it off with Herr Weber. Despite her seeming proclivity for vice and idleness, the Paris Hilton phenomenon exhibits no insubordination against the capitalist economy. On the contrary: her entire life and sexuality are being transformed, by devices of extreme surveillance, into work—into digital images that are transferable worldwide. Her triumph is having known how to recover her body and her sexuality as ultimate values on the global-exchange market of pharmacopornographic capitalism. In this sense, Paris Hilton could be a high-tech pharmacopornographic sex worker; and perhaps this worker dimension of her immorality is what disturbs Grandaddy Hilton the most.

9. For more on Paris Hilton as an expression of the porno future that is conscious of class, see Virginie Despentes, *King Kong Theory*, 99–100.

If Paris Hilton has asserted herself as a paradigmatic figure of the pharmacopornographic mode of production, it isn't—unlike for porn actresses from the 1970s through the 1990s, from Marilyn Chambers to Jenna Jameson—a result of her qualities as a sex bomb. Hilton is radically different from traditional porn actresses: she did not come to X-rated films out of economic necessity or an unstoppable social destiny but, on the contrary, decided and planned her transformation into a Google star while relying on her own financial empire. In addition, she generates no significant masturbatory interest, neither on the physical nor on the performing level, which suggests that, if it weren't for her fortune and a powerful publicity machine, she would never have been able to make any inroads in the pornographic market in competition with such actresses as Traci Lords or Katsumi. If the persona of Paris Hilton presents any indisputable theoretical-political interest (outside the masturbatory), it's because she is an illustration of the contemporary tendency of all forms of work and production of value to transform themselves into pharmacopornographic production, thus indicating a "porn future" for the production of worth in contemporary capitalism as a whole.

Under the Puritan values that Weber believed he had identified hide digitized images of the completely waxed vulva of Paris Hilton, the testosterone-infused muscles of Arnold Schwarzenegger, and the worldwide Viagra dosing of limp biococks after their reaching their fifties.

URBAN SEXODROMES

For the 2005 soccer World Cup, Angela Merkel's German government gave the green light to the building of Artemis, a thirty-two-thousand-square-foot multimedia brothel located at three subway stations of Berlin's Olympic stadium, accelerating at the same time the pornification of the city and the Fordization of the sex industry. The inside of the building has a decorative aesthetic that the promoters have deemed "worthy of Las Vegas." Endowed with four floors, the complex includes a swimming pool; several saunas; two movie theaters; and a large number of rooms, enough to hold one hundred sex workers and 650 customers. The German government's reasoning reveals the foundations of today's pharmacopornographic capitalism: "There's a necessity to offer the four million spectators who are coming to Berlin for the World Cup the best sexual services possible, just as they'll be offered the best amenities in terms of hotels and restaurants, and the best of our cultural and communications services."[10] Please note, in passing, that the brothel as a state institution, a public service offered the inhabitants of a city or its visitors by the government, is in no way Merkel's invention, but a facility that has existed from the time of the medieval city to the colonial establishments of the nineteenth and twentieth centuries. For example, in 1434, the municipality of Bern put the public brothels at the disposal of Emperor Sigismond and his court during his visit to the city. In 1769, French

---

10. Article appearing in the *Le Nouvel Observateur* (May 4–10, 2006): 13.

writer Restif de la Bretonne argued for the construction of state-run brothels in Europe to regulate the presence of street women in European cities and to prevent the spread of syphilis. Despite the many differences that separate the paleo-urban brothel of Bern, Restif's state brothel, and the sex mall Artemis, all of them have played a decisive role in the biopolitical and economic development of the modern pharmacopornopolis. This "socceristic" brothel also falls within the genealogy of the multimedia brothels pioneered by Playboy's hotels and clubs in the United States at the end of the 1950s; it's an example of the building-brothel transformed into a space of production, consumption, distribution of pornographic audiovisual signs, and offers of sexual services and functioning as a "heterotopia," to borrow Foucault's term—a space of politicosexual exception dominated by laws and values that are in apparent contradiction with those of the dominant public space.[11]

The modern city is a gender- and race-segregated brothel. When a political measure attempts to "end prostitution in the city," what it is really saying is: it's necessary to make what's "urban" about this city invisible. And this is equal, as we know, to pushing the city beyond the limits of the city.

According to *Le Nouvel Observateur*, Artemis is intended "for the hordes of male bachelors and their libido when it has been galvanized by the warfare of soccer." However, what characterizes the hordes of potential consumers of the sexual services offered by Artemis isn't so much their status as

11. For more on Playboy's multimedia brothels, see Beatriz Preciado, *Pornotopia: Sexualidad y Arquitectura en* Playboy *durante la Guerra Fría* (Barcelona: Anagrama, 2010).

"bachelors" (it's of little importance whether these "males" are part of a couple or not before they come to the World Cup), but the fact that they identify sexopolitically as heterosexual; and this is because these sexual services are to be provided solely and exclusively by forty thousand women coming from every corner of the world (for whom the European Economic Union will obtain a temporary work permit for the region during the World Cup). For the occasion, the German government, which recognizes sex work as legal, has published a "travel guide for the women" intended for the young girls from the old Soviet bloc who want to work in Germany as prostitutes. In France, Malka Marcovich, the national director of the Coalition Against Trafficking in Women–International, launched a petition—signed by Fadela Amara and Ségolène Royal, among others—under the slogan "Buying sex isn't a sport." Unsuccessfully—and naively—they tried to convince the German government to prohibit sex commerce during the World Cup.

The relationship between sports and prostitution could offer some keys to understanding the contemporary pharmacopornographic regime. Adding ironic understatement to Marcovich's slogan furnishes us with our own: "Buying sex *is* a sport." On the other hand, if there hadn't been a radical Fordization of the sex industry up until now, we would be able to say that a severe pornification of Fordist and cultural industries is at work. Rather than imagining prostitution as a practice on the margins of the soccer industry, we'd have to consider the sport in general, and soccer in particular, as being part of a worldwide pharmacopornographic industry that controls Internet networks;

clubs and discotheques; chains of pornographic production, distribution, and dissemination; pharmaceutical production industries of anabolic drugs and other molecules that supplement the athletic and sexual body and their marketing; and the chains of production and distribution for music, clothing, accessories, and derived products (such as figurines of Zidane or boxes of condoms).

In the milieu of professional sports, as in that of sex work, the problem is not the sale of the body, contrary to the affirmations of abolitionist feminists and Protestant and Catholic fundamentalists. Work in the post-Fordist society is always and in every case the sale of the force of communication and excitation produced by a living body—the sale of that body's *potentia gaudendi*. And what is specific about any form of pharmacopornographic production is found in the asymmetry of class, gender, race, and disability in the market at hand (nine out of ten sex workers are cis-females, and barely four out of ten are white), as well as the asymmetry of economic remuneration and professional status.

Despite the radical differences between Jenna Jameson's and Thierry Henri's thighs, it's interesting to observe that, quite often, athletes from the major European teams and sex workers engaged to serve soccer fans by Artemis belong to the same worldwide economic, political, and racial stratum: they come from the classes of poor workers or the former colonies of the European nation states, and they make their way through the contemporary pharmaco-pornographic market (winning European residency at the same time) by selling their somatic and affective capital, their *potentia gaudendi*. What the German pharmacoporno-graphic industry is making available to the spectators (both the physical and virtual kind) of the World Cup are the erot-icized and sexualized bodies of athletes and sex workers. The process of the pornification of labor, as present in the industry of the spectacle as it is in the sex industry, extracts a pharmacopornographic surplus value from racialized and pauperized bodies (nonwhite bodies from places referred to as "developing countries") that have been completely shut out of legal access to the West by any other means.

THE PHARMACOPORNOGRAPHIC WORKER

In every period of history, a certain type of work and worker define the form of production that is characteristic of that particular economy. Curiously, the work and the worker in question retrospectively appear as the most endangered, laboring under the most devalued working conditions. It is the body of the cotton-picking male and of the female worker and reproductive slave that defines the economy of the plantation, the body of the female that defines white heterosexual reproduction, the body of the miner that defines the economy of the steam engine, the body of the fungible male or female worker that defines the concentra-tion camp, the body of the male or female factory worker that defines the Fordist economy. The work and specific kind of exploitation that today defines the pharmacopor-nographic economy is sex work, and the paradigmatic body of this model of production is that of the migrating whore, the transgender sex worker, or the porn actress or actor.

The difference between ostensible production (the legal production of authorized merchandise) and real production (the production of excitation-frustration value) is so important in the case of the sex worker that throughout history no other category of producers of capital has been in such a precarious situation, except for the slave workers of the plantation economy and the fungible workers of the concentration camp economy. The real, ultrapauperized workers of pharmacopornographic capitalism are the whores, the "unchosen" emigrants, the petty traffickers, the nonwhite and transgender prisoners, the bodies fated for domestic work and care of the body, and finally, children and animals (the actual sources of raw materials for pharmacological production—bodies destined to take part in clinical trials or be consumed by the agrifood industries). All of them are just short of citizenship. And just short of being human. Therefore, referring to the "feminization of work" to describe contemporary capitalism's transformation of work is not only insufficient but also biased. It is advisable to speak of the *pornification of work* and the production of the racialized and transgender body and subjectivity in a global pharmacoporno political regime.

Until now, sex work and the work of reproduction were considered to be disinterested, the origins of the supposed dignity of the female subject, who would feel completely degraded by the commodification of sexual services. And this is where left-wing theorists of "the feminization of labor" bring up the unpaid services that women have performed in history, speaking about the hygiene of people and things, household management, the education of children, care for the sick and the elderly, the web of networks of cooperation and solidarity, but omitting sexual and reproductive services, which nevertheless are part of this unpaid labor; as if, intentionally or not, they are protecting the domain of sexuality from that of economic production, thereby making it a sacred zone of human activity. But how can it be possible that no one considers the fact that political responsibilities, school education, or musical creation are the free province of all, whereas we continue to believe that keeping sex work and reproduction free services (in other words, pauperized or politically obligatory services) is equivalent to preserving the essential dignity of women and, to a larger extent, the entire human population?

Most analyses of capital's process of transformation chastely avoid the sticky problem of pharmacopornographic production. The notions of the "feminization of work" or the "becoming-woman of work,"[12] as elaborated by Cristian Marazzi,[13] Maurizio Lazzarato,[14] Toni Negri,[15] and Judith Revel[16] obscure the real reason for the appearance of a gender predicate (in this case, gender incorrectly reduced to the feminine) to describe the current change

---

12. Antonio Negri, *Exil* (Paris: Editions Mille et Une Nuits, 1998).

13. Cristian Marazzi, *The Violence of Financial Capitalism*, trans. Kristina Lebedeva and Jason Francis McGimsey (New York: Semiotext(e), 2011).

14. Maurizio Lazzarato, *Les Revolutions du capitalism* (Paris: Les Empêcheurs de tourner en rond/Le Seuil, 2004).

15. Antonio Negri, *Fabrique de porcelain: Pour une nouvelle grammaire du politique*, trans. Judith Revel (Paris: Stock, 2006).

16. Judith Revel, "Devenir-femme de la politique," *Multitudes* 12 (printemps 2002): 125–33.

in the trajectory of capitalism. Nothing allows us to claim that the new post-Fordist model of work is more "feminine" than the industrial model was. Is it possible that women didn't work as slaves in the cotton fields? Is it possible that they weren't the first to pack sardines on an assembly line, or work in the textile industry, or manufacture smart cards for Microsoft? Saying "feminine" to describe the progressive casualization of work implies a presupposed heterocentricity, a metaphysics of sexual difference, and the precondition of a "rhetoric of gender" according to which, *sure, stable, and permanent* implies industrial and male and *flexible, changeable, mobile, and precarious* implies postindustrial and female.

Let us think out this gender relationship in terms of the contemporary pornification of work. Describing the current process of the transformation of work in terms of "feminization" can only be justified by the fact that it is the virtual or factual production of the cis- or trans-female body and the *performance* of femininity that makes the worldwide heterocock get hard. But it is also true that an important number of homococks get hard for guys' asses, for other cocks, and for lubricated anuses. Let us add to this the new masturbatory mechanisms working on the bodies of women. Although still underexploited, they could soon constitute a new platform for the production of pharmacopornographic profits. But, to speak more generally, the facts are oozing out in evidence and must be faced: until now, cis-females (and to a lesser degree, some transfemales and certain eroticized cis-males) were the ones who performed the task of making the world's cock hard. But nothing indicates or justifies requiring cis-females to continue to take care of it.

One of the indices of the degree of exploitation of sex work and pornography is the social immobility of its laborers, the impossibility of leaving that domain of production to attain other forms of work that are less pauperized. In the current conditions of production, sex and pornographic work are pushing the ontological force of all relationships of exploitation to its limit. At a time when work is becoming flexible and professional reinvention routine, sex work seems to most effectively reduce workers to a natural essence, branding them for the rest of their lives and making employment in other work markets very difficult. Workers in the pharmacopornographic industry are comparable today to a caste, a cursed species who remain devalued for all other work in the legitimate market, despite the short duration of their career in the field of pharmacopornographic services (five years on average).

I discuss this issue with Nina Roberts, preeminent French porn-terrorist actress. According to her analysis, "Certain porn actresses fatten up to a high degree when they stop making films, to avoid being recognized and to desexualize themselves, so they can go out and do their shopping without being taken for sluts in heat looking for hard cocks." The thought crosses my mind that it would be easier for them to take testosterone and change genders. That way, they could transform themselves into courteous and anonymous customers, with hairy arms and low voices. Such a metamorphosis would be a form of political indemnification: a cultural reparation for having served in the formation of your basic Hairy Arm heterosexual masturbator. No one would ever guess that a bitch in heat could be hidden behind the features of an anonymous porn consumer and treat herself to possession of the dominant gaze, for only a few milligrams of testosterone a month during a period of barely six months. Strangely, such an unheard-of transformation would simultaneously grant attainment of the place of the hegemonic subject of representation and the luxury of pornographic invisibility. A change in gender could also be envisioned as an occasion for a comeback of a career in porn, which is normally so short for cis-females. If we take into account the fact that the professional path of an X-rated actress is becoming ever shorter (it being rare to remain under the spotlights beyond the age of twenty-five), we can imagine Mandy Bright, Jesse Jane, Jenna Jameson, or Nina Hartley after their mastectomies, armed with "real-skin" suction-cup dildos, size XL, starting new careers as delightful dandies of porn who'd usurp all the Roccos and the Nachos . . . I'll refrain from a stream of commentaries on the pharmacopornographic pleasure there'd be in seeing a technoharder version of Nina Roberts having it off with all the porn stars.

For the moment, the restriction of prostitution from the category of work as it is defined by unions and laws to which government institutions in the West subscribe (with a few near exceptions that we can view as testing grounds of political dissidence) and the control of the circuits of production and distribution of pornography, which prevents pornography's assertion as a cinematic industry equal to any other branch of entertainment, are not the result of a desire to protect the rights of women facing objectification of their body on the market, which various voices from the left, the right, and feminism have claimed in unison. On the contrary. If it seems to be necessary (in right-wing as well as left-wing discourses) to deny that sex can be the object of work, of economic exchange, services, or contracts, it is because the potential opening of the category of work puts into question the so-called Puritan values of the spirit of capitalism, or even worse, makes visible the real porn values inherent in them.

Thus, what is at stake here is a particular way of avoiding the public emergence of the true engines of pharmacopornographic capitalism, of avoiding, by any means, the social panic generated by the following revelation: it isn't rationality and production, but *potentia gaudendi*, that sustains the world economy. And this is a panic that would trigger the total dislocation of work as a fundamental value of modern societies. Panic in admitting that behind the economy of the steam engine and Fordism hid and emerged the giant war-porn-drug-prison industrial complex.

ÜBERMATERIAL LABOR

The inheritors of Italian *operaismo* are debating among one another about the degree to which cognitive or "immaterial" work is truly *immaterial*. Perhaps they haven't made enough references to the movement of their hands along the length of their erect members while masturbating as they look at porn webpages over Wi-Fi on their cell phones, or the dampness between their legs, the stickiness of their secretions. Virno prefers to call immaterial work "linguistic," whereas Hardt and Negri, opting for the Foucauldian adjective, describe it as "biopolitical," thus emphasizing the relationship of such immaterial production to the body. But this body itself seems desexualized. None of them mention the effects on their philosopher's cocks of a dose of Viagra accompanied by the right image. None dare call a spade a spade: the crux of work has become sexual, spermatic, masturbatory, toxicological; and if you're expecting any economic benefit from work, it must produce the effect of a fix; and when all is said and done, we are talking about a type of work that must be called *pharmacopornopolitical*, rather than *biopolitical*.

Let's stop beating about the bush and say it: in a porn economy, there is no work that isn't destined to cause a hard-on, to keep the global cock erect; no work that doesn't trigger the secretion of endorphins, no work that doesn't reinforce the feeling of omnipotence of your basic hetero-macho consumer. Our current form of capitalism or production could be defined as an economy of ejaculation. The only authentic surplus value is the index of the cock's elevation, its hardness and rigidity, the volume of its spermatic ejaculations.

Contemporary pharmacopornographic work cannot in any case be described as immaterial. Nothing in reality is less immaterial than the work on which pharmacopornographic capitalism is based; rather than immaterial, we could call it *übermaterial*, supramaterial, technomaterial, or hypermaterial, because its texture is biological, molecular, as well as carnal and digital, irreducibly synaptic and capable of being digitized; and its ultimate objective is the production of erections, ejaculations, and spermatic volume. Besides, part of this work can be measured in liters and deciliters of flow, in the number of muscular reactions and chemical discharges. As a way of emphasizing this materiality, during a performance, Annie Sprinkle calculated in inches the number of cocks she'd sucked while she was a sex worker and compared them with the height of the Empire State Building.[17] There is no immaterial sex work just as there is no porn without the cum shot, whether it's semen, female ejaculate, or condensed milk. There is no work that isn't wet work. The simultaneous spread of urban sprawl and networks of prostitution, the colonization of populations able to be sexualized through war or sex tourism, the production technique of feminizing or masculinizing a living body, the control of physiological reactions by pharmacological compounds whose manufacture and sale are surveyed and controlled by state medico-legal organisms and by the pharmaceutical multinationals, the digital recording and intentional diffusion of fragments of life previously considered private, the production of pornographic material in the domestic space and its distribution through the

17. Annie Sprinkle, *Post-Porn Modernist: My 25 Years as a Multimedia Whore* (Berkeley, CA: Cleis Press, 1998).

Internet—all are so many signs of the appearance of a type of *übermaterial* production.

If contemporary work isn't immaterial, it also isn't the product of a process of "feminization," as has been claimed. It isn't possible to assert with Lazzarato that "the content and conditions of work today, the result of intense restructuring, are only the underlying extension of the characteristics of work, whether salaried or not, that has structurally and historically been assigned to women,"[18]—*unless and only if* we intend the term *women* as a signifier referring to all the toxicological, affective, racialized, and sexualized male and female workers (men and women, cis- and trans-). It will therefore be more relevant to claim that the content and the conditions of contemporary work are the extension of the toxicosexual and pharmacopornographic work performed by bodies that often appear labeled as *feminine* (independently of their gender) and that today are being extremely racialized and pauperized. Their common condition comes less from being the bodies of cis-females than from appearing as bodies that are penetrable (by capital), bodies that provoke ejaculation at the best possible price.

All the criteria that has been recategorized under the label *feminization of work*, such as flexibility, total availability, high level of adaptability, vulnerability, talent for improvisation, and so on are only the basic and previously

18. Maurizio Lazzarato, "Sobre la feminización del trabajo," in "trabajo<no trabajo: perceptivas, conflictos, posibilidades," special issue, *ContraPoder* 4–5 (2001).

unpublished curriculum vitae of any virtuoso sex worker. The characteristics of sex work—lack of security, sale of corporal and affective services at a low price, social devaluation of the body that performs the work, exclusion from the right to residency—are becoming central in the post-Fordist paradigm of the twenty-first century. Or more precisely, they were always there, but their character is becoming structural and explicit, revealing the slimy engine of production. Today, no structure of capitalist production functions without the aid of a masturbatory device and without a certain quantity of spilled sperm (spreading from the industry of culture and spectacle to telephony and telecommunications, by way of computer programming, the arms industry, the pharmaceutical industry, etc.). All these forms of work are becoming gradually pornified, and their casualization and apparent feminization are indicative of a new process that is making the orgasmic force of each body available to capital.

THE PORNOGRAPHIC DIVISION OF LABOR

The concept of the pornification of work takes us back to the orgasmico-affective dimension of production (traditionally performed as a salaried task by a limited number of men and women considered to be "whores"). This work is characterized by the transformation into capital worth (surplus value) of body contact (whether virtual or present); of the excitation of biochemical centers of hormonal production; of the production and transmission of affects; of the reception of an audiovisual impulse; of the connection of the neocrotex with blood vessels irrigating the erectile tissue of the penis, clitoris, or skin; of the reaction of the centers that produce endorphins and ocytocin; of a response to a certain substance by a particular biochemical metabolism, under the form of an immediate or deferred pleasure, and so on.

Until now, the feminist Marxist analysis of production used the notion of *sexual division of labor* to refer specifically to the work of reproduction for which cis-females as "egg carriers" took responsibility. However, such a notion needs to be qualified, to the point of being radically changed, if we wish to take into account the current conditions of pharmacopornographic production.

The concept of the "sexual division of labor" is a reference to the reproductive division of the species, which establishes a structural segmentation between bodies with uteruses capable of bringing to completion the development of a viable fetus and bodies without uteruses (having a uterus rather than producing eggs is today the determining difference, since a fertilized egg can be implanted within another uterus) that have no possibility of gestation. This division, according to which the difference between the work of production and the work of reproduction function as a sexual difference, takes for granted the coincidence between the body of a woman and a body provided with a fertilizable uterus capable of sexual reproduction. However, the relationship between femininity and reproduction is an asymmetrical one, first of all, because not every body that has been assigned female gender is endowed with a fertilizable uterus capable of bringing a viable fetus to completion and, second, because, even in the case of bodies that are capable of gestation, the time spent on reproduction is not equivalent to the total life of the subject. Therefore, it's more relevant to speak of the *techno-reproductive and technogestational division of labor* to refer to the segmentation of bodies in a way that is derived from the technologically constructed capacity for reproduction and gestation. On the one hand, the body of a trans man (who has kept his uterus and has simply stopped the administration of testosterone) can be inseminated and can bring to term a successful gestation. On the other hand, current research appears to be announcing the future possibility of gestation in an artificial uterus, or the implantation of an embryo in a pseudouterine gestational cavity inside the body of a cis-man.

In the concept of the sexual division of labor, the term *sexual* silently sanctions the normatively heterosexual—hetero *by default*—character of reproduction, assuming that it goes without saying that heterosexual reproduction is the only kind that is natural. What would be needed to begin with is the realization that the institutions of heterosexual breeding (the heterosexual couple, marriage, social recognition of "natural" kinship), as well as their practices (coitus as biopenis/biovagina penetration, followed by ejaculation), are techniques of culturally assisted reproduction that have been sociopolitically sanctioned and naturalized by tradition and law. Although it's more obvious when it comes to current practices of medically assisted reproduction, the nature of the political technology at work in any sexual reproduction accompanies and defines—both historically and culturally—all processes of filiation. In order to move away as far as possible from contemporary queer relational configurations and get closer to the founding myths of reproduction in the West, let's take an example from the Bible. The major patriarchs, often married to sterile women (were they cis-males presenting themselves socially as females?), used the living bodies of their slaves as reproductive organs, without such a practice modifying the relationship that the fruit of such unions would maintain with their "sterile" mothers. Such is the case, not only for the Holy Family but also for Jacob, whose wife Rachel was sterile, and who inseminated his slave Bilhah. Their children would be considered Rachel's. Here it would seem that the slave has the double task of providing sex and reproducing even if the weight of the sex work and care of the child falls to Rachel, in her role as sterile wife, but without it causing her to lose the recognition of her "natural maternity." In this case, "kinship," as Donna J. Haraway demonstrates, is a "technology for producing the material and semiotic effect of natural kinship, of shared kind."[19]

The mid-twentieth-century invention of the Pill, which separates heterosexuality and reproduction, differentiates and reveals the multiplicity and specificity of those services involved in reproduction: specifically sexual work, the production of spermatozoids and ova, the work of gestation (insemination, pregnancy, delivery), and work having to do with care of the newborn. All work of reproduction does not involve sexual work, and all sexual work does not involve

19. Haraway, *Modest_Witness*, 53.

the work of reproduction. If the Pill really has separated heterosexuality and reproduction, it clearly does not seem to have liberated heterosexual cis-females from these two other tasks. For cis-females, true liberation from heterosexual work and from the work of reproduction cannot come from contemporary methods of contraception (capitalist tools of control and pharmacopornographic consumption), but from a radial transformation of their gender status and of their sex and sexuality, and from a reappropriation of the sexopolitical techniques of subjectification.

WHAT FLARES UP FAST, EXTINGUISHES SOON

> *Would you like to have a stronger ejaculation? Come on in: Every man wants it. Great erection and inimitable pleasure. Use this tab regularly and you'll have the best. Increase your volume in just days. What flares up fast, extinguishes soon. The sacrifice of the wicked is an abomination to the LORD: but the prayer of the upright is his delight.*
>
> —MAIL-MARKETING CAMPAIGN FOR
> COUNTERFEIT VIAGRA IN 2006

One of the discursive bases of the pharmacopornographic regime takes the form of a fantastical, indisputable equation:

A cock = an orgasmic force = a consumer, or his complementary opposite: a feminized body = an orgasmic force = a sex worker.

Despite the profound technological transformations that have taken place during the past twenty-five years, the discourse concerning management of the social body persists in functioning with naturalized and disciplinary representations of the sexes and genders: the rhetoric of sexual difference dominates; heterosexuality is presented as the fundamental sexual orientation; the equivalencies between masculinity and erection and femininity and penetrability continue to prevail. Meanwhile, however, in the laboratories of pharmacopornism, capital has taken other paths and orgasmic force is being employed on other fronts. The marketing campaign for this Viagra counterfeit has spilled the beans: pharmacopornographic masculinity isn't defined by its capacity for masturbatory erection but, more precisely, by the difficulty of maintaining the erection. The market of chemical and audiovisual products are supplementing erections to the point of supplanting them. On graphs showing economic growth, the curve showing capital follows the rise of an erection. And vice versa. As we have seen, the mechanism at work in the equation *sexual difference = coitus = heterosexuality* became explicit with the production of the first synthetic hormones in the 1950s, when capitalism foresaw the advantages of working with a malleable and sexually polymorphic body that could be intentionally transformed into feminine or masculine, would react to any kind of sexual stimulation, could be a consumer as well as a producer and sexual worker, and could, at the same time, be the keeper of an orgasmic force and also the potential buyer of an exterior orgasmic force.

PENETRABLE ORIFICES AND PENETRATING EXTREMITIES

The global proletarization of sex, deprived of critical consciousness and political action, is increasing the occasions for and forms of oppression and submission. Nonetheless, the pornographic division of labor isn't disappearing; it's diversifying and changing. All workers are becoming part of production in the form of so many swollen chests and penetrable pussies, anuses, and mouths; in the form of so many flaccid, erectile, or turgescent cocks; in the form of so many estrogen-, testosterone-, serotonin-, and sperm-producing bodies; in the form of so many techno-organic connectors that can be integrated with the global digital pharmacoporno circuit. Each worker enters the pharmacoporn factory as "penetrable-penetrating," as a secretion facilitator or as a secretor, as a furnisher of something to shoot or as an addicted body, as a productive or dependent toxicological platform. Or both. These segmentations are not dependent on any type of innate, biological, or acquired predisposition; they are for all bodies that possess an anus, a mouth, or any otorhino orifices that are potentially penetrable. All bodies that possess a tongue, fingers, or arms are potentially penetrating or can become a port for prosthetic insertion (dildonic or cybernetic). All bodies are capable of producing sensorial excitation of some kind (speech, image, smell, touch); they can suck or be sucked. All bodies are at the same time toxic drug and addicted subject, fit and crip,[20] organic and supplemented by technology. Here,

20. "Crip" is a term used by disability activists to appropriate "crippled" or other derogatory words for "disabled."

the division of sexual work doesn't depend on a natural condition, but on a technical specialization of the body, a somato-political programming.

Nevertheless, we now find ourselves in a distinctive sexopolitical ecology: in our current configuration of gender dimorphism, only the bodies of cis-females, trans-females, and gays are considered to be *potentially penetrable bodies*, in the same way that only the bodies of cis-males present themselves and are represented as natural and universal penetrators. This biopolitical division of bodies produces successive segmentations of social space according to gender. However, these segmentations are gradually destabilized by the increasing technologizing of the production of pleasure and sexual reproduction. It follows that the sexual division of labor is currently becoming diluted, is subsiding, or is even reversing, since more and more cis-females have the possibility of achieving the position of universal penetrators. Similarly, a growing number of cis-males, finding themselves in an insecure financial position, will have to accede to the position of penetrated anuses, fellating mouths, and masturbating hands, eventually becoming pornographic signs or exciting prostheses, transforming into universal audiovisual masturbatory mechanisms. If we think of this technical division of sexual work in the current context of globalization and migratory flux, the following conclusion seems imperative: a majority of migrant bodies declared illegal and distinguished by lines of racialization and social exclusion have been put in the position of "global anuses" (and here the notion of "anus" indicates the position of pharmacoporno workers who are universally penetrable), whereas the Western white minorities (cis-males or cis-females) are attaining or preserving their position as universal penetrators.

What concerns capital is the ability of any body endowed with political subjectivity to experience pleasure and to produce it in other bodies endowed with masturbatory political subjectivity. But such a form of capitalism is not hedonism. For as Weber-Hilton's principles state, the goal is not the production of pleasure but the control of political subjectivity by means of the management of the excitation-frustration circuit. The purpose of porn, as is that for sexual work, is the production of *frustrating satisfaction*.

In this context of production and masturbatory control, talking about sexual liberation or the war between the sexes seems obsolete. What must be substituted for them are notions of pharmacopornographic domination, resistance, and hacking; what is at work here is a confrontation between pan-ejaculating subjectivities as well as a throng of subjectivities that perform the function of masturbatory prostheses (penetrated anuses and vaginas, fellating mouths, hands that jerk off, bodies that are dependent on chemical doses) struggling to achieve self-determination as technoliving bodies capable of joy and pleasure.

This new pharmacopornographic proletariat is not simply an economic subject engaged in producing sexual and toxicological surplus value; it is also a new form of political subject. Even if it cannot embody the promises of radical feminism (which was betrayed by white liberal feminism and state-backed censors and abolitionists), the promises of the queer and *crip* movements (betrayed by the gay and transsexual movements, as well as by the disability associations and by their alliances with the powers of medicine, law, media, and the troubled-persons industries), the promises of movements for nonallopathic medicine and the antispeciesism movement and the movement for the depenalization of drugs (betrayed by pharmacological agreements and threatened by state mafias and those of the drug traffickers), it finds its source directly in the ejecta of these exhausted movements. It is growing from their revolutionary dunghills.

GENERAL SEX

Here is a possible pharmacopornographic definition of sexuality: a techno-organic activity corresponding to the type of work praxis in which—to follow Marx's formulation—"production is inseparable from the act of producing" and is thus "an activity that has no end product," because it is "a practice that finds its own achievement in itself, without becoming objectified in any outcome that exceeds it."[21] Paolo Virno reminds us that Marx resorted to this category to conceive of those workers "whose labor turns into a virtuosic performance: pianists, butlers, dancers, teachers,

---

21. Paolo Virno, *A Grammar of the Multitude: For an Analysis of Contemporary Forms of Life*, trans. Isabella Bertoletti, James Cascaito, and Andrea Casson (New York: Semiotext(e), 2004), 54. Here Virno cites an unpublished, sixth chapter of Karl Marx's *Le Capital*, titled "The Buying and Selling of Labour-Power."

orators, medical doctors, priests, etc."[22] The supreme model for this type of "nonproductive production" is not only political work, as Virno suggests, but also sex work—which comes short of considering sexual work as the ultimate model for all political work.

No practice corresponds so well with Marx's description of nonproductive and virtuosic production as the one that serves as the foundation of the urban sexual market today: fellatio. Marx and Engels consider prostitution to be the structural complement of the bourgeois institution of monogamous marriage. Nevertheless, they are leaving out an essential form of nonproductive labor, performed by female and male sex workers whose virtuosic activity consists in exciting and producing pleasure.[23] Sex work must be thought of as pharmacopornographic *poiesis* and belongs to the type of activities that Marx calls "servile work" or nonproductive "labor in which no capital is invested, but a wage is paid (example: the personal services of a butler),"[24] work that is always living and corporal. As Virno observes, what characterizes virtuosic and nonproductive forms of work is their constituent dependency regarding a context that Marx calls "cooperation": there is no virtuoso and nonproductive work without "publicly organized space,"[25] without

22. Virno, *A Grammar of Multitudes*, 54.

23. Karl Marx, *Theories of Surplus Value*, 3 vols., (Amherst, NY: Prometheus Books, 2000); Frederic Engels, *The Origin of the Family, Private Property, and the State*, rev. ed. (1884; repr., New York: Penguin, 2010).

24. Virno, *A Grammar of Multitudes*, 54.

25. Ibid., 13.

an audience, (auditorium, theater, community of readers, space of domesticity, etc.), without *intellectual cooperation*, without *General Intellect*.[26] This is the case for sex work: the relationship between customer and sex worker can occur only in a publicly structured space; it is a relationship of spectacle, one involving representation and communication more than consumption. The customer doesn't consume anything (there is no object or outcome), nothing but a fantasy that is physically or virtually embodied by the worker through what Annie Sprinkle calls "performance," a dramatization of sexuality whose goal is to trigger the excitation-frustration cycle. As conceived by Roland Barthes in *Sade, Loyola et Fourier*, pornographers are "scenographers," manufacturers of a public context, a theatrical décor in which the ritual of excitation-frustration takes place;[27] a technical device for the publication of sexuality that connects bodies to audiovisual and telecommunication technologies. In a situation of this type, we ought to be speaking no longer about "intellectual cooperation" but about *masturbatory cooperation*.

Whereas the theorists of post-Fordism employ the Marxist notion of *General Intellect* to speak about the communicative potential for cooperation among brains as a new platform of capitalist production, we theorists of the post-porn era are emphasizing the notion of *General Sex*, or

26. A notion of Marx that, in a post-Fordist rereading, confirms immaterial work and the work of communication.
27. Barthes, *Sade*, 10.

"public sex," to conceive of the cooperation between bodies, desires, impulses, organic fluxes, molecules, and pleasures mobilized by pharmacopornographic capitalism. Pharmacopornographic labor cultivates, exploits, and produces the sexual technobody of the multitude. The new capital is put together by the array of corporal and sexual relationships and relationships of dependency, by modes of the production of circuits of excitation-frustration, which deposit layer after layer of the force of sexual work, affecting the entire length of the process of production. All pharmacopornographic relationships (whether sexual, or whether a matter of a body's relations with itself, or whether a matter of those dependencies that link a molecule to a living metabolism) can be transformed into (at least partially, but without being reduced to) fixed capital. And living sexual labor captured and converted into property by an enterprise can become productive and therefore competitive on an international level. In such a case, productivity cannot be measured on the basis of quantity of production per hour worked; it cannot refer to a single enterprise or specific sector, but must refer to the entire group of excitation-frustration factors that make up the technoliving body and that go beyond the individual worker. Seven minutes of high on cocaine or a twenty-five-second orgasm is well worth the existence of an efficient cybernetic system of distribution and exchange of documents, archives, and hypertexts and is enough to justify the covert chain of production and virtual distribution of molecules and bodies, images and sounds.

General Sex—public erection, global ejaculation, collective coming, orbital shooting—is the impulse for communal joy that travels through the multitude, convulsing the totality of excitable producer-bodies of capital.

General Sex is exciting communication, global masturbatory strength, the connecting of potentially joyful subjectivities. But beware, *General Sex* cannot be reduced, must not be reduced, to liters of spilled sperm, or to fixed capital: its practice occurs in the communication of excitation, in the forms of performative paradigms (of the theatralization of gender roles and sexual games) and psychotropic doses, by means of incessant molecular variations and hormonal modulations. *General Sex* teaches us that masturbation and the fix are never solitary activities but are vibrations coming from cooperating bodies, effects of the collective practice of sexual or pharmacological labor on the living orgasmic body that squirts capital everywhere. In this context of exploding sexual productive forces, cooperation between bodies absorbs all other types of productive labor, in a way that makes all commodities simultaneously an incitation to sexual pleasure and the frustration of that same pleasure. One of the keys of the productive circuit of excitation-frustration-excitation lies in the toxicological nature of sexual pleasure. When we speak of a pharmaco-pornographic economy, we must take into account the fact that the two tentacles (pharmaco and porno) are exploiting a common somato-political foundation: the toxicological dimension of pleasure. The pleasure (in its capacity as frustrating satisfaction) of the multitude is the ultimate source of the production of wealth.

THE SEX WORKER BECOMING CYBORG

In Marx's analysis of the different forms of exploitation in the industrial economy, the productive dimension of sexual and domestic services provided by the dominant classes of women, by the working classes, and by colonized bodies occurs nearly unperceived (in terms of its specificity of gender, class, and race). In an 1892 essay, Simmel develops a pioneering theory of sexual services: he contemplates the practice of prostitution as one of the components of the urban economy. For Simmel, the economic specificity of the prostituted body is to function as an "ejaculation mechanism."[28] This analysis allows him to compare the prostitute to other technical workers who perform "unrewarding" tasks, such as those who work "in the arsenic mine, or in the mirror-coating factory and in all the directly dangerous or slowly poisoning manufacturing plants."[29] Sex work, like work in mines, cannot be reduced to the simple act of taking a load or loading coal, or to the effort expended by the mouth or hand to accomplish such tasks, "but contains *implicitly* his entire previous training, his entire past. Similarly, the work of countless workers and that of prostitutes contains all its consequences and its relationships, the entire attitude toward life and the entire future of the worker."[30]

To Marx's definition of sexual work (with or despite Marx) as "nonproductive production" or "private service,"

28. Georg Simmel, *Simmel On Culture: Selected Writings*, eds. David Patrick Frisby and Mike Featherstone (New York: SAGE Publications, 1997), 262.
29. Ibid., 266.
30. Ibid.

we must now add the technical and mechanized dimension of sex work, whereby the way to a possible industrialization of sex is opened.

In the second half of the twentieth century, pharmacological intoxication, the production of sexuality and communication become mass-produced work. But unlike work in the information-communication and cultural industries, mass-produced sex and toxicological work are located in the framework of underground labor that is off the books, unsalaried, without union representation, and marginal or illegal. As a shadow of communications work (that is more invisible than it is immaterial), pharmacopornographic work supports and animates all other contemporary productive economy.

In a certain way, the pornographic and pharmaceutical industries conform to the Fordist criteria of Taylorization and seriality: pornographic audiovisual grammar has the goal of triggering an ejaculation with the minimal number of shots and scenes, the same way that the molecule sildenafil (Viagra's active ingredient) must initiate a lasting erection, accompanied by an always renewable sufficient dose of pleasure. Nevertheless, actuating a sexual assembly line that would permit the permanent industrialization of sex work seems difficult to achieve. Certainly pornography is upping its degree of technological serial processing thanks to programming and circulation by digital means. However, for the moment and at the start of the third millennium, there is no machine capable of performing fellatio assembly-line style that can supplant the biomouth or any robotic masturbator capable of distracting the attention of customers who can get a hand job from a humanoid for ten euros in the Parisian bois de Boulogne.

Until recently, the technological restrictions and hurdles for the processes of industrialization that were characteristic of domestic work were equally at play in sex work. In both cases, it was a matter of keeping the domestic and sexual workforce in the most carnal and vulnerable of states, of reducing these spaces of production to the "private" sphere, of removing domestic and sexual work from the world of paid activities and thus preventing their contact with principles of democracy and visibility.

If it is true that domestic space has been the object of a certain technologizing since World War II, we must still agree with Angela Davis's contention that this process has not led to any radical emancipation of the (unsalaried) domestic worker.[31] Davis asks us to imagine workers at high-performance, high-tech companies performing domestic work in a context of serial organization: cooked meals delivered to the home; laundry picked up, washed, and ironed; industrial cleaning of every domestic space, and so on, services that would make the tasks of the housewife obsolete. Nevertheless, these activities are still being performed today to a large extent by unpaid female bodies or by bodies in a precarious work situation (often, a legal, racialized immigrant or one without papers), those for whom access to other kinds of employment is checked

---

31. Davis, "The Approaching Obsolesce of Housework: A Working Class Perspective," chap. 13 in *Women, Race & Class*.

by immigration laws and by the racial segregation of legal work, and for whom access to the political space has been permanently blocked. In reality, male and female domestic workers occupy positions resembling those of male and female sex workers.

According to Marx's taxonomy, the whore, the housewife, and the domestic worker belong to the same category of service and nonproductive work, and such a classification owes nothing to chance. The whore is ceaselessly engaged in the work of excitation and production of pleasure, while the housewife is engaged in the never completed task of taking care of hygiene and bodies and producing relaxation (including the sexual type) for the inhabitants of the home. The domestic slave is merely a hybridization of these two forms of exploitation of the *potentia gaudendi*. In all cases, the work lacks a finished product, does not stand as an autonomous and defined accomplishment, and is a productive practice that corresponds to Marx's formula for "private services."[32] Culturally, these corporal practices are considered not possible to mechanize, not able to be entirely absorbed by technical production.

During modernity, the double-helix trajectory that led to the domestication of sexuality and the sexualization of domestic work brought with it an even stricter privatization of the two practices. Therefore, a possible philosophical pornology would encourage us to think of domestic activity (paid or unpaid) as part of the economy of sexual work in the broad sense of the term that brings together

---

32. Virno, *A Grammar of Multitudes*, 53.

the processes of breeding, culture, and care of masturbatory/ejaculating subjectivity.

In a counterintuitive way, the technologizing of sexual work is not revealed by the presence of technical tools for sexuality. It operates more subtly, by means of the biotechnological production of the cultural body of the sex worker, a process we could dub "sex-worker-becoming-cyborg," according to Klynes and Clyne's concept, as repoliticized by Donna J. Haraway.[33] Or, to put it another way: the ideal sex worker, the high-tech cock-sucking machine, is a mouth treated with silicone that is silent and politically subaltern and belongs to an immigrant cis-female or transsexual without access to administrative identity and full citizenship. The sex machines of the third millennium are living bodies denied entrance into the political sphere, deprived of public discourse, stripped of union rights and strikes, and lacking medical care or unemployment benefits. Unlike for traditional Fordism, there is no longer any competition between machine and worker. On the contrary: the worker is becoming a sexual biomachine.

True technologizing of sex work is accomplished through the production of sexual bodies as ejaculatory mechanisms and ejaculating sexual bodies. Most of the male and female sex workers of the twenty-first century are biopolitical,

33. See Donna J. Haraway, "A Cyborg Manifesto: Science, Technology, and Socialist-Feminism in the Late 20th Century," in *Simians, Cyborgs, and Women: the Reinvention of Nature* (New York: Routledge, 1990), 149–81. Originally published as "Manifesto for cyborgs: science, technology, and socialist feminism in the 1980s," *Socialist Review*, no. 80 (1985): 65–108.

lumpen-proletarianized, racialized cyborgs, adapted to the process of the mass production of pleasure at reduced price. But careful, for we must not see in this case any natural determination, not about sex, or gender, or race. This is solely a matter of differences resulting from the processes of sexopolitical specialization. Any cis-male or cis-female at all has the capability to follow a process of pharmacoporno-graphic transformation into a technically *performing* whore. Let's take the body of a cis-male as an example: such a transformation would necessitate regular doses of estrogen and Androcur, a certain amount of silicone to produce breasts and buttocks, and permanent body hair removal, and will probably also entail preserving a working biopenis (such a biotool is a precious instrument of work for professional activities and is equally valued by both homosexual and heterosexual clientele). When it comes to being a source of *potentia gaudendi*, any body can become a fairly expert multimedia technowhore in a relatively short space of time.

In pharmacopornism, the zones of pornographic production and sex work occupy a structural position that is similar to that of a prison. The cartography composed by the circuits of the sex industry, the penal-industrial complex, and domestic spaces is made up of enclaves of maximum exploitation, genuine oases of *übermaterial* capitalism, dystopic reserves of biopolitical experimentation existing at the heart of contemporary democratic societies.[34] Porn

---

34. See Angela Y. Davis, *Are Prisons Obsolete?* (New York: Seven Stories Press, 2003); David Ladipo, "The Rise of America's Prison Industrial Complex," *New Left Review* 7, (January–February 2001): 71–85; Loïc Wacquant, "De l'esclavage à l'emprisonnement de masse. Notes pour repenser la 'question raciale' aux Etats-Unis," in *L'Esclavage, la colonization, et après…*, eds. Patrick Weil and Stéphane Foix (Paris: PUF, 2005), 247–74.

and prison are the only two industries that function in our democratic and humanist societies in accordance with a pro-slavery regime that is close to the economy of the plantation: racial and gender segregation; minimal or nonexistent salaries;[35] prohibition of unions and the right to strike; an absence of paid holidays, sick days, or unemployment insurance. The sex industry[36] and the prison-industrial complex are the two domains in which workers are entirely deprived of civil rights, and any economic or moral entitlement over the products of their work are expropriated from them. The current European penal code (its condemnation of the marketing and consumption of drugs, sex work, and the distribution of certain pornographic audiovisual material) is one of the techniques of delegitimization and desubjectivization of the bodies of pharmacoporno workers. Once they are reduced to the category of criminal, their *potentia gaudendi* can be used freely or at a low price. Through such a biopolitical coup, the same historical and material subjects occupy the interior of a closed circuit that links the drug industry to the sex industry and to the penal-industrial complex. More than a ghetto, it should be thought of as a spatiotemporal wormhole inside contemporary democratic societies.

If Angela Davis's argument is transposed to the sex industry, the penal-industrial complex and the domains of

---

35. For example, a worker in San Quentin Prison in San Francisco earns twenty cents an hour, or $1.60 a day, a salary comparable to that given a worker in an industry that has relocated to Cambodia.

36. With some rare exceptions, in which the actors and directors of porn do sign contracts for traditional productions; for example, in the case of John B. Root and Marc Dorcel, or for Canal-Plus.

work in pornography and prostitution seem a fresh expedient for the continuation of the economy of slavery at the heart of Western democratic societies. That is, the porno-narco-prison wormhole is no exception as a space, but is a subterranean coil in which the new technologies of control and production of the technoliving are tested before their being extended to democratic society as a whole.

Therefore, in the context of the pharmacopornist economy, the war (which is an extreme form of the porno-narco-prison complex) isn't exterior to the economy of production and consumption in times of "peace," but a special laboratory for experimentation on the global scale for hard drugs, mass rapes, unpaid and obligatory sexual services, and programs of technobiopolitical extermination.

The pharmacopornographic regime is rising from the ruins of World War II. It towers upward like the nuclear mushroom of the H-bomb. The psychopolitical heritage (extreme violence, maximum excitation, collective drug addiction, posttraumatic symptoms, etc.) and technology (a network of communication through computer science, the digitization of data, the invention of molecules and synthetic materials, etc.) of the experimental industry of the war is permitting the implementation on a global scale of new technologies for the production of pleasure (excitation-frustration) in the technoliving body.

11. JIMI AND ME

VIRGINOLOGY

The new year. I get stoned. In every way possible. Always more so. The first time she fucked me with my own dildo-harness, she made me come as if I were a schoolgirl. Being taken by your own dildo-harness: an act of extreme humility, relinquishing all forms of my hormonal, prosthetic, or cultural virility. She induces me to produce a form of femininity I've never allowed myself. Not an essential femininity, or a nature hidden behind the drag king, but rather, a kind of "masculine femininity,"[1] a "drag king femininity." I'm her king bitch, her trans whore, a kid showing his vulva behind her big cock. I've become her slave, getting pierced angrily, a nymphomaniac who'd like to unzip every fly in search of sex organs to take into my mouth, for every orifice. Without her, I would have stuck to my insatiable instinct to penetrate. Only she, queen of the bitches, had the right to transform this body into a hole that's always open, at her disposal. *Gloriam penetrationis.*

It is at that moment that I define the principles of such pharmacopornographic knowledge:

1. See Judith Halberstam, *Female Masculinity* (Durham, NC: Duke University Press, 1998).

Concerning the queer perfection and that VD does every-thing in the most desirable way.[2]

The conception of VD that is the most common and the most full of meaning is expressed well enough in the words *VD is an absolutely perfect being.* The implications, however, of these words fail to receive sufficient consideration. For instance, there are many different kinds of perfection in pornography and in feminism, all of which VD possesses, and each one of them pertains to her in the highest degree.

We must also know what perfection is. One thing that can surely be affirmed about it is that those forms or natures that are not susceptible to *transgenerization* to the highest degree are not perfections. Consequently, pornography and feminism are perfections, and insofar as they pertain to VD, they have no limits.

From where it follows that VD, who possesses supreme and infinite wisdom, acts in the most perfect manner, not only metaphysically, but also from the moral standpoint. And with respect to ourselves, it can be said that the more we are enlightened and informed in regard to the works of VD, the more will we be disposed to find them excellent and conforming entirely to that which we might desire.

That love for VD demands on our part complete satisfaction and acquiescence without it being necessary inasmuch to be a cis-male.

To act conformably to the love of VD it is not sufficient to have an orgasm; we must be really satisfied with all that comes to us according to her will. Since she is the best of

2. See G.W. Leibniz, *Discourse on Metaphysics and the Monadology (1686)*, ed. Albert R. Chandler, trans. George R. Montgomery (New York: Dover, 2008).

all mistresses, she ever demands only the right intentions, and it is for her to know the hour and the proper place to let good designs succeed.

Of all beings, that which is the most perfect and occupies the least possible space, that is to say, that which interferes with another the least, is her love. The activity or the acts of will of VD are commonly divided into ordinary and extraordinary. VD desires everything that is an object of her particular intention. When we consider the objects of her general intentions, however, such as are the modes of activities of created things and especially of the unreasoning creatures and creatures in love with whom VD wishes to cooperate, we must make a distinction, for if the action is good in itself we must say that VD wishes it and at times commands it, even though it does not take place; but if it is bad in itself and becomes good only by accident through the course of events and especially after chastisement and satisfaction have corrected its malignity and rewarded the ill with interest in such a way that more perfection results in the whole train of circumstances than would have come if that ill had not occurred—if all this takes place we must say that VD permits the evil, and not that she desired it, although she has cooperated by means of the laws of sex that she has established. She knows how to produce the greatest good from them.

While I'm reading these precepts, she's caressing the space between my eyes, then between my ear and the roots of my hair; she kisses the hollows of my knees; puts my feet between her thighs to warm them. She is writing her book,

King Kong Theory, in front of me. Her back very straight. Tangled, blond rocker hair, a ring on each finger. On the right hand, a skull and crossbones, and on the left, a fake diamond. Every once in a while, she rolls a fake joint and smokes it as she writes, without looking at the keyboard, and with the speed of an electronic printer. I read the chapters as she finishes them, and I get them as if they were babies still drowsy, opening their eyes for the first time before me. A turn-on. I recognize the voice that excites me, fucks me: the voice of a teenage punk who has learned to speak using a cis-male program for the production of gender, the aristocratic brain of a futurist she-wolf lodged in the body of a hooker, the intelligence of a Nobel Prize winner incarnated in a street dog. A biopolitical miracle: the proof that new geneticopolitical and literary recombinations are possible. She gets up and dances in front of the curtainless window, to the glory of the neighborhood. All the new generations of dykes can be found in the body that harbors that voice, in its neuronal territory. Come, little girls, those who wear the veil and those who do not, those who have children and those who have none, those who suck cocks and those who don't, those who want to have a mustache and those who don't. Take and eat. Meanwhile, I'm reading Laplanche's text on the "general theory of seduction," in order to understand de Lauretis's fascination with the implantation of subjectivity.[3] The earliest seduction is a thorn planted in the somatic field of the mind, around which the subject develops like a callosity.

---

3. See Jean Laplanche, *Problematiques*, vol. 7, *Le Fourvoiement biologisant de la sexualité chez Freud suivi de Biologisme et Biologie* (Paris: PUF, 2006).

POLITICS OF CARE

As I submit my mind to the discipline of virile coaching and take testosterone, VD is gradually initiating me into the cultural rituals of femininity. As a result, after six months with her, I alternately occupy two extremes of the gender-cultural apparatus. On the one hand, there are my exercises in intentional masculinization, somato-political gymnastics brought to bear against received education, against the programs of gender that dominate social and political representation, sometimes even against my own desire; on the other is my feminine primping: hair styling, manicures, peels, massages, pedicures, removal of unwanted hair. In reality, testosterone belongs to neither of these two devices for the production of gender. Mixed with the other molecules in my body, it instead composes the somato-political context for the performative implantation of these practices. Both these devices belong to what we could call an aesthetic (in the dermatocosmetic sense of the term, the skin being the largest and most public organ of the body and therefore the main platform for somato-political and performative implantation and agency), or even ethic, of genders: the attention, the intentional care brought to the somato-political production of masculinity and femininity.

Having made up her mind to help me discover the ins and outs of feminization, VD invites me to go with her for some thalassotherapy. In a luxurious hotel complex in Bretagne, we spend a week in bathrobes and plastic sandals, soaking in baths of algae, floating in iodized and bio-energized Jacuzzis, eating oysters while reading *Le Figaro* (the French right-wing newspaper being the only paper available), and fucking. An unforgettable week. For the first time in my life, I agree to have a manicure. A translucent-glass staircase leads to the place where the treatments are given, a room in the shape of a shell, with walls and floor in pearly white. Several branches of red coral holding pendants, necklaces, Dior, Chanel, and Dolce & Gabbana watches are on display in a window; another has been converted into an aquarium in which a colony of little puppet fish are living with bracelets and pearls. The curious world of high-class white femininity. They call this strange universe a "center for marine beauty treatments." A young woman welcomes me, hands me a white bathrobe, a March issue of *Vogue*. There's a ten-minute wait, she tells me. I've brought my own book. I look around the place with contempt. The décor and the cis-females who are waiting for a skin cleansing seem terribly short on style, intelligence. A wave of anguish rises in me. My left-wing radical trans-lesbian culture puts me on guard against this form of gender hedonism. At the height of this political despondency, another young woman comes to get me. I think about warning her immediately that, contrary to what she may think, I'm not a simple cis-female, about telling her that I'm trans, that this is the first time that I've been here, that I don't even know what I'm doing there. I consider asking her if the procedure for a lady's manicure and a man's are the same, if they use the same products on both. She gives me a friendly smile and takes me into a private room, and I'm incapable of uttering the slightest sound. She has me sit down at a little table covered with a white towel on which

is a line of about a dozen cosmetics in flasks, several piles
of gauze compresses, boxes of colored cotton, a transparent
jar containing pink and blue files of various thicknesses.
Everything is organized with Leibnizian geometric strict-
ness. I sit on a small stool, and she settles in, facing me.
Asks me to give her my hands. First she touches my fingers.
Then she slides her palms under mine almost all the way to
the wrists. She takes my hands and raises them to the level
of her eyes. I feel exposed, naked. She places my right hand
in a small container filled with lukewarm, pink cream, the
color of white skin; then she files the nails on my left hand,
one by one. She takes my right hand out of the container of
cream, holds it between hers. She strokes it, massages each
finger, moves up to the wrist, then rubs the forearm with
the rest of the cream. The experience is completely lesbian.
An idea goes through my mind: she is aware of handling
one of my sexual organs; all the cis-females sitting in the
waiting room and reading *Vogue* know very well why they're
here and what they've come to do. Now I see them in a different way. They're the masked agents of a secret brigade
devoted to female pleasure. The young woman lets go of my
right hand, which no longer shows the slightest resistance
to being touched; it rests languidly on the table where she
has placed it. She begins to massage my left hand, enlaces
my fingers with hers, then pinches the tips, before moving
back down to the arch of skin at the base of the first pha-
lanx. She's giving me a countersexual hand job at the arm.
"How's that?" she asks. "Nice, very nice." I don't look at her
while she's touching me. I can understand what a cis-guy
must feel when he goes to a massage parlor and pays for

a girl to jerk him off. The difference is nominal: they call it "sex," and the women call it "beauty treatment." I come to a rapid conclusion about the functioning of the pharma-copornographic order. In heterosexual culture, well-to-do women can treat themselves to sensual services lavished on them by other women, whereas working-class women, immigrants, or ordinary contract workers are paid to take care of the bodies and erotic well-being of other women, as well as, to be sure, the erotic and sexual well-being of men. Deprived of that parallel homoerotic economy and the sensuality of children, heterosexuality in its capacity as an erotic and political regime would collapse. The only sexual services lavished by men on heterosexual women obviously wouldn't be enough to produce the endorphins and serotonin needed for survival of the body. One thing is clear: the work of taking care of bodies in our society has fallen to women. They take care of men's bodies as well as those of other heterosexual women. That is what is hidden behind the Marxist notion of the "sexual division of labor." It's not just about women being assigned to the sphere of reproduction and men to that of production. It seems a lot more complex than that. The women carry out a funda-mental task without which the eroticopolitical equilibrium of heterosexuality would crumble: bodies to which female gender has been assigned take responsibility for a gener-alized political dermatology. They take care of the skin of the world. One keystone of the heterosexual system is a scrupulous exclusion of the production of sexual pleasure from the framework of cares lavished on women by women. On the other hand, when women take care of men, all care becomes potentially able to be sexualized. It is even possible that the number of women who get manicures are comparable to the number of men who go to massage parlors to have their genitals touched. Absorbed in this eddy of thought, I realize with horror that the young woman is painting my nails red.

THE PROSTHETIC LUCKY STAR

I don't write a line without getting hard for her, without thinking that in one moment or other, my sex, my dick, my dildo, my hand, my arm will be able to have something to do with her mouth. With 250 milligrams in my skin, it's difficult to expect an adequate sexual response from an estrogen-filled body. A conclusion becomes obvious: everything would be easier if the heterosexual political imperative were put aside and the exchange of pleasure and sexual discharge were regulated only by molecular excitation. Teaching a hypertestosteroned body to desire hyperestrogened bodies: this is one possible definition of cultural heterosexual sadomasochism.

She tells me, "I had a lot of group sex when I came to Paris." I imagine dildos of every size have already burst through each of her goddess holes. She tells me, "No, never," while half opening her rubber-duck lips. I had forgotten that cis-guys don't wear dildos when they're having heterosexual group sex. I know nothing about straight sex. I belong to another species: the boy-girls. Since that's the way it is, blond giant, welcome to the planet trans dyke.

Women abandoned by virile poets come to trans world. The possibility of fucking her for the first time with a megadildo triggers a wave of T in me, and heat spreads through my skin, from the coccyx to the neck, flows through my arms and seeps to the point of my tongue. I know the value of my dildos, and I glide molecule by molecule into artificial islands while I evaluate which will have the privilege of fucking her first. I take hold of these centimeters of pure pleasure with my five fingers, the same ones that will later explore the center of her loins, go back up and into her mouth, caress the internal walls of her throat and descend into the digestive tube to the colon. She wants the anatomically realistic blue one. She moans and opens up while lifting her legs. At high speed, I steer the bright-blue Aston Martin DB5 to the inside of her tunnels. VD doesn't want me to fuck her with the dildos I've been using up to now to fuck Victor. Victor doesn't want me to fuck VD with the dildos I was using with him. I understand such heightened sense of prosthetic exclusivity. Both of them demand a scrupulous form of plastic fidelity. It pleases me. I go to the sex superstore on the boulevard Magenta; it's hetero, but less expensive than the sex shops in the Marais. On the window, on the bodies of three worn mannequins, is heaped an eclectic collection of chains, handcuffs, black boas, metal brassieres, nurse's rubber costumes, red hooded capes, and Cat Woman masks. Like any other store in the neighborhood, this one is composed of poor-quality shelves holding porn videos arranged by category, dildos, inflatable dolls, and boxes of pasta shaped like cocks. I pick up a small basket as I enter, then zigzag among the customers bent over shelves. Hello, sir, one of the two salesladies who has been chatting behind the counter greets me. A fake blond with white skin and a childish face, a hetero look. The other one has black eyes edged with long, thick, curled eyelashes. They make me think that she's Franco-Arab, and she seems older, but is certainly not more than about twenty. I take a student tour of the different sizes, materials, colors, prices. The sex accessories superstore is a commercial apotheosis of the straight sexopolitical imagination. A woman is a body, her entire body is material that can be sexualized; a man is a cock, his sexualized material is reduced to his penis.

A few days ago, I asked V to make a list of cis-guys whose cocks she would have liked to suck if her becoming lesbian hadn't been mistimed. Jimi Hendrix was the first name on her list. Cock Number One. The prophet of rock before whom whites kneel. I think of playing a joke on her. I'm still walking around the superstore, and I find a black dildo easily: 8½ inches and very kitsch, with visible veins, the same color as chocolate with a milk chocolate head. Hey, Jimi, can I borrow your cock to plow my blond's ass? Without wanting to be too arrogant, I bet that mine is bigger and better at getting hard.

She calls me "chérie, chéri" when I drive Jimi in. It doesn't make a difference, but I know that she said it twice—one for each of my sexes. That's how she writes it in the text messages she sends me: chérie, chéri. She is certainly going through a reprogramming of her sexual configuration. I show her my prosthetic being: a body with its two little breasts, an 8½-inch silicone cock emerging from my loins, two multifunction arms. I'm installing a "become-my-dyke-whore" file in her sexual hardware. We're reconfigured. My body levitates ten inches above hers. The right distance to mine an image of her in the framework delimited by my outstretched arms. Outside this framework, the world fades to nothing. In close-up, her brassiere, green and red. A silk flower lies between her breasts. My black-leather harness compacts the Jimi against my clit, my nerve endings innervating my dildo all the way to the end. She wants more. Slow, deep fucking. *You got me floatin' round and round. You got me floatin' never down. Vamos hasta el final.*

VD's sex speaks the language of revolution.

FUCK BEAUVOIR

We've been fucking for more than two months. Almost as much time as I've been taking testosterone. Recently, she's been playing with my feelings. She lets herself be fucked like a whore, but afterward, she weeps, because she misses this, or that, because she can't forget n, n + 1 . . . Four days go by without my giving myself a dose of Testogel. When she rejects me, I feel a rise in estrogen and realize that I could cry at any moment. But I hold back, to keep from seeming like an idiot in love. Under my skin, the monster of the female cultural program is awakening: my body has been trained to produce the affects of a woman, suffer like a woman, love like a woman. Testosterone isn't enough to modify this sensory filter. Fuck Beauvoir. Fuck feminism. Fuck love.

To avoid sinking into an ordinary episode of female masochism, amplified by a rise in estrogen, I force myself into
the strict discipline of a program of virile coaching that I've
devised for urgent situations: avoiding all romantic thinking, I practice several exercises for becoming an elite macho
and enduring her absences. When she comes back to me,
I'm ready for her.

It begins like that. Her body is lying on its side on the
bed, her hair hiding her face. The light is a diaphanous white,
like her skin. She doesn't remain in that position for very
long. She makes a 180° turn on her axis, purrs, in a halting
voice says, Chéri, come, come to me, give it to me. I don't
see her mouth right away. The image of her lips emerges
gradually, with her words. First, everything is color. We
are made of red alveoli. A second later, her mouth becomes
sound, and I perceive it by hearing; "Foxy Lady" pours out
of the iPod speakers. The music and her voice construct
two parallel plateaus. The melody circulates at the upper
level, skimming past our heads. Her voices glides, spreads,
into the lower stratum, where our bodies are resting, and
a circular, gyrating shelf serves as our floor. We haven't
entered the sexual stage yet. I'm certain it will arrive right
after these sounds. After this note, to be more precise. I
prepare myself for it. By stages we climb up to the platform
of music, from which the sex emanates. When the rotation
of the plate makes my arm coincide with the bedside table,
I reach out to open the drawer. It contains four dildos, a
hairdrier, a small bottle of lubricant, size XXL condoms, a
tube of Biafine, and some hand cream. The outer surface
of my eyes caresses these objects in its peripheral vision,

rapidly, takes all of it in, in a flash. Next, my eyes stop to extract a single thing from the whole. I take the Jimi, which is already in its harness; I'm kneeling, caught between the wave of her voice and that of the music. She's telling me, *Je suis ta pute*, I belong to you. Everything is spinning. I take off my shirt, lower my jeans without taking them all the way off. I thread one of the leather straps between my legs, then hitch Jimi to my pelvis, locking the buckles on each side of my hips. A piece of skin gets stuck in one of the buckles, and I pull harder; the metal leaves a trace of red, a perfect half-circle at the top of my right thigh. I'm hooked up to Jimi. Superstable sex. I exist in the organic-inorganic continuity offered by this sex. I pull my pants back up, putting Jimi to the side, against my left leg. Her hand reaches for my jeans, confirms the pressure of the straps on my thighs, intensifies the suction effect of Jimi on my clitoris, detects Jimi's shape, its contours. Now we're having sex: the platforms join, making up a single spongy volume. She takes Jimi out of my fly, jerks me off with her hand, then, with her mouth, takes it halfway in, sucks the tip; she goes no further, because what she wants is for me to fuck her deeply with Jimi, and come on her. So yes, yes, take me like a bitch. I'm not afraid of anything. I'm on my knees between her legs. That's where you belong, chérie, only you. Yes, this is my space. She's a mutant virgin crossing the synthetic line of evolution to meet the chief of the clan of the boy-girls. Fucking with her is going back to each knot of my life—the straight girls who kissed me and then left me to go out with cis-guys, the dykes who were disgusted by my dildos; hetero knots, lesbian knots, transphobic knots, androcentrist knots—biting into them until they become undone. I'm her trannie, her monster. I'm not afraid of not being a cis-male. I fill my right palm with lube. I wait, before touching her. The music takes charge of us, everything is moving. I start jerking off my dildo. She watches me, sticks out her tongue. Her head turns three times from one side to the other. In that movement, our vision coincides briefly. My Jimi is bursting her open, butting against the bones of her pelvis before moving backward again. She squeals a bit, her face is near mine. I plunge into her farther, more gently, gliding inside at her rhythm. I feel the effort my arms are making, the traction of my dildo, which lifts her hips, bends her body slightly upward. When her pelvis bears my weight, I no longer need to support myself with my hands. I cling to her clavicles, digging my fingers into the hollow space between her neck and her bones. The eye's surface allows the image to touch it: sex is videographic. Now we are coming in green. Then the impression becomes more olfactory than visual, more haptic than auditory. It's universe mating. A connection made of human phenotypes, language, electronic sounds, and dildos, which I accept during the duration of the penetration as part of my consciousness. I breathe deeply, feeling the electricity rising from my feet to my chest and spreading through my fingers. This is the power of love. The power of digging a hole in her body through which the music flows. The power of knowing that she'd do anything at all to have me between her thighs. The power I extract from her sex.

12. THE MICROPOLITICS OF GENDER IN THE PHARMACOPORNOGRAPHIC ERA: EXPERIMENTATION, VOLUNTARY INTOXICATION, MUTATION

The old hegemonic grammarians—including the sexologists—had lost control of gender and its proliferating siblings.

—DONNA J. HARAWAY

So now we're standing on the side of freaks. Now what? If we can't call the freaks names anymore because we realize we're one of them, then we have to look back at our position as a former insider, and we begin to devalue that. We've now officially become activists. But outside or inside, it's still a side; and taking a side usually means taking the identity of a side, and there you have identity politics as one more rendering of a game called us-versus-them. In "transgender politics," as in any other identity politics, we look around for a "them." From the standpoint of the transgender person, there's no shortage of "them," no shortage at all.

—KATE BORNSTEIN

We want to reclaim our gender, redefine our bodies and create free and open networks in which we can realize our potential, where anyone at all will be able to construct hirs security mechanisms against the injunctions of gender. We aren't victims, our battle wounds are our shields. . . . We do not come forward as terrorists but as pirates, trapeze artists, warriors, gender dissidents. . . . We champion uncertainty, believe in the possibility of "looking back" as if it were a step forward; we think that no process of construction should be imposed as irreversible. We want to make the beauty of androgyny visible. We believe in our right to get rid of our bandages to be able to breathe, or never to remove them; in our right to be operated on by good surgeons and not by BUTCHERS; *in free access to hormonal treatments without having to resort to psychiatric permission forms; in our right to self-medicate with hormones. We demand the right to live without getting anyone's permission.*

—GUERRILLA TRAVOLAKA, BARCELONA

POSTQUEER MICROPOLITICS

The frontiers of contemporary metropolises (Los Angeles, London, New York, Bombay, Paris, Berlin, Singapore, etc.) don't coincide with the geographic limits of modern cities. You can think you're outside them when you're inside, or believe you're inside without having been in contact for a single moment with the virtual density of the pharmaco-porno-megalopolis. I went to New York in 1993 to escape the educational and cultural institutions of post-Franco Spain, where a lesbian feminist (which was how I defined myself at the time, using the limited political and discursive references that were available to me then) had little to do. At the turn of the past century, New York was one of the centers of the sprawling pharmacopornographic empire. But it was also a vortex of networks of emerging critical and political strategies that transcended frontiers and languages in their attempts to resist and dismantle the dominant order.

When I moved to Paris in 1999, I came to live in an eastern suburb of the pharmacopornographic empire, where people speak French. And I came to transcribe in that language (which wasn't mine either) some of the queer dialects I'd seen emerging a few years before. To begin with, this consisted of transferring to other parts of the world the power of discourses of resistance that were fermenting on the fringes of the pharmacopornopolis. Thus, one might also say, New York is not a place but, to put it in Spivak's words, a regime of cultural translation. And therefore, paradoxically, I began living in New York when I left that city.

The austere, sick, and disenchanted 1990s, which lacked the radicalism of the 1970s and the disco glamour of the early 1980s, would be the decade of the proliferation of queer micropolitics. At the end of the 1980s, an array of dyke, fag, drag queen, transgender, and transsexual groups (Queer Nation, Gran Fury, Fierce Pussy, Radical Fairy, ACT UP, and the Lesbian Avengers, to name the best known) scattered throughout the United States and England were rebelling against efforts at assimilation into the dominant heterosexual society by gay and lesbian identity politics. They transformed the street into a space for the "theatricalization of political rage"[1] and adopted a hyperbolic performative style as a way of contesting the heterosexual norm.[2]

1. Butler, *Bodies That Matter*, 233.
2. cf. Front homosexuel d'action revolutionnaire (FHAR), *Rapport contre la normalité* (Paris: Champ Libre, 1971); Guy Hocquenghem, *Homosexual Desire*, trans. Daniella Dangoor (Durham, NC: Duke University Press, 1993); Guy Hocquenghem, *The Screwball Asses*, trans. Noura Wedell (New York: Semiotext(e), 2009). The first of these shifts came from early French queer theorists such as Guy Hocquenghem, René Scherer, and Monique Wittig. Despite the diversity of their critical backgrounds, from Marxism to Foucauldian genealogy, their interpretation of the normalization of bodies and practices in the Western democracies result in a definition of "heterosexuality" as a "political regime."

At the same time, feminism mutated through a decentering of its political subject that simultaneously and transversely questioned the natural and universal character of the female condition.

Judith Butler shed light on the processes of discursive cultural signification and stylization of the body through which the differences between the genders become normalized, while Donna J. Haraway and Anne Fausto-Sterling questioned the existence of two sexes as biological realities that are independent of the technoscientific processes of the construction of bodies and their representation. Moreover, in conjunction with the emancipatory struggles of African Americans and the decolonization of the "Third World," critical voices had just been raised against the presuppositions of white, colonial feminism. Angela Davis, bell hooks, Patricia J. Williams, Gloria Anzaldúa, Cherríe Moraga, Gayatri Spivak . . . were defining projects to decolonize feminism, which obliged theorists and activists to think about complex systems of the unequal distribution of life chances and of violence involving race, gender, sex, sexuality, illness, class, migration, disability . . .[3]

Dissident forms of feminism were becoming visible as

---

3. Gloria Hull, Patricia Scott and Barbara Smith, eds., *But Some of Us Are Brave: All the Women Are White, All the Blacks Are Men* (New York: The Feminist Press, 1982); Cherríe Moraga and Gloria Anzaldúa, eds., *This Bridge Called My Back: Writings by Radical Women of Color* (New York: Kitchen Table: Woman of Color Press, 1983); Gayatri Chakravorty Spivak, "Can the Subaltern Speak?", in *Marxism & the Interpretation of Culture*, eds. Cary Nelson and Lawrence Grossberg (London: Macmillan, 1988), 271–313; Gloria Anzaldúa, *Borderlands/La Frontera: The New Mestiza* (San Francisco: Aunt Lute Books, 1987); Ranajit Guha and Gayatri Chakravorty Spivak, ed., *Selected Subaltern Studies* (New York: Oxford University Press, 1988); Avtar Brah, *Cartographies of Diaspora: Contesting Identities* (New York: Routledge, 1996); Chela Sandoval, *Methodology of the Oppressed* (Minneapolis: University of Minnesota Press, 2000); Chandra Talpade Mohanty and Jacqui Alexander, *Feminist Genealogies, Colonial Legacies, Democratic Futures* (New York: Routledge, 1997).

the subaltern subjects excluded from liberal white heterosexual feminism began to denounce the processes of normalization and repression inherent in their political and discursive strategies. Such purges had led to a colorless, normative, and puritanical form of feminism that saw cultural, sexual, or political differences as threats against the heterosexual, Eurocentric feminine ideal. From such issues, a host of new forms of feminism emerged—feminisms for freaks, collective projects of transformation for the twenty-first century. In a return to Virginie Despentes's thesis,[4] we could speak of the critical awakening of the "proletariat of feminism," populated by nonwhite women, dykes, raped women, gender-dissidents, the HIV-positive, transgender and transsexual people, fat people, immigrants, crips . . . most of us, in fact.

While queer theorists formulated gender performativity and queer activists resisted the disciplinary side effects of gay and lesbian identity politics, activists in ACT UP invented the first strategies of what, in the context of neoliberalism, could already be called "anti-pharmacopornographic activism": fighting AIDS became fighting the biopolitical and cultural apparatuses of the production of the AIDS syndrome—which include biomedical models, advertising campaigns, governmental and nongovernmental health organizations, genome-sequencing programs, pharmacological industries, intellectual property, bio patents, trademarks, definitions of risk groups, clinical assays and protocols . . .

4. Despentes, *King Kong Theory*, 10.

One of the most productive shifts will emerge directly from circles formerly considered to represent the dregs of female victimization, from which feminism was hoping that no critical discourse could arise. The circles in question were composed of sex workers, porn actresses, and the sexually rebellious. The movements created by sex revolts achieved discursive and political structuring in the 1980s when feminist debates against pornography exploded in the United States, a phenomenon that came to be known as the "sex wars." Enter Catharine MacKinnon and Andrea Dworkin, spokeswomen for antisex feminism, who'll label pornography the prime example of the political and sexual oppression of women.[5] Using a slogan created by Robin Morgan, "Pornography is the theory, and rape is the practice," they will condemn the representation of female sexuality as a practice that promotes gender violence and the sexual and political submission of women; and they will call for the legal abolition of pornography and prostitution.[6]

In 1981, Ellen Willis, one of the pioneers of American feminist rock journalism, critiques the complicity of such abolitionist feminism with the patriarchal structures in heterosexual society that repress and control women's bodies. For Willis, when abolitionist feminists ask the state to regulate the representation of sexuality, they are granting

---

5. Catharine MacKinnon, *Feminism Unmodified: Discourses on Life and Law* (Cambridge, MA: Harvard University Press, 1988); Andrea Dworkin, *Pornography: Men Possessing Women* (London: Women's Press, 1981); see also MacKinnon, *Pornography and Civil Rights: A New Day for Women's Equality* (Minneapolis: Organizing Against Pornography, 1998).

6. Robin Morgan, "Theory and Practice: Pornography and Rape," in *Going Too Far: The Personal Chronicle of a Feminist* (New York: Random House, 1978). Cited in Alice Echols, "The Taming of the Id: Feminist Sexual Politics, 1968–1983," in *Pleasure and Danger: Exploring Female Sexuality*, ed. Carole S. Vance (New York: Routledge, 1984), 50–72.

too much power to a patriarchal institution whose historical goal has always been the subjugation of the female body and the reinforcement of the masculine gaze and enjoyment. The perverse outcomes of the antipornography movement will become apparent in Canada, when laws based on feminist criteria that are used to repress the representation of sexuality are applied to the first censored films and publications, which turn out to be about sexual *minorities*[7]—more specifically, about lesbians (because of the presence of dildos) and about S&M sexualities (regarded by the state commission as violent and hurtful to women). On the other hand, stereotypical representations of women in heterosexual porn are not condemned by the commission.

The sex workers movement reacted to antiporn feminism by declaring the state incapable of protecting us from pornography. The decoding of representation is always an open semiotic task that does not require protection; rather it is something that must be approached with reflection, critical discourse, and political action. Willis would be the first to call "pro-sex feminism" the sexopolitical movement that categorizes female pleasure and the female body as political spaces of resistance to the control and normalization of sexuality. In parallel, the Californian prostitute Scarlot Harlot will use the expression *sex worker* to define prostitution, demanding professionalization and equal rights for whores in the labor market. The prostitutes of

7. The meaning of minority I'm using here is not a reference to the statistical meaning of the term, but to that of a revolutionary reservoir of political transformation, as conceived by Deleuze and Guattari.

San Francisco (who have gathered together to form COY-OTE, a movement to defend the rights of whores founded by the sex worker Margot Saint James), members of PONY (Prostitutes of New York), some HIV activists from ACT UP, and some radical lesbians and sadomasochists (calling themselves the Lesbian Avengers, SAMOIS, etc.) quickly form a coalition with Willis and Harlot. Beginning in the 1990s, in Spain and France, the sex worker movement, led by the groups Hetaira (Madrid), Cabiria (Lyon), Grisélidis (Toulouse), and LICIT (Barcelona) and represented by such activists as Christina Garaizabal, Empar Pineda, Dolores Juliano, Raquel Osborne, Grisélidis Réal, Claire Carthonney, and Françoise Guillemaut, form a European unit to defend the rights of male and female sex workers.

This "post-porn"[8] and self-reflective feminism was able to find a space for activism within audiovisual productions, literature, and performance. With the feminist postporn films of Annie Sprinkle; the documentaries and fictional films of Monika Treut; the literature of Virginie Despentes, Dorothy Allison, and Kathy Acker; the comic strips of Alison Bechdel; the photography of Del LaGrace Volcano and Axelle Ledauphin; the performances of Diana Pornoterrorista, Post-Op, and Lady Pain; the queer performances of Tim Stüttgen; the zines and ready-made politics of Dana Wise; the wild concerts of Tribe 8, Le Tigre, or Chicks on Speed; the neo-Goth sermons of Lydia Lunch; and the transgender science fiction porn of Shu Lea Cheang, an entire transnational postporn trans-feminist aesthetic was

8. I am using here Annie Sprinkle's politicization of Wink van Kempen's notion "post-porn" modernist. See Annie Sprinkle, *Post-Porn Modernist* (San Francisco: Cleis Press, 1998).

created that trafficked in signs and cultural artifacts and critically resignified normative codes considered by traditional feminism to be inappropriate for femininity. This aesthetic and political discourse drew its references from horror or porn films; Gothic literature; sex toys; vampires and monsters; mangas; pagan divinities; cyborgs; punk music; political interventions in public spaces; sex with machines; anarcofeminist icons like the riot grrrls; ultrasex lesbian parodies of drag king masculinity like Diane Torr; Océan LeRoy, Shelly Mars, and Antonia Baehr; and transsexual performers and artists like Lazlo Pearlman and Hans Scheirl.

However, the word *queer*, which was culturally translated and served for several years as a name that referred to various struggles occurring in Anglo-Saxon and European countries, has been subjected today to a growing process of reification and commercialization (processes belonging to the pharmacopornographic order). In the past few years, *queer* has been recodified by the dominant discourses.[9] We are currently facing the risk of turning the term into a description of a neoliberal, free market identity that generates new exclusions and hides the specific conditions of the oppression of transsexual, transgender people, crip, or racialized bodies. It is not a matter of choosing an oppositional biological or historical subject (whether it be *women*, *homosexuals*, *blacks*, etc. . . .) that could function as a mainspring for revolutionary transformation and the statistical sum of multicultural minority differences. Nor do I mean

---

9. To mention only one of these rehabilitations of the term: In 1998, the TV producer Thierry Ardisson registered the term queer at the Institut National de L'Industrie in France.

that we already can no longer use the term *queer*; I merely mean that it has lost a large part of its subversive energy and can no longer serve as today's common denominator to describe the proliferation of strategies of resistance to categories of gender and the normalization of sexuality as well as to the processes of industrialization and privatization of the body as "product." In reaction to this process of the capitalization of genderqueer identities, inside minority subcultures, transsexuals, transgender, and crip people and racial minorities are asking us to pay attention to the body's materiality, to the management of its vulnerability, and to the cultural construction of possibilities for survival within processes of subjugation and political organization.[10] Today we can understand the enunciation of *queer* as a critical moment in a wider process of the production of a trans-feminist critical politics and the construction of dissident subjectivities within the pharmacopornographic regime. The trans-feminist movement that has come out of the queer critique is spreading through fragile but extensive networks, leading to strategic alliances and synthetic links; it circulates like a political antidote that infiltrates the very circuits of global capitalism.

Tony Negri and Michael Hardt have described the contemporary world as a single, delocalized, interconnected city with centers of intensity; circuits through which capital, bodies, and information circulate; zones of luxurious comfort and pauperized zones; and remote places for the

10. See Judith Butler, *Bodies*, 27–55; see also chaps. 3, 4, and 8, in *Undoing Gender*. Butler herself, whose texts were read at the beginning of the 90s as critical foundations of "queer theory," is qualifying her performative interpretation of identity to emphasize the specificity of the material and discursive processes that produce intersexual or transsexual corporality.

production and evacuation of material and semiotic detritus. We live in a sort of punk cyber-Gothic Middle Ages of the bio-information empire. During a certain time, our gurus defined as "postmodernity" that planetary invagination, although it was a techno-porno-punk zenith of modernity. We are at a point of historical inflection in which modernity is puking up its repugnant ejaculatory potential; we're swimming in nuclear semen in which we are learning to breathe like mutant beasts. The difference between the Roman Empire and our techno-porno-punk global empire is that we no longer possess any ontotheological foundation. Some will think that contemporary civilization has substituted an industrial or ergot-like foundation for ontotheology. However, neither work nor production is enough to explain the present-day functioning of our societies. The contemporary techno-porno-punk empire relies on new slogans: "Consume and die," "Have an orgasm and make war." And don't forget to continue to consume and to come after your death. This is the thanato-pornographic foundation of this new empire.

We are not talking about a dark age—not living in some dim postmodernity—but are talking, rather, about the glittering age of porn. It's already not about the dawn of time but about an atmosphere that is completely illuminated, a pervasive gas saturated with moist images. In the middle of this dazzling confusion, concepts such as "lucidity," "illumination," "clarity," and "obviousness" blaze with a new obscurity. According to neurobiologists, there are four states of consciousness: lucidity, obnubilation, somnolence, and coma. When lucid, the subject is present to itself and to the surrounding environment; when obnubilated, the subject's eyes are open, but he or she is disoriented in terms of space and time and relatively indifferent to self and environment; when somnolent, the subject's eyes are closed but he or she still reacts to direct stimuli. In a coma, the subject reacts neither to direct nor indirect stimuli but may remain present to self. Our presence to ourselves as a species could be described today as prosthetico-comatose. We've closed our eyes, but we continue to see by means of an array of technologies, political implants that we call life, culture, civilization. It is, however, only through the strategic reappropriation of these biotechnological apparatuses that it is possible to invent resistance, to risk revolution.

SNUFF POLITICS

The fact is that we're being fucked right off the bat: becoming a punk civilization. The sudden emergence of the punk movement in 1977 was not a simple microphenomenon, but the last lucid explosion of what seems today to be the only ideal shared by the members of what has been called the human species: the pleasure instinct as a death instinct. At the beginning of the twenty-first century, no cultural production has entailed such a punk dimension as much as snuff has—the filming of death (or its representation) as it happens. In popular culture, *snuff* refers to those films that show the murder of a person or animal with the unique objective of making that death visible, transforming it into public, marketable representation.

Everything, in fact, begins as something sham. In 1971, Z-series directors Michael and Roberta Findlay made *The Slaughter*, a small-budget film production that combined erotic scenes with horror scenes. That same year, Ed Sanders interviewed Charles Manson. Manson claimed to have recorded some of the celebrity murders perpetrated by his followers under his authority. No trace of such films were found, but the myth of snuff was born. In 1972, the distributor Alan Shackleton got ahold of *The Slaughter*, added a last scene in which one of the actresses is disemboweled (fictionally) in front of the camera, and rereleased this new edit under the title *Snuff*. The premiere of the film took place in 1976 and provoked an unprecedented debate over the verity of the actress's death. Antiporn groups, pro-censorship feminists, and the media took part in this debate. The film, which had no other cinematographic or narrative interest outside the evisceration scene, would garner unexpected profits.

As a questioning of representational limits, snuff has served as a pornographic paradigm for both pro-censorship feminists and antiporn Christians, and also as a formal model of realism to which the dramatization of sex in pornography must tend: a film is that much more pornographic if the sexual scene that is filmed is real, in the same way that a representation is snuff when the crime has *actually* taken place. Radically postmodern, the notion of snuff is opposed to the dramatic or simulated and mimetic quality of all representation. On the contrary, it affirms the performative power of representation to modify reality, or a desire for the real to exist in and by representation. This brings us to the theatrical relationship between pornography, snuff, and politics. Today, some snuff film catalogs offer images filmed by Allied or Nazi soldiers in concentration camps, Zapruder's film of the John F. Kennedy assassination, the film of the assassination of Yitzhak Rabin, videos of the executions of prisoners of war in Afghanistan and Iraq, videos showing the American army destroying Iraqi villages, images of the destruction of New York's Twin Towers and of the execution of Saddam Hussein. Politics has become snuff: extermination by and for representation.

The mushroom cloud left in the sky by the atomic bomb, the photograph of the completely naked little girl running away from the Vietnam village Trang Bang in flames after a napalm attack, the sperm-filled lips of Linda Lovelace, piles of mutilated limbs in Rwanda, double penetration, the terrifying feats performed in *Big Brother* and the surgical scenes in *Nip/Tuck*, the liters of fat suctioned from the buttocks of American housewives for the cameras of *Extreme Makeover*, murders at the maximum-security San Quentin State Prison filmed by security cameras—all of them say more about the current state of our species than any philosophy book of the twentieth century, from Husserl to Sartre. The distinctive feature of the *techno-porno-punk* moment is *snuff politics*: rip away everything from life to the point of death and film the process, record it in writing and image, distribute it live over the Internet, make it permanently accessible in a virtual archive, an advertising medium on the global scale. By the beginning of the twenty-first century, our species had literally stuck good philosophical intentions up our ass, filming the thing before marketing the images from it. The philosophy of the pharmacopornographic regime has been reduced to an enormous, dripping butt-plug camera. In such circumstances, the philosophy of such high-punk modernity can only be autotheory, autoexperimentation, auto-techno-penetration, pornology.

When surmising about the future of the planet, Donna J. Haraway encourages us to avoid two kinds of narrative traps of the metaphysical and semiotico-fascist kind. First, there is the messianic temptation: someone will come to save us—some unique religious or technical force, an all-powerful understanding that possesses all the answers needed to transform the human condition. Second, there is the apocalyptic temptation: nothing can be done, and the disappearance of the species is imminent. Haraway tells us, "We might profitably learn to doubt our fears and certainties of disasters as much as our dreams of progress. We might learn to live without the bracing discourses of salvation history."[11] The problem resides precisely in the fact that no one will come to save us and that we are still some distance from our inevitable disappearance. It will thus be necessary to think about doing something while we are on the way out, undergoing mutation or changing planets, even if this something consists in intentionally accelerating our own disappearance, mutation, or cosmic displacement. Let us be worthy of our own fall and imagine for the time left the components of a new pornopunk philosophy.

11. Haraway, *Modest_Witness*, 45.

THE PRINCIPLE OF THE AUTO–GUINEA PIG

The first principle of a trans-feminism movement capable of facing *porno-punk* modernity: the fact that your body, the body of the *multitude* and the pharmacopornographic networks that constitute them are political laboratories, both effects of the process of subjection and control and potential spaces for political agency and critical resistance to normalization. I am pleading here for an array of politics of physical experimentation and semiotechnology that (in the face of the principle of political representation, which dominates our social life and is at the core of political mass movements, which can be as totalitarian as they are democratic) will be regulated by the principle that—in accordance with Peter Sloterdijk's intuitions—I will call the "principle of the auto-guinea pig."[12]

In China, in 213 BC, all books were burned by order of the emperor. In the fifth century, after a series of wars had ransacked and decimated the library at Alexandria, it was accused of harboring pagan teachings contrary to the Christian faith and was destroyed by the decree of Emperor Theodosius. The greatest center of research, translation, and reading disappeared. Between 1330 and 1730, thousands of human bodies were burned during the Inquisition, thousands of books were destroyed, and hundreds of works related to the expertise and production of subjectivity were relegated to oblivion or to the underground. In 1813,

12. In his interview with Hans-Jürgen Heinrichs, Peter Sloterdijk evokes "voluntary intoxication" and "auto-guinea pig" techniques in reference to Samuel Hahnemann; see Peter Sloterdijk, *Neither Sun Nor Death*. With Hans-Jürgen Heinrichs, trans. Steven Corcoran (New York: Semiotext(e), 2011).

American soldiers took York (now Toronto) and burned the parliament and legislative library. A year later, the Library of Congress was razed. In 1933, one of the first actions of the Nazi government was the destruction of the Institut für Sexualwissenschaft (Institute for Sexual Research) in Berlin. Created in 1919 by Magnus Hirschfeld, this center had for years played a role in the research and dissemination of progressive ideas and practices concerning sex and sexuality. Twenty thousand books from the Hirschfeld Institute were burned on May 10, 1933, on Opernplatz on a gigantic pyre whose flashing flames were imprinted on the camera film of Hitler's reporters. On the night of March 9, 1943, an air raid on a library in Aachen destroyed five hundred thousand books. In 1993, Croatian militia destroyed dozens of libraries (among them, those in Stolac). In 2003, American bombs and Saddam loyalists sacked and destroyed the National Library of Baghdad[13] . . .

The theorico-political innovations produced during the past forty years by feminism, the black liberation movement, and queer and transgender theory do seem to be lasting acquisitions. However, in the context of global war, this collection of scholarship could be destroyed also, as fast as a microchip melting under intense heat. Before all the existing fragile archives about feminism and black, queer, and trans culture have been reduced to a state of radioactive shades, it is indispensible to transform such minority knowledge into collective experimentation, into physical

13. On the destruction of the books, see Fernando Baez, *A Universal History of the Destruction of Books: From Ancient Sumer to Modern-day Iraq*, trans. Alfred MacAdam (New York: Atlas & Co., 2008).

practice, into ways of life and forms of cohabitation. We are no longer pleading, like our predecessors in the 1970s and 1980s, for an understanding of life and history as effects of different discursive regimes. We are pleading to use discursive productions as stakeholders in a wider process of the technical materialization of life that is occurring on the planet. A materialization that each day resembles more and more a total technical destruction of all animal, vegetable, and cultural forms of life and that will end, undoubtedly, in the annihilation of the planet and the self-extinction of most of its species. Alas, it will become a matter of finding ways to record a planetary suicide.

Until the end of the eighteenth century, self-experimentation was still a part of the research protocols of pharmacology. Animal experimentation was not yet called into question, but an ethical precept dictated that the researcher take on the risk of unknown effects on his or her own body before enacting any test on the body of another human. Relying on the rhetoric of objectivity, the subject of scientific learning would progressively attempt to generate knowledge outside him- or herself, to exempt his or her body from the agonies of self-experimentation. In 1790, the physician Samuel Hahnemann self-administered strong daily doses of quinine in order to observe its effects in fighting malaria. His body reacted by developing symptoms that resembled the remittent fever characteristic of malaria. The experiment would serve as the basis for the invention of the homeopathic movement, which, based on the law of similars, maintains that it is possible to treat illness using minute doses of a substance that, in much larger amounts, would provoke the same symptoms of that illness in a healthy body, in the manner of a therapeutic mirror. Peter Sloterdijk, inspired by Hahnemann, will call the process of controlled and intentional poisoning "voluntary auto-intoxication" and will sum it up as follows: "If you intend to be a doctor, you must try to become a laboratory animal."[14]

In order to transform conventional frameworks of the "cultural intelligibility"[15] of human bodies, it is necessary to evolve toward practices of voluntary autointoxication. From Novalis to Ritter, the romanticism from which Sloterdijk draws his inspiration for a counterproject to modernity will make autoexperimentation the central technique of the self in a dystopian society. Nevertheless, romantic autoexperimentation carries the risk of individualism and depolitization. On the other hand, two of the discourses around which the critique of modern European subjectivity will develop—those of Sigmund Freud and Walter Benjamin—will begin under the form of the invention of new techniques of the self and repertories of practices of voluntary intoxication. But the dominant discourse of disciplinary modernity will brush them aside; the process of institutionalization that both psychoanalysis and the Frankfurt School will experience will go hand in hand with the pathologizing of intoxication and the clinical industrialization of experimentation.

"It would be a good thing if a doctor were able to test many more drugs on himself," declared the young doctor

---

14. Peter Sloterdijk, *Neither Sun Nor Death*. With Hans-Jürgen Heinrichs, trans. Steven Corcoran (New York: Semiotext(e), 2011), 8.

15. I'm reclaiming Judith Butler's term here. See *Undoing Gender*, 35–46.

Mikhail Bulgakov in 1914, in "Morphine," a text in which the protagonist describes the effects of morphine on his own body.[16] Likewise, it seems urgent today, from the perspective of a trans-feminist project, to use our living bodies as biopolitical platforms to test the pharmacopornopolitical effects of synthetic sex hormones in order to create and demarcate new frameworks of cultural intelligibility for gender and sexual subjects. In an era in which pharmaceutical laboratories and corporations and state medico-legal institutions are controlling and regulating the use of gender and sex biocodes (the active molecules of progesterone, estrogen, and testosterone) as well as chemical prostheses, it seems anachronistic to speak of practices of political representation without going through performative and biotechnological experiments on sexual subjectivity and gender. We must reclaim the right to participate in the *construction* of biopolitical fictions. We have the right to demand collective and "common" ownership of the biocodes of gender, sex, and race. We must wrest them from private hands, from technocrats and from the pharmacoporn complex. Such a process of resistance and redistribution could be called *technosomatic communism.*

As a mode of the production of "common" knowledge and political transformation, the auto–guinea pig principle would be critical in the construction of the practices and discourses of trans-feminism and the coming liberation movements of gender, sexual, racial, and somatic-political

16. See Mikhail Bulgakov, "Morphine," in *A Country Doctor's Notebook* (New York: Melville House, 2013), 134.

minorities. To echo Donna J. Haraway's expression, it will consist of a positioned, responsible corporal political practice, so that anyone wishing to be a political subject will begin by being the lab rat in her or his own laboratory.

NARCOANALYSIS: THE PSYCHOTROPIC ORIGINS OF CRITICISM IN FREUD AND BENJAMIN

Freud was born at the heart of psychotropic Europe in 1856, just a year after Friedrich Gaedcke extracted an alkaloid he would call erythroxyline, a substance from which cocaine would then be isolated for the first time.[17] At the end of the nineteenth century, there was traffic in Europe in dozens of psychoactive substances, through colonial networks, and these were marketed and consumed without any precise regulations; they included opium, laudanum, hashish, marijuana, heroin, cocaine, and other well-known substances. Freud became aware of the existence of cocaine through an article in which the physician Theodore Aschenbrandt described the use of the first doses of pharmaceutical cocaine, produced by the German laboratory Merck as a treatment for fatigue in Bavarian soldiers. There can be no war without biochemical supplements to subjectivity that compel the body and consciousness beyond themselves, in the same way that there is no postwar situation without

17. I am indebted here to the work of Avital Ronell and to her use of "narcoanalysis" as a notion of literary criticism. Avital Ronell, *Crack Wars: Literature, Addiction, Mania* (Lincoln, NE: University of Nebraska Press, 1992), 47–64.

biochemical supplements that induce amnesia.[18] Aschenbrandt's 1883 article made a strong impression on Freud, who referred in a letter to his fiancée, Martha, at the beginning of April that year to a future "project" involving the consumption of cocaine.[19] "Martha, I have a project," he wrote. Certainly, he thought he had found El Dorado, would become rich, and would discover hitherto unknown medical uses (raising blood pressure, combating fatigue, inducing sexual excitement, and effecting local anesthesia), but he was also hoping to produce another form of knowledge.

For the young Freud, cocaine is an epistemological project as much as an economic one. Less than a year later, he orders a package of 99 percent–pure cocaine hydrochloride[20] from Merck laboratories and on April 20, 1884, inhales his first line, a week before his twenty-eight birthday. In 1885, he writes in "Über Coca:" "One has the general impression that the mood created by cocaine in such doses has been caused not so much by direct excitation as by the absence of depressing elements in the general state of feeling. One might perhaps be permitted to assume that the euphoria that occurs in the state of health is nothing other than the normal mood of a well-nourished cerebral cortex that is 'unaware' of its bodily organs."[21] However, Freud's project does not get off to a good start. The first idea that comes to

---

18. On the use of pharmacoporn techniques for contemporary war see Naomi Klein, *The Shock Doctrine: The Rise of Disaster Capitalism* (New York: Penguin, 2008), 26–49.

19. Sigmund Freud, *On Cocaine*, ed. David Carter (London: Hesperus Press, 2011), 3–6. Letter to Martha, April 21 and June 19, 1884.

20. This is a very different substance than the street cocaine being sold today, which sometimes can contain only 5 percent pure cocaine hydrochloride. See David Cohen, *Freud on Coke* (London: Cutting Edge Press, 2011), Kindle edition.

21. Freud, *On Cocaine*, 23.

his mind is to treat his friend Ernst von Fleischl-Marxow's morphine addiction with cocaine. The result of the undertaking: Ernst becomes "our first European cocaine addict"[22] and suffers from sharp pains after being injected subcutaneously with a cocaine-based preparation. It should also be mentioned that Freud's intentions regarding Fleischl-Marxow were certainly not the clearest: he would oscillate between an amorous passion for his friend and jealousy. In reality, Ernst could have been a better suitor for Martha, Freud's fiancée, but he could also potentially have served to offer an anus for the pansexual pleasure of Freud. It's necessary, then, to open up to experimentation, but not too much.

Two years later, Freud is still not convinced that regular injections of cocaine also produce addiction. In his "Remarks on the Craving for and Fear of Cocaine," he defends the point of view claiming that the prolonged use of cocaine does not lead to addiction, except for those subjects who take it to replace a previous addiction to morphine (since Fleischl-Marxow's case has become too notorious to be swept under the rug). What it actually leads to, he thinks, is something he'll call "aversion."[23] Freud is right, but, as always, too optimistic: to take cocaine is to hate cocaine, to fear the letdown that follows ingesting it . . . but it is also to continue to take it. Mikhail Bulgakov, who becomes hooked on morphine and cocaine, writes, "I, the unfortunate doctor, who became addicted to morphine in February of this year, warn anyone who may suffer the same fate not

22. Ronell, *Crack Wars*, 53.
23. Peter Gay, *Freud: A Life for Our Time* (London: W. W. Norton, 1998), 62.

to attempt to replace morphine with cocaine. Cocaine is the most foul and insidious poison."[24]

In the meantime, the pharmaceutical industry is reinforcing its status as the "jewel of the capitalist crown" in Europe and the United States.[25] It should be remembered that we were still in the antechamber of the pharmaceutical boom, which would increase full throttle thirty years later with the marketing of antibiotics and sulpha drugs. Dominated by a new technocapitalist imperative, the stirrings of the budding pharmaceutical industry would gradually demonstrate that there is no precise causal relationship between therapeutic certainty, liberty of production, and the consumption of bioactive substances.[26] During the last years of the nineteenth century, Merck laboratories produced hundreds of kilos of cocaine destined for medical or dietary uses. Between 1886 and 1901, cocaine was one of the ingredients for the first formula for Coca-Cola; and Pope Leon XIII was a regular consumer of it. While Merck was marketing cocaine for use as an anesthetic and MDMA (Ecstasy) to suppress appetite, Bayer was marketing heroin as a treatment for dependence on morphine.

Before turning to hypnosis or posthypnotic suggestion, Freud tries narcoanalysis. Avital Ronell writes, "The cocaine drama broke the ground for the study of hysterical neurosis."[27] Freud would conceive of therapy by hypnosis using the model of substance addiction, paying attention

---

24. Bulgakov, *A Country Doctor's Notebook*, 142.
25. Pignarre, 13.
26. On the advent of bacteriology and the commercialization of antibiotics, see Bruno Latour, *Pasteur: guerre et paix de microbes* (Paris: La Découverte, 2001).
27. Ronell, *Crack Wars*, 53.

to the *dependence* between the hypnotizer and the hypnotized in Charcot's practice. Morphine and the hypnotizer resemble each other in that both provoke an altered state of consciousness, a transformation of the mode under which the ego is present to the self, thereby permitting the emergence of other forms of perception, knowledge, and action. The psychoanalytic theory of transference itself seems to be derived from a model of the traffic and transport of a substance between the analyst and the analysand. For Freud, a reader of Krafft-Ebing's studies on psychopathology, masturbation, and the chemical production that it implies is the model for all addiction.[28] Alcohol, tobacco, morphine, and cocaine are masturbatory substitutes, exogenous practices of the production of surplus toxicity in the body. There's little difference between a substance being produced by injection and one produced by the body itself. There is no libido without toxicity. Sexuality, like the ingestion of psychotropic substances, is a search for the production of a state of neuronal intoxication.

Freud's penchant for the absorption of new technologies of the modification of subjectivity isn't limited to the trying and use of drugs. Not hesitating to transform his own body into a field of surgical experimentation, Freud brought his own testicles into play. Between 1923 and 1924, under the direction of his doctor, Hans Pichler, he undergoes two invasive operations, as well as more than thirty minor operations and a variety of more or less pain-

---

28. Freud to Fliess, in *The Complete Letters of Sigmund Freud to Wilhelm Fliess, 1887–1904,* trans. Jeffrey Moussaieff Masson, letter 79. See Peter Gay, *Freud*, 103.

ful fittings of oral prostheses to combat cancer of the jaw. Despite an unfavorable prognosis, Freud decides to undergo one additional operation: the "Steinach procedure," that is, the tying of the seminal tubes, or a vasectomy, and thus becomes our first European male-to-male transsexual.[29] As we have seen, Eugen Steinach was the most celebrated researcher in the field of hormones at that time. He had already researched the masculinization of female rats by implanting testicles, and by blocking seminal fluids, without, however, having yet isolated the molecule of testosterone with certainty. Although his experiments were no more than summary, they led him to conclude that there is a relationship between hormonal production, sexual vigor, and aging. Steinach's idea was more dependent on concepts of sexual hydraulics or the physics of vital fluids than it was on a molecular understanding of excitation: obstructing external sperm ducts would produce an increase in sexual power and a generalized rejuvenation. Freud underwent Steinach's operation on November 17, 1923. As he would explain in a letter to his friend Ferenczi: "I'm hoping to improve my sexuality, my physical condition in general and my ability for work."[30] After the surgery, Freud said that he felt better, but above all, he confessed to Otto Rank, the operation had aroused in him a desire for Dr. Pichler—Freud's surgeon and the maker of his jaw prosthesis, which Freud called "the monster."[31]

29. Later, Onassis, General de Gaulle, and even Pope Pius XII would also undergo Steinach's procedure.

30. Freud to Ferenczi, *The Correspondence of Sigmund Freud and Sándor Ferenczi*, vol. 3, 1920–1933, eds. Ernst Falzeder and Eva Brabant, trans. Peter T. Hoffer (Cambridge, MA: Belknap Press, 2000). See Gay, *Freud*, 426.

31. Gay, *Freud*, 426.

A philosophy that doesn't use the body as an active platform of technovital transformation is spinning in neutral. Ideas aren't enough. "With 42,000 dead, art is not enough."[32] Only art working together with biopolitical praxis can move. All philosophy is intended to be a form of autovivisection—when it isn't a form of dissection of the other. It is an exercise in self-cutting, an incision into subjectivity. When enthusiasts of vivisection escape from their own body and head for the body of others, the body of the collective, the body of the earth, and the body of the universe, philosophy becomes political. This political extension of philosophical vivisection can take the form of a thanatology of the species (as in the proliferation of technologies of war) or of universal and utopic autoimmune therapy (religious, democratic, or scientific); moreover, thanatological management and utopic therapy often communicate with each other, one leading to the other by unexpected pathways (e.g., through the American democratic industrial-military complex).

Freud was a *cloaca maxima*, a sewer mouth who absorbed all the substances and techniques of the self produced in his time. Inhaling everything that passed by, he would not spare any exposed cell, neither his nor others'. Therefore, it would be erroneous to say that Freud's psychoanalysis had uniquely, and as a matter of priority, been a treatment technique based on words. The distinctive feature of the Freudian sewer mouth was the ingesting of all the somato-semiotic techniques, incorporating all prostheses

32. "With 42,000 dead, art is not enough," was a slogan of ACT UP New York, a direct action advocacy group working to address the AIDS crisis.

of his era and transforming them into living bodies and cultural discourses. Through his own practices of injecting psychotropic substances, through the poisoning of his friend Fleischl-Marxow, Freud learned that it was possible to modify psychic cartography only through a certain toxicity. Chemical substances that can be assimilated by an organism function like *potentia*: they provoke a substantial modification of the body and consciousness—provided that subjectivity allows itself to be affected, that it makes itself dynamic in the Greek sense of the word *dynamis*, which is to say, it allows its potentiality and its capacity to pass from one state into another to emerge. The transference that is understood to be the cornerstone of psychoanalytic therapy depends on a model of substance transport, a traffic in images, memories, and emotions that will modify a network of somatic links. Similarly, alcohol, tobacco, hash, cocaine, or morphine, as well as estrogens and androgens, are neither synthetic tunnels for escaping from reality nor mere links from point A to point B. Rather, they are technologies of the subject, microtechnologies of the mind, chemical prostheses from which will issue new practices for defining frames of human intelligibility. Modern subjectivity is the management of self-intoxication in a chemically harmful environment. Smoking in the plastic-electric-nuclear metropolis can be seen simply as one way of vaccinating yourself against environmental poisoning by means of homeopathic inoculation. The battle for modern subjectivity is a struggle for immunological equilibrium. The ingestion of drugs or psychoanalysis is the experimental ground on which we learn how to live in a somatic and semiotic environment that is becoming ever more toxic.

Self-analysis, as practiced by Freud, is above all a practice of somato-semiotic experimentation. The theory of the interpretation of dreams and the talking cure must be understood as methods of intoxication by images and language, while keeping in mind their chemico-material nature. It was only after having admitted that resorting directly to the ingestion of chemical substances will have unexpected side effects (dependence, the need to increase the dose, cellular degeneration) that Freud went back to the talking cure, the interpretation of dreams, or accounts of hallucinations as ways of producing a degree of neuronal toxicity—using memory, imagination, and free association to induce a psychic impact that is comparable to the ingestion of poisonous chemicals in small quantities. Psychoanalysis is semiotic homeopathy. The unconscious is a virtual terrain of extreme chemical hypersensitivity, and the mind is a fog through which run electric pathways and pernicious molecular combinations that can be reached only at the risk of modifying an interior psychotropic equilibrium. Knowing yourself by yourself means poisoning yourself by yourself, risking self-mutation.

Paris. Barcelona. Seville. Barcelona. Paris. Barcelona. Paris. New York. New Jersey. Paris. New York. Paris. Berlin. Paris. Montparnasse. Montparnasse. Montparnasse. It's your city today and always will be. Montparnasse. My life goes on, like the illusion of movement. Vauvert. Montpellier. Vauvert. Nice. Vauvert. Paris. Barcelona. Paris. Barcelona. Paris. Barcelona. Paris. Madrid. Paris. Bourges. Paris. Bourges. Paris. London. Paris. Metropolitan addiction. London. Donostia. Burgos. Donostia. Paris. London. Paris. Bourges. Paris. Every city is a different narcotic terrain. Paris: V + T. Barcelona: C, cannabis, alcohol. New York: C + speed + Prozac. New Jersey: Ritalin + Prozac. Berlin: X. Hong-Kong: C, cannabis, cortisone. Madrid: C. Vauvert: *sex*.

Between 1927 and 1932, Walter Benjamin and several friends, including Ernst Block, Ernst Jöel, and Fritz Fränkel, engage in a series of chemical impregnations: they eat hashish, smoke opium (which they called *crock*), inject mescaline and morphine.[33] In every case, the substance must enter the body, penetrate the skin, the digestive tract, the blood, the cells. You must assail the mind by the synthetic route. A series of practices involving intentional infection. Benjamin, Block, and Fränkel wanted to find the key to universal therapy beyond the urge for individual intoxication. The political principle for such therapy is elementary: you cannot intend to hold forth about the real without first poisoning yourself with what you plan to administer to the other person next. This guinea pig principle stands today as a requirement for the possibility of any future micropolitical action.

In 1927 in Europe, the ingestion of hashish, opium, or mescaline was still a bizarre, marginal, and little announced experiment (as administering testosterone to cis-females is today). What's interesting about Benjamin's case isn't his consumption of hashish but his psychoaesthetic transcrip-

33. Max Milner, *L'Imaginaire des drogues: De Thomas de Quincey à Henri Michaux* (Paris: Gallimard, 2000).

tion of the experiment. As Henri Michaux would later do with mescaline,[34] Benjamin recorded his detailed impressions (in the strict sense of the term, they were mental inscriptions produced by the effects of these substances) in a series of letters and aphorisms that he described as the protocols of drug experiments carried out with the drugs.[35] Each of these protocols, which sometimes extended over time, was associated with a city (Marseille, Paris, Moscow, etc.), with a space that displays itself and is transformed under the effects of the substance. Modern metropolises are on drugs. The production, trafficking, and consumption of drugs mirror the circuits of colonial trade, the processes of sublimation, and the phantasmagorias characteristic of industrial pharmacopornographic cities.

Conceiving of this guinea pig principle in relation to the politics of gender and sex implies that it is impossible to advise you to try it or not, to fuck with a condom or not, to get surgery or not, that it is impossible to tell you which porn is supposed to excite you, whether lesbianism is a better sexuality than S&M, whether I should eat you out or the opposite, whether it's better to have it one way or another, whether it's better to take hormones or not. In the face of the conservatism and moral indoctrination that have dominated American feminist, gay, and lesbian politics and most nonprofit anti-AIDS organizations one must develop a micropolitics of gender, sex, and sexuality based on practices of intentional self-experimentation that are defined by their

34. Henri Michaux, *Miserable Miracle: On Mescaline*, trans. Louise Varese (New York: New York Review Books Classics, 2002).

35. Walter Benjamin, *On Hashish*, ed. Howard Eilan (Camrbidge, MA: Harvard University Press, 2006).

ability to resist and dismantle the somato-semiotic norm and to invent collectively new technologies of the production of subject.

THE DRAG KING PLAN OF ACTION

The first time I take part in a drag king workshop is in 1998 at the Lesbian, Gay, Bisexual, and Transgender Community Center on West Thirteenth Street in New York. I sign up for the workshop with a mixture of voracious curiosity and confusion, characteristic of someone who comes from post-Franco Spain. I also participate in some lesbian sadomasochism workshops for fist-fucking, public sex, and coming out via writing; some workshops for pre-op and non-op transsexuals and NOHOs (those who take no hormones) and their partners; and some workshops to promote the visibility of sexual minorities. During the years when I inhabited the city of the living dead, I turned, in my struggle against an endemic loneliness, to a system for that training and construction of identity techniques developed by queer and trans micropolitics that, I am now convinced, not only helped me overcome the depression common to metropolises but also ended up as elements of a discipline of the mind, replacing the *exercises* of Saint Ignatius de Loyola from my Catholic childhood. This technique of the self is what would next allow me to resist being disappointed in politics, to resist succumbing completely to disenchantment and to your death.

My first drag king workshop is an initiatory exercise, the first step in an open process of mutation. There are a dozen of us cis-females, assigned the female gender at birth; each of us gives her name and explains where she comes from and what her experience with gender and sexual norms has been. The organizer is a butch woman with short hair who is wearing leather pants, with the face of a young boy and a soft voice. She listens attentively to our stories, but without awarding them too much psychological weight. Although we are in the LGBT Community Center, not all of us identify as being lesbian, butch, or bisexual. There are also some cis-females who go out with transsexual men and a hetero actress who has come for theatrical training on how to construct a male role. Going around the group twice produces enough talk to verify the fact that dealing with cultural and political codes of femininity and masculinity is not exclusively a lesbian or transsexual matter. The group members speak about their first time, rape, abortion, incest, the difficulties of having to feel different from other girls, the shame experienced at being pointed at in school for being a tomboy, or having too large a chest, or not having enough of one, or having one too early or too late, about not being able to sit the way they want or where they want, about not being able to spit or shout or hit back when others hit. I talk about never having felt like a woman, about thinking at the age of seven that I'd travel from Spain to Sweden like Christine Jorgensen with my first savings and get a penis grafted on, then about the operation on my chin when I was eighteen, about the feeling of not recognizing my body or my face. Little by little, a denser and denser fabric of voices is created; it surrounds us and allows us to cover ourselves with shared words, creating a collective second skin. Under that protective membrane, through a political magnifying glass, we can see that femininity and masculinity are the gears of a larger system in which every single person participates structurally. Knowledge liberates. It produces a certain political joy that I have never experienced before.

This first part of the workshop could be defined as a collective induction into *gender suspicion*, in reference to the hermeneutics of Marx, Nietzsche, and Freud as described by Paul Ricoeur.[36] It encourages us to examine what we assume are stable foundations of our identity (sex, gender, and sexuality) and see them as the opaque effects of cultural and political constructions and, consequently, as potential objects for a process of intentional, critical, and insubordinate intervention. This shared gender suspicion provokes a subjective shift that Teresa de Lauretis and José Muñoz have called "disidentification."[37] The drag king workshop doesn't begin with dressing or making up our face to look like a man, but in becoming aware of the cultural orthopedics that construct everyday femininity, and by disidentifying from the normative nature of politically assigned gender.

Transformed by this knowledge, we put on men's clothing and learn how to fashion a *packing* with condoms filled

---

36. Paul Ricoeur, *De l'Interprétation: Essai sur Freud* (Paris: Editions de Seuil, 1965), and Paul Ricoeur and Olivier Mongin, *Le Conflit des interpétations: Essais d'herméneutique* (Paris: Le Seuil, 1969), 149–50.

37. On disidentification, see José Esteban Muñoz, *Disidentification: Queers of Color and the Performance of Politics* (Minneapolis: University of Minnesota Press, 1999).

with cotton and how to bind our chest. By flattening the chest and making the pelvis bigger, you can modify the axis of the body and the balance of proportion between the shoulders, arms, and legs. Thus, the body's center of gravity—culturally located in cis-females at the level of the breasts (the sexualizing site par excellence and focal point of the hetero-male gaze)—is displaced to the pelvis. The legs are slightly spread, thus changing the distance between the feet and providing a more stable support for walking. Once verticality has been reinforced, freedom of movement of the trunk and extension of the arms is increased.

Following the instructions of our drag king orchestrator, I clip off a lock of hair and cut it into smaller pieces, then rearrange it on a sheet of creased white paper so that the hairs are aligned in the fold. I create my first beard. At first, I don't know exactly what kind of beard I want or which kind suits me, the one that goes the best with my face or with the type of drag king that I am. It will be the same thing with testosterone later on; the transfer of the hair pertains to illicit trafficking, to the smuggling of a political signifier. Subject fiction in a flash: these hairs applied to the face of a cis-female offer a glimpse of the possibility of another life. It's a certainty that wearing a beard provides an accelerated image of what the administration of testosterone produces in a cis-female's body after four to six months. Such artifice is therefore not merely a masquerade, a disguise, pure exteriority, but a revelation of a pharmacopornographic possibility already existing in my genes, and it has the ability to take on a cultural and political signification. On my face I outline the shape into which the beard will need to fit: a

Mexican-style mustache that descends from the corners of the mouth to the edge of the chin. I think of Pancho Villa, of Walter Benjamin. I think of you. Suddenly I see it in the mirror out of the corner of my eye: Bob. No mystery to that; it's just me, but it's also a man. I'm not inventing it; he's not a stage character; he is emerging out of what I am, the way I've always seen myself. The difference between now and before is that from now on it's visible to others. I'm not hiding any longer behind the name that was given to me, or the weighty supposition that I am or ought to be a woman.

The important thing is not to be dressed as a man— anyone at all can do that in his or her private space—but to have had the *collective experience* of the arbitrary and constructed dimensions of our gender. During the first drag king workshop, we're not trying to produce a theatrical effect or a caricatured stereotype of gender, but to construct a commonplace, all-purpose form of masculinity. Surprisingly, from this perspective, a minimal transformation produces an effect of maximum realism. Obviously, it's possible to think about the varieties of kitsch or camp in a drag king performance, in which the goal is to bring out the constructed dimensions of masculinity with hyperbolic style, as would be the case in drag king incarnations of Elvis Presley, the over-the-hill skirt chaser, the vulgar macho guy, or the cliché of a plumber in porn. In any case, the drag king destiny of each participant is an insoluble enigma until the moment when the transformation is produced. The process evolves in the course of performative exercises in the workshop and often extends into daily life. What struck me about that first experience was the power of the workshop as a collective plan of action for the reprogramming of gender, its potential to function as a political laboratory, its denseness in its capacity as public space. I immediately knew that I wanted to do it with others, reproduce this plan of action, and that a single time wasn't enough for me. There is a ritual dimension, a psychopolitical magic in the drag king workshop and its performative process of becoming, something that I cannot shirk, that intrigued me from the beginning, and that led me with the passage of time to become the drag king MC.

This is how I was given access to a culture of resistance against the normalization of gender organized around an array of drag king micropolitics that generated platforms to create and distribute knowledge. Drag king culture made its appearance in New York and San Francisco in the mid-1980s, in the workshops of Diane Torr, Annie Sprinkle, and Jack Armstrom;[38] the performances of Moby Dick, Dred, Split Britches, and the Five Lesbian Brothers; and the photographic work of Del LaGrace Volcano.[39] This culture hasn't found its niche in universities or archives; it has spread through a network of bars, clubs, and organizations that today reaches from San Francisco to Istanbul.

Drag king practices create a space of visibility peculiar to fag, dyke, and trans culture by recycling and by parodic declension and deconstruction of models of masculinity coming from dominant popular culture. Man and woman, masculine and feminine, and also homosexual and hetero-

---

38. Sprinkle, *Post-Porn Modernist*, 131.
39. See Del LaGrace Volcano and Judith "Jack" Halberstam, *The Drag King Book* (London: Serpent's Tail, 1999).

sexual seem to be insufficient codes and identity locations for describing the contemporary production of the queer, trans, and crip body. Performative politics will become a field for experimentation, a place for the production of new subjectivities, and, as a result, a true alternative to traditional ways of doing politics that surpasses resignifying or resisting normalization.

2000. I spend six months at Princeton University and six months at the École des Hautes Études en Sciences Sociales in France. Drag king practices are nearly nonexistent in France, Spain, and Italy; I decide to start organizing workshops. Obviously, this takes me to the heart of the drag king mafia: Diane Torr and Del LaGrace will become my first mentors. When I do a workshop with Diane Torr in France or in Spain, I'm the one who takes care of the commissions and acts as translator, the kid who picks up the cigarette butts and shines the shoes; and Danny King becomes the "master." I'm there to learn from the boss and, according to the ethic of "drag king *oblige*," to make him feel that he is the boss. In my workshops, obviously, I'm the boss. And this power is not to be shared; if you share it with another person or several others, you've lost your cachet as a *king*. This is one of the first lessons about masculinity—everything depends on the way power is managed: making another person believe that he has the power, even if, in reality, the person has it only because you've conceded it to him. Or else making the other believe that power, as something natural and nontransferable, is yours, and that you and only you will be able to endow him with the status of masculinity, which he needs to belong to the dominant class. Foucault put it best when talking about sovereignty: power doesn't exist beyond the techniques involved in its theatricalization. Masculinity, an old biopolitical fiction constructed within the sovereign society before the eighteenth century, depends on an orchestration of power and body techniques, on a system in which power circulates through shared performative codes that are transmitted from body to body via semiotic signs and material rituals.

Diane Torr's technique of the deconstruction of femininity and apprenticeship in masculinity depends on a theatrical analytic method, on the breaking down of learned body gestures (a way of walking, speaking, sitting, getting up, looking, smoking, eating, smiling) into basic units (distance between the legs, opening of the eyes, movement of the eyebrows, speed of the arms, fullness of the smile, etc.) and examining them in their capacity as cultural signs for the construction of gender. In a second synthetic moment, different cultural codes are rearranged to construct a different gender fiction.[40] The goal of Diane's workshops is to experiment physically and theatrically with the ways in which masculinity is produced by an array of performative cultural codes learned and incorporated through what Judith Butler has called "regularized and constrained repetition of norms."[41]

---

40. See Diane Torr and Stephen Bottoms, *Sex, Drag, and Male Roles: Investigating Gender as Performance* (Ann Arbor: The University of Michigan Press, 2010).

41. Judith Butler, *Bodies that Matter*, 95.

In order to construct my own workshops, I have learned from Diane's performative analysis of action, combined with a psychopolitical method that is closer to posttraumatic reeducation of the body and to the training of political minorities for survival, starting with *gender suspicion* and the elaboration of a collective narrative. There is no anatomical truth independent of the cultural and political practices of constrained repetition that lead us toward being men or women. From this perspective, which I would call postqueer—because it has experienced Butler's performative theories but also AIDS, Dolly the sheep, and the intentional consumption of hormones—desire, sexuality, and erotic and political pleasure reside precisely in *having access* to these performative biocodes. I suppose it's a matter of my generation and the fact that I've had it up to here with the dominant feminist politics and their restrictions: prohibitions about using dildos, prohibitions about watching pornography, prohibitions about fucking with everything, prohibitions about wanting money and power, prohibitions about succeeding, prohibitions about amusing yourself at the expense of those close to you, prohibitions about destroying the house of the master with the tools of the master. For me, being a drag king is inhabiting the potential that it is my prerogative not to deny, without apologizing, and fulfilling my sexual and political desire to be the master, to incorporate those performative codes, to attain this type of specialization of power, to experiment with the city, the body, sex, public speech the way a cis-male would. Without excuses. Without naturalization.

Once the initial construction of a drag king impersonation is over, a performative practice guided by exercises of self-observation, recodification, and improvisation can begin. Becoming a drag king is a process that could be called a gender "chance operation," using the well-known technique developed by Merce Cunningham: finding a way between norm and improvisation, between repetition and invention. When the participants have succeeded in constructing a masculine fiction that is sufficiently convincing and commonplace, they can confront the "naturalistic" gender ecology in the outside world. One of the most intense and transformative workshop techniques is experienced when you explore the city as a drag king. Walking around, getting a coffee, going down to the subway, hailing a taxi, sitting on a bench, smoking a cigarette leaning against a school wall . . . A new cartography of the city takes shape; for the first time you can enjoy the pleasure of the public space of the male flaneur, nonexistent for a body culturally encoded as female until that moment.

Once the drag king virus has been triggered in each participant, the hermeneutics of gender suspicion extend beyond the workshop and spread to the rest of daily life, causing modifications within social interactions. Drag king knowledge isn't the awareness of being an imitator of masculinity surrounded by anonymous male and female bodies, businesspeople and mail carriers, mothers pushing baby carriages, young guys mainlining next to garbage cans; rather, it resides in the fact of perceiving others—all others, including oneself—for the first time, as more or less realistic biofictions of performative gender and sexual norms that are decodable as male or female. In strolling around among these anonymous bodies, all these masculinities and femininities (including one's own) appear like caricatures that, thanks to a tacit convention, are seemingly unconscious of being so. There is no ontological difference between these embodiments of gender and mine. All of them are performative products to which different frames of cultural intelligibility confer various degrees of legitimacy. The difference is found in the degree of self-reflection, of consciousness, of compulsion, of the performative dimension of these roles. Becoming a drag king is seeing through the matrix of gender, noticing that men and women are performative and somatic fictions, convinced of their natural reality. This vision of the world makes you laugh, blows a current of buoyant air under your feet, makes you float—political ecstasy.

With time, from one workshop to another, my other drag king egos appear: Bruno (the name I gave myself when I was a kid to get into a boxing club with my father), Miguel, Alex. But it is Pedro Lemebel who gives me my drag king name, while I am organizing a workshop in Santiago, Chile, in 2004. Pedro Lemebel had organized a party at his house to welcome me. He received me wearing a long black dress and a strand of blue plastic beads around his neck; he was bare-chested on a winter day with a red turban on his head, à la Simone de Beauvoir. "I burned my head trying to rid it of boldness," he said me. I had never seen anyone like him. He kissed me and told me, "*Ya llegó la niña revolucionaria.*"[42] I loved him from the first moment I saw him. "Lemebel

42. Translates to "Here comes the revolutionary kid."

doesn't need to write poetry to be the best living poet of my generation,"[43] said Roberto Bolaño. He is not only the best poet but also the most radical political queer performer of his generation—you have to be a brave poet to face Pinochet's police naked and riding a white horse.[44] Pedro called me Beto: his will be done. As if the phantom of Bolaño was speaking through him. These are my names: Roberto, Bob, Beto, Beatrizo, algebraic variations of a phonetic constellation. We organize the workshop at MUMS (Movimiento Chileno Unido de Minorias Sexuales) with the Queer MC, the first French drag king hip-hop group, who have come with us to Chile.

Chile has barely come out of its period of military dictatorship and has been undergoing the most radical neoliberal transformation, which was imposed by the Chicago School during the mid-1970s and 1980s and which has brought hyperinflation, free trade, the privatization of social services, and growing social inequalities. The country has gone from being a playground for Spanish colonialism and caciquism into becoming a lab for Milton Friedman's fundamentalist capitalism. The idea of a conference, a seminar, or a workshop in that context has a special intensity; but I am white and Spanish, have earned a PhD at Princeton University, and talk about dildos, testosterone, and trans and queer politics. During my first talk at the University of Chile, a group of Chilean feminists come to my conference to accuse me of being a "representative of the

43. Roberto Bolaño, *Entre paréntesis* (Barcelona: Anagrama, 2004), 65.
44. I refer here to the performances of the group "Yegüas del Apocalipsis," formed by Pedro Lemebel and Francisco Casas between 1987 and 1995.

hetero-patriarchal and colonial order." But the accusation slowly transforms into debate and the debate into dialogue. Finally, thirty-five women appear at the workshop on the winter day of August 27. They are militant mothers from the feminist Left of the Allende period, and with them are their grandmothers, daughters, and nieces, some sixteen-year-olds, some elderly lesbian couples, some working-poor women who will never leave the country and some girls from the bourgeoisie who will one day go to study in an American university. The Andean cold is freezing on our backs as we have our discussions; we dress and work on the unheated premises of MUMS, which is in a Santiago neighborhood behind which flow the polluted waters of the Mapocho. Thirty voices come forth, forging links to the point of creating a narrative of survival. The story that emerges from all these words isn't about male domination or female submission but about resistance to domination, about refusal to surrender. Making each of them a drag king is a rite of investiture that the Queer MC and I carry out with more devotion and respect than ever. We prepare beards and mustaches, slick back hair, bind chests, and size up sports jackets. In most cases, there's not much to do; these women *are* kings. They've never bowed their heads to anyone, they haven't been afraid of torture or death, and they could face any little cock of the walk. There isn't much to teach them, and I'm the one who learns from them, about living with pride and believing in gender revolution in a country where all revolutions have been violently crushed. That night, after eight hours of workshop, we go out in a group of forty drag kings, as if we were in a postqueer remake of *Mad Max*, and walk through the streets of Santiago toward one of the rare gay bars in the capital. Pedro Lamebel is waiting for us there with his fag and trans pals. The Queer MC sing a Spanish version of one of their hip-hop pieces, "A New Gender Has Come." A small pack of drag kings and their friends invade the stage while the fags cruise the unattached drag kings. In the disco, we're breathing in so much coke that there is no need to snort it. Around four in the morning, the police arrive, we start keeping a low profile, and no one notices that there are cis-females in king drag in the room. The party lasts until the wee hours. I wake up in a bar with whores, fags, and trannies, and I'm in Pedro's arms.

In the face of the upsurge of corporate production and distribution of biocodes of heterosexual masculinity and femininity and gender violence, it is urgent to work to proliferate drag king workshops as spaces for the creation of urban brigades that, in their turn, will set off more workshops, decode the dominant gender grammar, invent new languages. Creating *global* counterhegemonic networks for reprogramming gender. No genuine drag king knowledge can be obtained from merely reading about a model for a workshop. Following the principle of the auto–guinea pig, it is necessary to take the risk of giving corporal and collective practices their chance. Such an experimental form of the production of knowledge and subjectivity renders obsolete the figure of the "professional" drag king guru going from place to place to initiate the process of the denaturalization of gender. The best organizer of a drag king workshop is the person who has participated in another drag king workshop and has decided to continue the experiment with a group of people within hir own local context.

After having experienced a variety of psychoanalytical or psychodynamic therapies, I have come to understand the drag king workshop as a new practice of political therapy, part of an array of techniques of criticism, reprogramming, and psychopolitical care that we might call *queeranalysis*. The Brazilian Guattarian psychoanalyst and art critic Suely Rolnik has taught us to consider modern clinical practices—those of psychiatry starting in the eighteenth century and psychoanalysis at the beginning of the twentieth—as techniques that arose precisely for the management of "the collateral effects of this mode of historically dated subjectification that is characterized by the reduction of subjectivity to its psychological dimension and the proscription of its aesthetic dimension."[45] Similarly, we could say that the problem of contemporary clinical opinions has to do with the reduction of gender to individual psychology. Psychoanalytical or psychodynamic therapy often attempts to reduce the processes of the construction of political subjectivity to a psychological account. Psychology and psychoanalytical institutions use a colonial and Western epistemology, based on strongly racialized and heterocentric accounts of the Oedipal complex, castration, or penis envy as syndromes and pathologies, in order to diagnose and treat the frustrations generated by resistance or submission to the political imposition of gender, sex, and race

45. Suely Rolnik, "El arte cura?," *Quaderns Portàtils* 2 (Barcelona: MACBA, 2006).

norms. Moreover, during the Cold War psychology became the discursive support of the pharmacopornographic industry, providing scientific legitimacy to the normative production and distribution of chemical prostheses. It is imperative to understand our sexual identities as the traumatic effects of a violent biopolitical system of sex, gender, sexuality, and race and to work out new myths that will allow us to interpret psychopolitical harm and give us the courage needed for collective transformation.[46] Critical accounts of the hormonal and surgical treatment of "intersexual" babies should be substituted today for the myth of the Oedipal complex, just as a drag king workshop, in its capacity as a corporal, collective, and political laboratory of production of genders (an ensemble of techniques that we could describe—in opposition to the clinic—as depsychologizing gender) would be a more effective place than the psychoanalyst's couch to work on identity. Queeranalysis isn't against psychoanalysis, but it goes beyond it by politicizing it, triggering an anticolonial and trans-feminist critical reading of its analytical narratives and therapeutic techniques. Queeranalysis develops the insights of Franz Fanon and Francois Tosquelles, of Jean Oury and Félix Guattari at La Borde. Queeranalysis is a practice that, instead of conceptualizing gender and sexual dissent through a lens of psychological pathology and identity dysphoria, would conceive of normalization and its effects as biopolitical

46. Judith Butler, *Antigone's Claim: Kinship Between Life and Death* (New York: Columbia University Press, 2002). Butler, for example, in reinterpreting the discourses of psychoanalysis and legislation, has suggested the irreverent and suicidal Antigone—a child of incest who is more faithful to her brother than to the State—as a political figure that epitomizes the contradictions of heterosexual filiation.

apparatuses and forms of political violence. Queeranalysis does not reject all techniques of the production of subjectivity derived from Freudian psychology or from neurolinguistic programming—the analysis of dreams, the talking cure, hypnosis, and so on—but it attacks their model of "subject" as well as the rhetoric of gender, sex, race, disability, and class at work in these psychotherapeutic practices and their complicity in the pharmacopornographic regime. Finally, queeranalysis calls for a collective reappropriation of "common" biocodes (discursive, endocrinological, chemical, visual, etc.) for the production of subjectivity.[47]

GENDER BIOTERRORISM

The Techno-Lamb Model

In October 1958, a young woman of nineteen comes to the department of psychiatry at the University of California at Los Angeles. She's seen by a team composed of Robert Stoller, Harold Garfinkel, and Alexander Rosen, a psychiatrist, sociologist, and psychologist, respectively, who are researching sexual identity. The medical register describes her as "a white female working as a secretary in an insurance company."[48] The report adds, "Her appearance is convincing. She is tall, slender and shaped like a woman. . . . Her body displays male genital organs and a normally

---

47. Teresa de Lauretis, *The Practice of Love: Lesbian Sexuality and Perverse Desire* (Bloomington, IN: Indiana University Press, 1994). In this text, see the critical reinterpretation of psychoanalysis for further study.

48. Records of race (white) and class (worker) function as conditions of normality that authorize any other diagnosis whatsoever in terms of gender.

developed penis as well as secondary sexual characteristics of the female sex: breasts of average size, no facial or body hair." [49] If she seems to satisfy the taxonomic expectations of the group of sex technocrats who are examining her, it's perhaps because—as they put it—she presents no sign of "sexual deviance, transvestism or homosexuality. Nothing could differentiate her from a young woman of her age. She has a high voice, doesn't wear clothes that are exhibition-istic or in bad taste like those characteristic of transves-tites or men with sexual identity problems." In the medical history, Garfinkel assigns her the fictional name Agnes, unaware that he is naming the seeds of a rebellion to come, a future *politics of sacrificial lambs* (from the Latin *agnus*) that will infiltrate the pharmacopornographic order.

After more than thirty hours of interviews, the entire medical team, armed with a detailed endocrinological and hormonal analysis, unhesitatingly establishes the same diagnosis. They affirm that they are dealing with a case of "genuine hermaphroditism": Agnes is suffering from "tes-ticular feminization syndrome," a rare type of intersexu-ality in which the testicles produce elevated quantities of estrogen.[50] Following the protocol for the treatment of intersexuality, which provides for the reassignment of gen-der by means of hormonal and surgical techniques, she is

49. Harold Garfinkel, *Studies in Ethnomethodology* (Englewood Cliffs, NJ: Prentice-Hall, 1967), 123.

50. Robert Stoller, cited in Garfinkel, 120–22. See also the discussion of the case of Agnes in Hausman, *Changing Sex*; Norman Denzin, "Harold and Agnes: A Feminist Narrative Undoing," *Sociological Theory* 8, no. 2 (1990): 196–216; Norman Denzin, "Back to Harold and Agnes," *Sociological Theory* 9, no. 2 (1991): 280–85 ; Mary F. Rogers, "They All Were Passing: Agnes, Garfinkel, and Company," *Gender and Society* 6, no. 2 (June 1992), 169–91; D.H. Zimmerman, "They Were All Doing Gender But They Weren't All Passing: Comment on Rogers," *Gender and Society* 6, no. 2 (1992): 192–98.

granted the right to therapeutic vaginoplasty, which is the surgical construction of a vagina using her own genital tissues in order to restore the coherence between her "hormonal identity" and her "physical identity."[51] Agnes will be operated on in 1959, the erectile tissue of her penis and her testicles amputated; a vagina will be fabricated for her using the skin of her scrotum. Somewhat later, Agnes will have the right to legally change her name, and her female first name will appear on her identification papers.

From the viewpoint of traditional medical discourse, Agnes's story seems to speak of the management of a problem of intersexuality to which medicine understood how to respond successfully. On the other hand, if we apply what Sedgwick might call "a paranoid hermeneutics "[52] to a reading of this story, we will be inclined to consider the hypothesis that the mechanisms of control of the body and sexuality characteristic of disciplinary medico-legal institutions of the pharmacopornographic regime have displayed all their effectiveness in acting on Agnes's body. Let us compare Agnes's clinical history with the tragic story of Herculine Barbin (the autobiography of a so-called hermaphrodite at the end of the nineteenth century who committed suicide when faced with the obligation to choose a single sex); we could conclude from this comparison that, in Agnes's case, the apparatus of repression, having been transformed into a program of the public health system, was endowed with a new endocrinological and surgical sophistication to accom-

51. See John Money and Anke Ehrhardt, *Man & Woman, Boy & Girl: Gender Identity from Conception to Maturity* (Baltimore: John Hopkins University Press, 1972).
52. Eve Kosofsky Sedgwick, *Touching Feeling: Affect, Pedagogy, Performativity* (Durham, NC: Duke University Press, 2003), 123–51.

plish in virtuoso style something that Herculine Barbin's epoch was only capable of dreaming about; and this was to establish a linear axiomatic relationship between sex, gender, and sexuality, turning the body into a legible and referential inscription about the truth of sex.[53]

The memoirs of Herculine Barbin (which were published in the late 1970s and became a best seller in France) will function as a foundational fiction for Foucault in order to construct his own history and theory of sexuality. If Herculine was pushed toward death (or rather, toward suicide), it was, for Foucault, because she/he was exactly located at the breaking point between two epistemes of sexuality. Herculine exists in a rift between two frameworks of the representation of sex, as if her/his body had fallen into the crack separating two divergent fictions of the self. Herculine isn't a man imprisoned in the body of a women, or vice versa, but actually a body caught between conflicting discourses about sexuality. According to Foucault, whereas hermaphrodites before the end of the nineteenth century lived in a world without sexual identities where the ambiguity of organs allowed for a plurality of social identifications (which was the case for Marie Madeleine Lefort, who lived during the nineteenth century and whom we can conceive of as a woman with a beard and penis as much as a man with breasts), the new modern episteme of sexuality, forced Herculine Barbin to choose a single sexual identity and, as a consequence, to reestablish a coherence between

53. Herculine Barbin, *Being the Recently Discovered Memoirs of a Nineteenth-Century French Hermaphrodite*, trans. Richard McDougal. With an introduction by Michel Foucault (New York: Pantheon Books, 1980).

the organs, the social expression of sex (male or female— the terms of gender don't exist yet), and sexual identity (heterosexual or perverted).[54] Ultimately, in this causal chain of the production of sex, Herculine Barbin becomes the source of a series of insurmountable discontinuities that will transform her/his body into a medical spectacle and her/his subjectivity into a moral monstrosity.

Remaining faithful to Foucault's model of analysis, it would seem logical to be inclined to extol Herculine Barbin's resistance to integration and to be critical about the ease with which Agnes seems to have been absorbed by means of 1950s biopolitical apparatuses.

Nevertheless, such a Foucault-inspired reading of the case of Agnes—in which subject formation is an effect of a normalizing apparatus—is complicated. Seven years after her operation and change of legal identity, Agnes produced a new account of her process of physical transformation in which she defied and ridiculed the contemporary medico-legal and scientific techniques of psychiatric and endocrinological diagnosis to which transsexuals have been forced to submit. This second account is a relatively humble but very effective example of the bioterrorism of gender, and it shows how a sacrificial techno-lamb can devour a pack of pharmacopornographic wolves. Agnes was no a victim of the medico-legal system, but rather a fine cartographer who managed to map out the new pharmacopornographic power relationships emerging during the Cold War.

---

54. For a discussion of the historical construction of the bodies of hermaphrodites, see Alice D. Dreger, *Hermaphrodites and the Medical Invention of Sex* (Cambridge, MA: Harvard University Press, 1998).

A few years after her vaginoplasty, Agnes goes back to a doctor for a gynecological problem and introduces herself as a young boy of anatomically male sex who at the start of adolescence began secretly taking estrogen-based Stilbestrol, which had been prescribed to treat her mother following her hysterectomy. In this new version of the story, it all began as a game; when her elder sister began to take the pill, Agnes, who was still a child at the time, decided to do the same thing and took her mother's hormones. Agnes had always wanted to be a girl, and thanks to the estrogen, her breasts began to grow, while certain undesirable signs of puberty (such as facial fuzz) grew milder. The boy began by stealing one or two pills from his mother, now and then. Then it became whole boxes of them.

Agnes's second account presents some questions about Foucault's theory of power and subjectification, but also, by extension, puts into question certain readings of Judith Butler's analysis of performative identity to which her theory is often reduced. In the first place, Foucault describes a power regime in which a diffuse, tentacular array of disciplines of biopolitical normalization determines forms of subjectivity. However, in accordance with Maurizio Lazzarato, I think it is useful to offset this notion of biopower with the Spinozan idea of *potentia*; in analyzing Agnes's account, we will see that, far from being docile, abnormal bodies today have become imbued with political power and, consequently, present possibilities for creating forms of dissident subjectification.

From a Butlerian perspective, Agnes's case can be understood as an example of performative resignification and reappropriation. What Agnes learned is that gender identity, whether it's cis-gender, intersexual, or transsexual, is nothing other than *script*, narration, performative fiction, rhetoric in which the body acts simultaneously as scenario and as principle character.[55] Agnes strategically omits certain details in her account to the psychiatrists. For example, she avoids references to her relationships with women, which could suggest the possibility of a lesbian orientation after the sex change. On the other hand, her story emphasizes the tropes that belong to the script of an intersexual diagnosis: her desire to wear skirts, her sensitivity, her love of nature.

Agnes effectively uses a process of reappropriation of the performative techniques of the production of sexual identity, until then used to construct the gay, lesbian, intersex, transsexual, or transgender body as pathological. In this sense, we could categorize as *queer* performativity such trafficking in fictions by means of which certain terms for gender are severed from the authority of medical discourse (even at the very moment of its intervention) and used by a new subject of knowledge presently claiming for itself the status of "expert."

We can understand Agnes's case only through an analysis of the technological processes of inscription whereby her "imitation" of both femininity and intersexuality becomes able to pass for natural. This involves not only drawing attention to the constructed quality of gender but, more important, also claiming the potential to intervene in

55. See Judith Butler's analysis of a case of intersexuality in "Doing Justice to Someone: Sex Reassignment and Allegories of Transsexuality," in *Undoing Gender*, 57–74.

this construction to the point of creating forms of somatic representation that are *alive*.

Agnes defies the logic of impersonation according to which a transsexual woman is a cis-male who is imitating femininity. She seems to have undermined the relationships of femininity to drag queen, of original to copy, of natural to artificial, of serious to irreverent, of content to form, of discretion to flamboyance, of structure to decoration. In such a case, Agnes is already no longer imitating, or claiming to make herself pass for, a woman by means of a performance that is to some extent stylized. By ingesting hormones and the production of a specific narration, Agnes is becoming an intersexed body "physiologically" in order to gain access to sex reassignment therapies without going through the psychiatric and legal protocols for transsexuality.

Through her intentional enlistment of intersexuality, Agnes is effectively critiquing not masculinity or femininity in themselves, but (by a tongue-in-cheek understanding of the complexity of the technologies of gender) the very pharmacopornographic apparatus of the production of the "truth of sex" itself. If the camp aesthetics emanating from the culture of transvestism and transsexuality has been defined by Susan Sontag[56] as a critique of the original through the process of producing a copy or counterfeit version, then we can say that, in a certain way, Agnes is pushing the very notion of camp to its limits, to the point of rendering it obsolete. In camp practices, aesthetics supplants

56. Susan Sontag, "Notes on 'Camp'," in *Against Interpretation and Other Essays*, rev. ed. (New York: Picador, 2001), 275–92.

ethics and theater supplants life. In Agnes's case, somatic technology supplants aesthetics, and life supplants theater.

Agnes is practicing biodrag: it is her body that achieves the process of imitation and thus puts an end to the traditional metaphysical oppositions that seem to produce so many problems in performative theory (facade vs. interior, performance vs. anatomy, mind vs. body, psychological gender vs. chromosomes, social identity vs. genetics). Agnes is a biocultural artifact composed of organic substances, a fiction whose very contours are somatic.

If we accept the fact that Agnes is a living pharmacopornographic biopolitical fiction, we must also say that her mother (hooked on the seemingly slightly chaotic ingestion of a hormonal technology of substitution) and her sister (who has been taking the birth control pill since adolescence) are as well. In taking their innocuous pills, both of them are allowing themselves to live biotechnological fictions of identity. The difference is that Agnes seems to reappropriate the techniques of subjectification and *genderization* of her body, whereas her sister and mother unconsciously ingest each of these technologies as if they were supplements to their "natural" femininity.

Agnes's body is neither the passive material acted on by a series of biopolitical mechanisms of normalization nor the performative effect of an array of discourses on identity. Her body, truly a sexual colossus of self-design, is the result of the reappropriation, use, and collective arrangement of certain technologies of gender with the goal of producing new forms of subjectification.

Agnes allows imagining a cheap, auto-experimental form of do-it-yourself bioterrorism of gender that we—in reference to the politics of free software management[57]— could call *copyleft gender politics*, a cellular micropolitics that looks beyond the politics of representation for leakage points in the state's control of fluxes (hormones, sperm, blood, organs, etc.), codes and institutions (images, names, protocols, legal inscriptions, architecture, social services, etc.), and the privatization and marketing of these technologies of production and modification of gender and sex by pharmacopornographic corporations. The axiom of the lamb: the principle of the auto–guinea pig. The objective of the lamb: to struggle against the privatization of the body and the reduction of the *potentia gaudendi* to a workforce, a brand, a copyright, and a sealed biocode. The mode of functioning of the lamb: the pirating of hormones, texts, body techniques, knowledge practices, codes, pleasures, fluxes, chemical substances, cartographies . . . The transformation of the body of the multitude into an open living political archive: the common *somathèque*.[58]

Traps of Pharmacopornographic Neoliberalism

Contemporary biodrag activism is confronted, fifty years after Agnes, with a new set of violent neoliberal economic and politic strategies, including the privatization of the

57. See the texts of Lawrence Lessig, the founder of the creative commons movement; Lessig, "Code and the Commons," (keynote address, given at a conference on *Media Convergence*, Fordham Law School, New York, NY, February 9, 1999).
58. My notion of *somathèque* in French refers to somatic technologies and to the body as techno-living cultural archive, as in the word *bibliothèque*, which means library.

health system, government deregulation, deep cuts in social spending, and the militarization of social life. In the present context, it's possible to imagine (at least) two tracks of development for the pharmacopornographic economy in the face of which different modes of activism could be articulated.

The first is the preservation of theological-humanist political states that regulate the action of the neoliberal (meaning free trade, either democratic or totalitarian in the context of globalization) pharmacopornographic economy. Current pharmacopornographic corporations would function as free market tentacles inside contemporary nation-states (which would continue to see themselves as sovereign and patriarchal) and would negotiate with them to determine the directives for the production, use, and consumption of chemical prostheses and semiotic gender and sex codes.

The second transformation is one into an abstract deterritorialized nation-state of the pharmacopornographic industry. We could also be witnessing a process of privatization of contemporary nation-states, which would be progressively absorbed by the pharmacopornographic industry. This would be the strategy employed by the pharmacopornographic companies to escape pre-1970s regulations imposed by states (to avoid the gradual transformation of pharmaceutical patents into generics, the more or less severe regulation of the production and distribution of pornographic audiovisual material, and attempts to abolish prostitution), as these companies engage in the political direction of new national entities (via the FDA; the

International Monetary Fund; the European Union; and the governments of the United States, China, or India) and purchase state institutions (for example, the Department of Health or Department of Justice or the prison-industrial complex) and put them to work to their benefit, refilling such archaic institutions with new content whose only objective would be increasing consumption and pharmacopornographic profits.

In fact, the pharmacopornographic industries are already in competition with the domestic affairs of the old nation-states . . . The war to come isn't a war between states (Israel vs. Palestine or the United States vs. the oil-producing countries) but more probably a war of pharmacopornographic multinationals against the multitude of vulnerable bodies, a war of the pharmaceutical multinationals that hold the copyright for active principles against the traditional gatherers of plants and their specific forms of knowledge, a war of the military-prison-industrial complexes against the racialized and pauperized populations, a war of mafia states against the users of "illegal" drugs, a war of the multinational conglomerates that coordinate the management of medical and legal institutions and free market consumption against bodies deprived of nationality, a war of the systems of control that construct docile sexual subjects to achieve the total and limitless exploitation of their *potentia gaudendi*.

The history of the transformations of production, distribution, and consumption of heroin offers several leads about the probable evolution of the legal and political management of sex hormones. Although their common origins don't seem obvious, heroin and aspirin were synthesized in the same year, 1897, and in the same laboratory, by Hoffman and Eichengrun, by means of the same process. It involved the simple acetylation of morphine (in the case of heroin) and salicylic acid (in the case of aspirin). Heroin and aspirin were legally marketed by Bayer the following year for the treatment of various pulmonary affections, because of their analgesic properties. Although restrictions on the production and distribution of heroin went into force in the 1920s, it was still possible to find heroin-based pills in an English pharmacological catalog in 1949.[59] After fifty years of the repression and criminalization of the marketing of heroin, which resulted in the deterioration of fields, which weren't being tilled, the adulteration of the substance, and the corruption of its trafficking networks, medical specialists today are developing a gradual reintegration of heroin into the legal pharmaceutical market. For example, Macfarlan Smith Limited in Edinburgh is making yearly advances in the experimental and therapeutic use of this substance.[60]

The changes in the legal status of a substance and the description of a consumer as criminal or mentally ill (addicted in the case of heroin, and gender dysphoric in the case of sex hormones) facilitate the establishment of a political relationship between illegal drugs and biocodes of the production of gender. Sex hormones, whose consumption is strongly regulated by the state, are drugs whose use is, if not illegal, at least politically controlled; and their use, considering their potential for transforming gender and

59. Carnwath and Smith, *Heroin Century*, 31.
60. Ibid., 30–31.

sex, is subject to specific restrictions that espouse administrative criteria and channels of distribution comparable to those of narcotic substances.

How to react in the face of states' resistance to legalizing the sale of pharmaceutical heroin or removing the consumption of sex hormones from psychiatric protocols? If we consider the close relationships maintained by the neoliberal nation-states, the pharmaceutical corporations, and the networks of drug trafficking, it appears urgent that those dismissed as junkies (the users of illegal drugs) and those diagnosed with gender dysphoria (the potential users of sex hormones) must organize into associations of copyleft drug consumers and force the state-industry-pharmaceutical-drug-trafficking networks to facilitate free access without restrictions to these biocodes of the production of subjectivity. Just as the users of Agreal prosecuted Sanofi-Aventis laboratories for the serious side effects[61] of this medication (originally intended to disguise the symptoms of menopause by blocking the action of the dopamine neurotransmitters), the users of heroin could prosecute the state in instances of withdrawal or overdose for that state's having prevented the production, distribution, and consumption of that substance for users in a trustworthy and legal manner. This political pressure would lead gradually to the production and distribution of heroin (or cocaine, MDA, etc.) as generics that could be first bought freely on the pharmaceutical market and, in the long run, be produced and managed collectively as *chemical prostheses*

61. Some side effects include Parkinsonian syndromes, symptoms of anxiety, and depression.

commons. This would ultimately entail a process of a multitude-in-the-making, not only of a lobby of consumers of gender and sex biocodes but also a network of trans-junkie experts, a monster-multitude-in-the-making.

Gender and Sex Hackers

The cis-males and cis-females (indiscriminately heterosexual or homosexual), as well as transsexuals, who have access to surgical, endocrinological, or legal techniques of the production of identity, are not simple economic classes in the Marxist sense of the term, but genuine "pharmacopornographic factories"—existing simultaneously as raw materials, producers (but rarely proprietors) of biocodes of gender, and pharmacopornographic consumers.

Porn actors; whores; the transgender; genderqueers; and producers, traffickers, and consumers of illegal drugs inhabit different cultures, but all are used as living pharmacoporn laboratories. All of them sell, buy, or get access to their biocodes as pharmacopornographic property. The sudden emergence of new gender statuses is creating a novel type of conflict between owners and managers of the patents of the microtechnologies of subjectification (sex hormones, psychotropic molecules, audiovisual codes, etc.) and the producers and traffickers of these techno-biocodes. The pharmacopornographic entrepreneurs, who are among the contemporary leaders of global capitalism, are trying to restrict and privatize the biocodes of gender and convert them into rare and naturalized objects by means of legal and market techniques.

Computer hackers use the web and copyleft programs as

tools of free and horizontal distribution of information and claim that they should be in reach of everyone. The pharmacopornographic *gendercopyleft* movement has a technoliving platform that is a lot easier to gain access to than the Internet: the body, the *somathèque*. Not the naked body, or the body as unchanging nature, but the technoliving body as a biopolitical archive and cultural prosthesis. Your memory, your desire, your sensibility, your skin, your cock, your dildo, your blood, your sperm, your vulva, your ova . . . are the tools of a potential gendercopyleft revolution.

The various producers of sexual biocodes are very different from one another. Some get off on economic and social privileges, such as the models through whose bodies the dominant codes of male and female beauty are produced. Others, such as porn actors or sex workers, suffer from the lack of regulations for the open market of their biocodes. But all of them depend on the pharmacopornographic industry and its local alliances with the police forces of the nation-states. One day, they will all become hackers.

Agnes, mother of all the techno-lambs: Del LaGrace Volcano, Kate Bornstein, Jacob Hale, Dean Spade, Mauro Cabral, Susan Stryker, Sandy Stone, King Erik, Moises Martínez—all are master hackers of gender, genuine traffickers of semiotico-technological flux, producers and *tinkers* of copyleft biocodes.

Gender copyleft strategies must be minor but decisive: the survival of life on the planet is at stake. For this movement, there will be no single name that can be transformed into a brand. It will be our responsibility to shift the code to open the political practice to multiple possibilities. We could call this movement, which has already begun, Postporn, Free Fuckware, BodyPunk, OpenGender, FuckYourFather, PentratedState, TotalDrugs, PornTerror, AnalInflation, UnitedUniversalTechnoPriapism . . .

This book, a legacy of Agnes's self-experimentation politics, is a protocol for self-tests carried out with testosterone in gel form, exercises of controlled poisoning on my own body. I am infecting myself with a chemical signifier culturally branded as masculine. Vaccinating yourself with testosterone can be a technique of resistance for bodies that have been assigned the status of cis-females. To acquire a certain political immunity of gender, to get roaring drunk on masculinity, to know that it is possible to look like the hegemonic gender.

Little by little, the administration of testosterone has ceased to be a simple political test and has molted into a discipline, an asceticism, a way of restoring my spirit by means of the down growing on my arms, an addiction, a form of gratification, an escape, a prison, a paradise.

Hormones are chemical prostheses. Political drugs. In this case, the substance not only modifies the filter through which we decode and recodify the world; it also radically modifies the body and, as a result, the mode under which we are decoded by others. Six months of testosterone, and any cis-female at all, not a should-have-been-boy or a lesbian, but any girl, any neighborhood kid, a Jennifer Lopez or a Rihanna, can become a member of the male species who cannot be told apart from any other member of the hegemonic class.

I refuse the medico-political dose, its regime, its regularity, its direction. I demand a virtuosity of gender; to each one, its dose; for each context, its exact requirement. Here, there is no norm, merely a diversity of viable monstrosities. I take testosterone like Walter Benjamin took hashish, Freud cocaine, or Michaux mescaline. And that is not an autobiographical excuse but a radicalization (in the chemical sense of the term) of my theoretical writing. My gender does not belong to my family or to the state or to the pharmaceutical industry. My gender does not belong to feminism or to the lesbian community or to queer theory. Gender must be torn from the macrodiscourse and diluted with a good dose of micropolitical hedonist psychedelics.

I don't recognize myself. Not when I'm on T, or when I'm not on T. I'm neither more nor less myself. Contrary to the Lacanian theory of the mirror state, according to which the child's subjectivity is formed when it recognizes itself for the first time in its specular image, political subjectivity emerges precisely when the subject does not recognize itself in its representation. It is fundamental not to recognize oneself. Derecognition, disidentification is a condition for the emergence of the political as the possibility of transforming reality. The question posed by Deleuze and Guattari in 1972 in *Anti-Oedipus* remains stuck in our throat: "Why do the masses desire fascism?" It's not a question here of opposing a politics of representation to a politics of experimentation, but of becoming aware of the fact that the techniques of political representation always entail programs of the somatic production of subjectivity. I'm not opting for any direct action against representation, but for a micropolitics of disidentification, a kind of experimentation that doesn't have faith in representation as an exteriority that will bring truth or happiness.

In order to accomplish the work of therapy for the multitudes that I have begun with these doses of testosterone and with writing, I now need only to convince you, all of you, that you are like me, and not the opposite. I am not going to claim that I'm like you, your equal, or ask you to allow me to participate in your laws or to admit me as a part of your social normality. My ambition is to convince you that you are like me. Tempted by the same chemical abuse. You have it in you: you think that you're cis-females, but you take the Pill; or you think you're cis-males, but you take Viagra; you're normal, and you take Prozac or Paxil in the hope that something will free you from your problems of decreased vitality, and you've shot cortisone and cocaine, taken alcohol and Ritalin and codeine . . . You, you as well, you are the monster that testosterone is awakening in me.

13. ETERNAL LIFE

After a seminar on Spinoza, taking advantage of the eleven subway stops separating the station Saint-Germain-des-Prés from the station Pryénées, a disciple of Toni Negri tells me the story of the drug-addicted loves of Félix Guattari and Gilles Deleuze. I don't know if it's true, but I believe it. I think of my love for VD. Of my relationship with testosterone. He tells me that Félix, who was abstemious and depressive, operated as a connector, a toxin filter, between his lovers' addiction to psychotropic drugs and his friend Gilles's alcoholism. The cis-male who's telling me this story is obviously jealous of the indestructible chemical link between these "white-powder ladies," envious of the postal passion between Félix and Gilles. I'll learn later that this version of the facts is partly guesswork. But what I retain from it is the understanding that writing and love emerge from an entheogenic cybernetics, a narcotic feedback during which the person hooked isn't always the one who ingests the substance.[1]

In the La Borde clinic, Guattari was researching modes of political therapy, not to treat individuals (modern fic-

---

1. I've turned up no trace of any addicted quality in the relationships between Guattari and his mistresses and Deleuze; cf. François Dosse, *Gilles Deleuze and Félix Guattari: Intersecting Lives*, trans. Deborah Glassman (New York: Columbia University Press, 2010).

tions that are the exclusive domain of psychoanalysis), but rather to treat the systems, institutions, and configurations of power. His space for experimentation was the cybernetics of his own love life, a form of reasoning according to which affect—in the course of an amorous or sexual relationship—creates circuits, designs new electrical connections in the highly specialized zones of the cerebral neocortex, and determines by means of associations and mental images the specific regions of pleasure and pain.

Love is a map of connections (movements, discharges, reflexes, convulsions, tremors) that for a certain time regulate the production of affects. The functioning of this electrocellular circuit is similar to the tonic and clonic phases of an epileptic fit, on the one hand, and to the muscular spasms and tensions of the heart, on the other. The transmission of an electric current from membrane to membrane. It's a matter of a rhythmic movement, the necessarily regular production of intense affects, and it matters little whether they are positive or negative. Love, a prosthetic system of psychosomatic information, transforms us into addicted, cybernetic animals. The lover is like the laboratory cats on which Norbert Wiener was working at the Rockefeller Foundation after World War II. The brain of a cat, removed under local anesthetic, was replaced by a microchip electronically connected to a technoliving external organism. In the time of Proust, the mechanism of writing/reading was the only virtual means of prosthetic implantation of subjectivity. After the H-bomb and the saturation of the body, house, and entire city by media and information, these prosthetic systems now contain the worldwide amplified cybernetic network. Being in love today is inevitably communicating with the entire planet. Feeling the consciousness of the planet.

Love is always a cybernetics of addiction. Ending up with an addiction to someone, for someone, making someone the object of the addiction, or becoming addicted to a third substance for someone. To her, to me, to testosterone. Testosterone and I. She and I. She or the testosterone. She = the testosterone. Producing or consuming testosterone. Stopping testosterone for her. Absorbing her testosterone.

I'm not surprised that Guattari was the one who—entering a philosophical cybernetics once again—would have brought the anorgasmic Deleuze to the cooings of *Anti-Oedipus*. Like Hanemann, the inventor of homeopathy, and Bateson and Ericson, psychosomatic experimenters in Palo Alto, Deleuze and Guattari had become masters of a form of biosophy that could be called political homeopathy, or molecular political exorcism. Beyond philosophy.

Philosophy—perambulation, dialogue, writing technique—was to the Greek world what shooting up is to post-Fordist Western society. In a context in which the wheel and writing were the fundamental technologies, philosophy excelled as an exercise of the virtual production of subjectivity. Language was enough to produce a residual (individual or collective) political fiction that did not exist before the dialogue was begun. The advent of technological masturbation in the seventeenth century, using at first mechanical and then electrical devices for the control of the body and surveillance of the mind inaugurated a new era in philosophy as a form of self-abuse. In the twenty-first cen-

tury, after the H-bomb, electric guitars, the transmission
of telegraphic and telephonic waves, cybernetics, the integrated circuit, viral contagion and design, and irreparable
pollution of the atmosphere, philosophy must become a
form of pharmacopornographic ecology.

HAIRY ARM

She and I: two days of fucking without a break. Testogel and
lubricant turning into architecture: a brilliant, viscous edi-
fice, lavished on us. This is the mind in its moist, adhesive
state. The highway system of her body feeds the functions
of entrance and exit, under the form of an elastic, semiliq-
uid wall, performing like a sequential whole. Her body is a
posh club. It's called the HardPlay Space. I've never tried
anything better. A cellular Las Vegas. Testosterone in gel
form and lubricant impregnate the air, enriching it, stream-
ing through my hair. I breathe its aqueous consistency
without difficulty; my lungs have recovered their amphib-
ian ability from the fetal state. The lubricant reduces the
index of friction, limits conflict, stress, difference, thins the
walls of the ego. Restricts individuality to its thinnest state
at the place where the mind is confused with the prevailing
milieu.

VD is editing the *Mauvaise étoile* video clip. Patrick Eude-
line's voice winds around the tattooed bodies of dykes and
rocker boys, around Daniel Darc's black arm, and around
the tattoo of the relic of Busty's disillusioned love and
Axelle Le Dauphin's tattoo of an octopus devouring little

girls. VD has plunged into the alchemical process of cutting the images to blend them with the music. She sends me a text message: I can come see her. I can buy some OCB rolling paper if I find any—and if I'm nice enough to. I can come when I want. The production company is on the second floor of premises on the rue Saint-Martin. I punch in the door code. Pass the first door and ring at the second. VD comes to let me in. She has put polish on her nails, has made up her eyes. She's my whore. She kisses me, grabs me by the belt and pushes me through the premises. A film production office is a post for the manufacture of masculinity: maximum technology, minimum domestic comfort. Dirty gray carpeting, shelves filled with cassettes, computers, monitors, editing tables. At the back of the place, the layout extends beyond the limit that separates the inner space from the dumping area, a table full of scratches and empty beer cans, a refrigerator, a coffee machine, a row of potato chip packages, some full and some empty. At first, there's only VD, the film editor, and me. Little by little, other boys arrive. The head of production, a cool type with a beard and long hair, handsome but a little slovenly. Another, who is young, has just produced HPG's last film. Then there's another producer who is half elegant, half sexy, half sure of his impending success. Another dude, who is working as an agent and is with his Japanese girlfriend, who's single celled, docile, and ultrafeminine, an amoeba of high design. And there's another ambitious guy there, who's preparing his first film.

VD is a guy among guys. She's in her element here. No need to justify herself. The guys revere her. She's one of them, at the same time as being above them all. The possibility of their putting their tender cocks in her pussy and, above all, the possibility of her taking them by the ass—all of which seems likely, but which in reality is not—elevates her to the upper level of the male hierarchy. The half-sexy boy keeps flattering her. He loves *Baise-Moi*, but *Les chiennes savantes* is really her best novel; if he met a girl like Gloria from *Bye Bye Blondie*—he says, without knowing what he's talking about—he'd immediately fall in love with her. One of these days, he adds, they've got to have a drink together. With his male insularity, he doesn't even realize that, while they're conversing, VD is fondling my ass, under the material of my pants. VD is ignoring him and at the same time attaching him to an invisible chain, the way a genuine literary diva does, feeding on the narcissistic contact high she gets from her fans.

All together, there are five or six dudes in the room, smoking, talking about the Cannes Film Festival, about the money that the new Avid system costs, about HPG, who's a cool guy, about swimming pools in Los Angeles. One of them takes out a cassette and says to HPG's producer that he needs to see the casting he's doing to find the actress for his next film. Of all the guys there, this one is the most unattractive; he's barely five feet three inches tall, is bald, has a beard and mustache and a nasal, slobbery voice. He leaves his script on the table. The title is the first name of an Arab girl. Maybe "Leila," or "Farida," or "Salma" or "Gamila". . . In less than ten seconds, all the guys are gathered in front of the monitor on which the cassette is playing. The Japanese girl goes to sit on a chair at the back of the room;

she's smoking a cigarette and making a phone call; perhaps such a high level of testosterone in the surrounding atmosphere could be harmful to her amoeba-like purity. And clearly, this is a men's ritual. They're straining toward these images as if they were going to be served entire pieces of heterosexual knowledge-power. VD gets up and positions herself in the middle of them. I, too, join the group and stay standing behind them. I can see well from here, and I'm a head higher than all of them. Only VD is on a level with me. Hairy Arm, the baldie, is disturbed. He wasn't expecting the two of us—two cis-chicks in his eyes—to come and see these images. Like hardcore porn, these stolen images are reserved for the elite little roosters. On the screen is a sixteen-year-old girl, who looks eighteen and is apparently French with an Arab background; she has thick lips, prominent cheekbones, pink lipstick, long, frizzy hair. She's sitting on the ground, wearing a little black top with thin straps; her low-wasted jeans reveal a couple inches of delicate fat, which still looks sexy at sixteen, and all of it is perfected by the black Pumas she's wearing. She's looking at the camera with an expression that says she's waiting to be told what to do. She's laughing foolishly, as if she doesn't know how to present herself to the camera. You hear a guy's voice: "We're going to see how you do a sex scene, if you had to seduce the character; and we'll pretend it's me; now go ahead." She says, "I don't know." Smiles again. Lowers her eyes, closes them. She puts her hands in front of her face. "Go ahead," repeats the voice. Again, she says, "I don't know," but begins to come up with an idea. She lifts her hair while raising her arms, opens her mouth, closing it as if she were pronouncing the sound *oh*, bites her bottom lip, sticks out her tongue and licks her upper lip with its point, then closes her mouth again, while saying, "Oh." "Go on, very good, that's it, you see, you do know." The camera pulls back, and we see the girl on the ground, leaning on both hands, turned with her back facing the camera. Then a short, fat, hairy arm enters the frame, tugs at the neckline of the little top, touches first one breast, then the other. No one speaks. You can't see the girl's face, only her torso. Then the husky voice again: "Come on, show me what you know how to do, how you'd do a scene." The girl looks at some point outside the frame, as if to be certain that there's no one there. Then she stares directly into the lens, licks her lips again, sticking out her tongue, removing her top at the same time. She takes off her brassiere. Her hair fills nearly all of the frame. "Good, good, very good like that," says the deep voice while the hairy arm reappears in the frame, pushes back the hair to free the girl's breasts. They're enormous, bio- and a bit droopy—but almost not, considering their volume—with large aureoles, and very dark, protuberant nipples. The hairy arm now occupies half the frame. In the upper part is the girl's mouth, her bare shoulders, her breasts; and in the lower part, the hairy arm. For the first time, the girl leaves the frame, and you can see other sneakers, the girl's jeans lying on the ground, her Pumas, another pair of jeans filmed from above; then, an abrupt movement of the camera reveals a window, a reproduction of Van Gogh's *Sunflowers*. Next, rapidly, we can see the girl again, lying on the ground, naked. Her parted breasts are hanging slightly to either side, and the hairy arm is gripping her neck. A short, thick cock moves across the frame for a brief moment, immediately disappearing under the girl's body. She is sitting on a body that seems to be the anatomical continuation of the hairy arm. We can't see her cunt, nor the mini-cock, and we don't know whether it's going in or out; all we can see are her moving breasts, a little of her hair, her swinging head, and the hairy arm gripping her neck. The guys watching the cassette don't miss a pixel of it. On the outside of the screen of the monitor, the same hairy arm is pressing fast-forward and saying, "That's more than enough; figure out the rest yourselves." The images goes by in fast motion; the girl's body careens faster and faster, attached to the hairy arm. He presses "play," returning the video to normal speed. The girl doesn't try to simulate an orgasm. But she imitates the expression of a bitch in a porn movie, the kind of face she appears to have seen a thousand times and has no trouble simulating. Pressing the fast-forward button again, Hairy Arm explains, "They're ready to do anything to get a part, and the worst is when they call me back and ask me to see them again. That one is a good actress, but she's all wrong for the film. The girl in the film isn't like that. It's a very beautiful, very high-class, pure girl." His is the voice of the Western cis-guy's porn consciousness. The chief subject is a white hairy arm and a mini-cock without a body. A white arm masturbating a cock with the help of an image. In this case, the girl is a simple masturbatory bio-device, a body that Hairy Arm couldn't know a thing about.

The name Hairy Arm is born of that image. Hairy Arm has the same relationship to the contemporary pharmacopornographic condition that Oedipus has to modern consciousness in Freud's imagination at the beginning of the century. In order to embark on political therapy in the West, the Hairy Arm complex must be discussed. Today it's no longer a question of an intersected desire for the father or for the mother. No cis-girl from the poor suburbs of Paris wants to kill her mother to do it with her father. With racial and social exclusion to be endured from the get-go, any further desire, above and beyond the demands of the market, to go to bed with the old man is highly unlikely. The Oedipal complex has ceased to have any political validity. Oedipus has been overthrown by the Hairy Arm. The father and mother are already dead. We are the children of Hollywood, porn, the Pill, the TV trashcan, the Internet, and cybercapitalism. The cis-girl wants to transform her body into a consumable image for the greatest number of gazes. To get out of the shit pile. And come into the money. To know digital glory, be it only for a split second. She wants to be converted into digital merchandise, in order to be eternal. She wants her pornification, not to produce any pleasure (a form of pleasure that is not only indifferent to her but also continues to turn her off), but to transform her body into abstract capital, into indestructible virtual code: to become an *e-body*. She desires, with repulsion, to do it with Hairy Arm, and at the same time—with a bit of coaching—to transform herself into the Hairy Arm.

I can't avoid thinking of the fact that in Spanish, "Hairy Arm" is called Brazo Peludo, which has the same initials— BP—as my name. Will I become a Hairy Arm if I keep on taking testosterone?

10½ INCHES

During a whole year, long before I began taking testosterone, you were still alive, AB/CS, we were discussing how and when we were going to begin the process of changing sexes. Back then, we were thinking about changing only our sex, not our gender; AB wanted a vagina instead of a cock, and I wanted a cock as well as a vagina. AB was imagining what it would be like to fuck after vaginoplasty, and I was thinking about how to get the money needed for a phalloplasty—but not just any kind: a high-tech one. That meant a lot of money. For both of us. His vaginoplasty and my high-tech cock; they'd cost as much as buying an apartment in the center of Paris. I didn't want to have chest surgery or have my vagina sealed off. I'd studied the different operations available on the European medical market. The most standard consisted in using the skin and muscle of the forearm and a vein from the leg to construct a tube-penis out of it. There is a penis in each arm; in each leg there's a vein that could become erectile. The medical texts call this operation the "suitcase handle" technique, influenced, no doubt, by surrealist rhetoric. Dada surgery.

A penile graft, in the form of a handle, is detached down the length of the body, transforming the body into a suitcase. First, a flap of skin is removed from the arm and is grafted across the hip area. The body is now a suitcase with a lateral handle. It isn't yet completely masculine, with the unusual exception that a future penis is attached to the side of the pelvis. Thus far, the result is an asexual geography, with an adjoining penis. I like it this way. Next, the handle is shifted until it reaches the point at which one of its extremities is grafted to the lower abdomen. At this point the body's landscape has begun to be masculinized, but still subtly: the body has a penis, but the end of it is attached to the abdomen. If we were to interpret this image using codes from S&M porn, we'd say that it's an erect penis sewn to the stomach. An architectural reading of the body would allow us to call these proportions a prêt-à-porter suitcase with a vertical penis-handle that cannot be used for penetration. Finally, the handle is detached from the abdomen by cutting it, and the graft is allowed to hang, being attached from now on only on one end to the pelvis. I am describing in detail the photos and surgical descriptions published by a Dr. Wolf Eicher in 1984.[2] Compared to Eicher's documents, a Cronenberg film seems as gentle as *Winnie-the-Pooh*. At the foot of a photo, a caption reads, "All of them have found mental stability thanks to the operation." But I myself don't want mental stability; I just want the cock of the century.

I measure my forearm. Exactly 10½ inches. Wild! I can already imagine myself with at least a 10½-inch cock, expecting that they'll have to cut off a bit, here and there. In the worst of cases, 8½ inches, if I lost two inches because of blood circulation problems or any necrosis during the grafting process. I enjoy nothing but thinking about it. On the Internet, almost all the pages dedicated to phalloplasty, put together by post-op trans boys, are insistent about

2. Wolf Eicher, "*La transformation génitale en cas de transsexualisme*," *Cahier de sexologie clinique* 10, no. 56 (1984): 97–105.

two problems, regardless of the possibility of a graft being rejected: loss of pleasure and difficulty in getting an erection. One of the conceivable surgical techniques consists in leaving the new cock hollow, in order to be able to insert a hydraulic aerosol erectile device through the bottom, near the testicular implants. Any one of my dildos seem hotter to me than a hydraulic cock. Apparently, medical institutions and surgical teams are respectful about one pharmacopornographic prohibition: avoid the production of any kind of luxury cock.

I speak with the technoguys in various transsexual groups in Paris and Barcelona. They show me their technococks. Some are incredibly well made, but small. Most of them opted for metoidioplasty, reconstruction of a micropenis with the hood of the clitoris. Some of them have testicular implants; others have opted for a maximum of pleasure by keeping their testosterone-enhanced macro-clitoris and their open vaginas. To me this seems top-notch, the ideal solution. I go to the meeting of a trans group in Paris. They invite me to see an Australian maker of prostheses, a Dr. Arienzo, who makes prêt-à-porter penises in silicone, at affordable prices. He calls them "sexual-prosthesis camouflage." He brings out a box full of samples: a large range of skin colors, shapes, sizes. They're white, black, rigid, semi-rigid, flaccid, circumcised or with a foreskin. They're glued to the pelvis with an adhesive gel that keeps them attached for as long as fifteen days. "What's distinctive about these penises is that the silicone skin is filled with a semi-hard gel that gives them a feel and a weight that is close to those of a natural penis," explains Dr. Arienzo. Testosterone in gel form, a sexual-prosthesis camouflage in gel form, gel adhesive for attaching the cock to the body.

I start thinking that the distinctive feature of sex, including the cock, lies in gel. Being isn't matter, but gel. "Foam"— and not planetary mega-ejaculation issuing from a heroic biocock, as Sloterdijk implies—but rather, a synthetic compound desiring consciousness, a sticky molecular network trying to force its way into life.[3] *Dasein* is a "fermentation of subjectivity,"[4] a viscous subversion of matter, of course, but it cannot emanate from a will to power. It only discovers itself at the price of its own monstrous transformation. Being a subject, at the price of becoming a gel.

SIZES

It isn't the size of my dildos, but that of my trousers, that unleashes a normative temptation in VD. They're too big, she says. She says that my trousers are too wide for my thighs, too wide for her hand to reach my clito-cock directly. It's hard for me to believe that it's a question of inches, especially because her hands—I know because I measured them with my dildos—measure 8½ inches long. Actually, the problem comes from the fact that she obviously does not yet fully participate in the dyke aesthetic. But she is coming toward me. You're not fifteen anymore, she says. Yes, baby, I'm exactly fifteen years old. They call me the "little kid with the big cock." That's exactly what you like

3. Sloterdijk, *Sphères*, 28.
4. Ibid., 26.

about me, so don't lecture me about the size of my pants. Pants that are large enough to be able to wear a dildo with an erection inside them.

Years ago, my mother was working at home for a store that made bridal gowns. That's when I learned everything about sizes from her. Her specialty was making articles of lingerie that the virgin would reveal to her possessor during their wedding night, just before she was converted into an honest housewife. Before becoming ugly and frigid, young brides had the brief chance to feel my mother's hands busy in the most remote recesses of their still untouched bodies. I'd go with her to hold the chalk and set the pins. That's how I learned the subtle difference between a size and a half size. That is also how I learned to open brassieres and cut panties.

She's looking at me. She parts her thighs. She's writing a manifesto with her vulva. Come. Her hands move up from my feet to my waist, verifying that the seams of my jeans are adjusted to my body. They're two sizes too large, she says. She asks me, And what about me? I don't know, I'll have to see. She gets undressed, moves away, and dances in front of the window.

SEX PICTURES

At ten, after having doubts all evening, I give myself a dose of fifty milligrams of Testogel. I take some photos as we fuck. Her hair on my clito-cock. While she sucks Jimi. Her blue eyes, her mouth, the reflection of the red lamp on her chest. A tattoo: a heart closed with a lock, framed by two black roses, on her hip. Another: a bomb with an electric fuse, about to go off on her shoulder. Another: a row of black flowers surrounding her left breast, like a harness supporting the seriousness of her heart. Images and sex, two ways of catching time in matter. She asks me to erase them from my digital camera. I take even more. Her right hand slipping into my trousers: short fingernails painted red, a ring around her index finger with a skull and Hell's Angels wings, three multicolored plastic rings from Africa, which draw three circles on my skin, like Olympic rings. She asks me to erase everything. She says, photos are like tattoos. An image inscribed on the skin of reality forever. Each photograph bears the possibility of magic for her, conjuration, the evil eye, and influence from a distance. Erase them. I show her the photo of one of her tattoos. Justine, the dog, is sleeping on the black heart. If you find the key to my heart, you can tattoo it on yourself, she says.

She could leave me at any moment. Love is magic, evil eye, influence from a distance, tele-endocrinal transmission. At any moment, she could say, *I was a trannie's whore for three months*, the way Christine Angot said she'd been a lesbian for three months, citing Hervé Guibert's desperate litany: *I had AIDS for three months. More precisely, for three months I believed I was condemned to die of that mortal illness called AIDS.*[5] Guibert was writing this knowing that hundreds of worms were already weaving a sheet of white silk for the day of his death. The worms would enter through

5. Hervé Guibert, *To The Friend Who Did Not Save My Life*, trans. Linda Cloverdale (London: Serpent's Tail, 1991), 1.

his ass and spread a soft fabric around his entrails, without making the slightest noise. The heavenly retrovirus had fallen in love with a young blond angel, as he would next fall in love with you.

DEATHS TOO SHAMEFUL TO MENTION

I'm going with VD to the publisher Grasset, on rue des Saints-Pères. She's dropping off her finished book. We come back to my place loaded with books and films for the weekend. She is laughing while imitating Lemmy Kilminter's howls, hitting her chest like a gorilla out of its cage. We're in a state of exhilaration common to the euphoria felt by the author who has finished a book, when S calls. Eric has died of an overdose. Sextoy, Karen, Toi, Eric. A book = a death. Each new stage begins with a death. Mourning, as the only alternative to melancholia. VD tells me that the only thing she remembers about reading Blanchot is that the generations take shape around unavowable deaths. She is weeping. I caress her. Her skin is as soft as that on the stomach of Justine.

How to mourn your death? In 1935, the Spanish poet Miguel Hernández writes to his dead friend Ramon Sijé: "*Yo quiero ser llorando el hortelano / de la tierra que ocupas y estercolas, / companero del alma, tan temprano.*"[6] This book is not enough to mourn your death. I also want to tear up

6. Miguel Hernández, "Elegía," *The Selected Poems of Miguel Hernández*, ed.Ted Genoways (Chicago: University of Chicago Press, 2001), 29, lines 1–3. Translates literally to "I want to be, as I weep, the farmer / of the earth that you are occupying and fertilizing / too early, my soul mate."

the earth until I find you, I want to kiss your noble death's head, I want to suck the bone of your cock until you plunge into my digestive tract, I want to explode your anus with my best dildo, I want to take you back to the orange trees in blossom on the streets of Valencia, where you talked to me for the first time about how you had masturbated while reading the *Manifeste*.

We're together in a taxi. While we pass the Lonja de los Mercaderes, you tell me, "You smell good. Your book is the best philosophy book that I've read since Sade." You tell me that this kind of intelligence makes you hard. I didn't know you were filming the trip to Valencia. Both of us were invited to a colloquium on the new Franco-Spanish literature. Everything was gray and academic, except us. I see the edit made by Philippe and Tim for the first time since your death, on October 22. You are filming yourself in your hotel room, the hotel where I was, too. You take your cock out of your pants, put it on the night table and fondle it as if it were a wounded animal. You film the neighboring balconies, the wash hanging in the sun, the peeling walls, the faded patios. You film yourself as you're giving your presentation. You're wearing a khaki camouflage Spanish army shirt, as if queering the Franco uniform. You're speaking English, despite the fact that I've warned you that nobody will understand you. You didn't want to speak to them in French. Actually, you didn't want to speak to them. You're speaking for a future species of bilingual Euro-alien-Asiatics. If you could have, you'd have spoken in Japanese or in a metalinguistic, mathematical, or musical code. You're speaking about sex, drugs, techno music. The relationship between all that and this academic colloquium isn't very clear. In fact, you have an idea: since the 1970s, the only major revolution has been carried out by gays listening to music while getting high and fucking. You're afraid to speak about literature, about your literature. You say that literature was invented to weep about lost love. What is your lost love? Where are your tears? Whom are you crying for? What are you afraid of? What's killing you? What could save you? But you go back to sex, drugs, techno music. At one point, you talk about dykes; you say that we (and you count me among them) are also part of this history of sex, drugs, and techno music; you turn the camera around and film me. Now I'm looking at the images you shot. You're dead. I see myself on the screen, just opposite you, like a ghostly reflection. It's as if you were speaking to us from the eternal hereafter. And here I am, on the other side of the eternal hereafter.

PHARMACOPORNOGRAPHIC GENIUS

The 1990s are so far away. They were different years, and we were close to the death that had bound us in its viral laces; and this would next be replaced by a little red ribbon and a domino game of dollars and pharmaceutical molecules before us, allowing us to forget death while politics was dying.

Queer politics as you understood it was nothing other than a preparation for death: *via mortis*. A politics primarily about death, without any vitalistic populism: a reaction in the face of the biopolitics and passion of the decaying body, in the process of decomposition, cultural necrophilia. Queer politics has died with those who initiated it and succumbed to the retrovirus. Like you. Therein you were perhaps right to commit suicide, if that's what you really did, although according to the autopsy what happened is that, without knowing it, you mixed too many synthetic molecules, like Jimi Hendrix and Janis Joplin did. "Drug overdose," is what they all say, including your mother and the few newspapers that reported on your death. Were you the victim of an overdose of biopolitics, of a lethal cocktail of tritherapy and antidepressants, or did you voluntarily escape this implacable political game to transform your body into stardust, to take it out of the market of life so that all of your body that would remain was words, like legible molecules?

You gambled with your body, as well. You were playing with death. That is definitely why you allowed yourself to take the venom of writing. Before me, you'd already taken everything. What the government calls hard drugs, the illegal ones, for certain, as well as the others, those hard drugs that are marketed by the government, such as tritherapy, and testosterone, before me, to get hard. Because this barebacking[7] wasn't just a political bitch-slap invented by a handful of San Francisco kamikazes to pull the bottom out of anti-AIDS preventive politics or to spoil the funda-

---

7. From the term "barebacking," a collective and consensual practice of penetration without a condom that was coined in the United States gay community during the years following the AIDS crisis as an alternative to the control and surveillance of sexual practices. Today, the term is at the center of a biopolitical controversy surrounding the management of the HIV-positive body and its fluids. It currently refers to all sexual practices of penetration without a condom, whether consensual or not.

mentalist Left of ACT UP; it was the only way to sock it to somebody during three short good minutes. You can't roll a condom onto a flaccid cock. Nobody has the balls to tell the truth, you were telling me one day in a basement on the rue Keller, while tracing the outline of a cock on my chest with your finger. The problem was to keep getting hard on winter days for dead lovers, for the books you didn't have the time to write. Keeping hard—that's what's good about dildos, being able to stop worrying about an erection, having it always hard, you were repeating to me as your were sticking your tongue into the hole of one of my nostrils and complaining that ACT UP wanted your hide, that they'd decided to skin you alive and that one day you were going to give them what they wanted, your hide. And I didn't believe you.

SHOOTING THE HAIR OF THE DOG

The end of innocence does not begin the moment we become aware of the fact that we're mortal, and that others are, as well. It begins with the intuition that we kill to survive. That we are predators, carnivores. Savagely omnivorous, devourers of everything that lives. Survival depends on our ability to kill the beauty around us. Lately, I see the death of an animal every day. First the whale that swims up the Thames and dies without having found its way back to the sea. Then the disemboweled horse in Gaspar Noé's *Carne*, the dog bitten to death in Iñárritu's film, the chickens in Turkey that were infected by the H5N1 virus and put into sacks of lime. In *Santa Sangre*, the Jodorowsky film, the little girl, who is like a human variation of the animal, and whose two arms are cut off, after which she is smothered in a bath of her own blood. Next, an elephant is emptied of blood through its trunk and quartered by an entire village. I'm not ready for such violence. I don't know how to defend myself. I'm not ready for love with VD. I'm not ready for T. I'm the whale, the horse, the dog, the chickens, the elephant, the little girl. I'm entering the adult age when I understand that no one will be able to do anything for my happiness: not my mother or my father, or society, or the state, or my girlfriend, or a whore, or testosterone. At such moments, I turn to Justine and I find a canine solution to a cosmic problem.

I apply a dose before going to bed. Taken outside a protocol for changing your sex, Testogel proves to be, in fact, a dangerous game. The problem isn't dependence. There's a slight dependence that you couldn't even call "testomania" . . . The problem comes from the management of your own identity: man, woman, transsexual, transgender person, and so on. A few more days and the testosterone in my blood, following a rule that no pharmacology book lists, changes into something new. I know it: the devil is in my blood.

We spend all Sunday in bed, VD, Justine, and me. Sleeping and reading. As soon as she wakes up, she finds my sex with her mouth. VD is sleeping in a brassiere, and I'm sleeping with a black dildo that is 9 x 3 inches. She reads the last volume of Simone's memoirs, *Tout compte fait*,[8] and I,

---

8. Simone de Beauvoir, *All Said and Done*, trans. by Patrick O'Brian (New York: Paragon House, 1993).

Guibert's *Les chiens*. Simone writes about her relationships with women—first Zaza, Bianca, Violette Leduc; and then she informs us that, during a certain time, her friendship with Sylvie Le Bon "had an important place in her life." Not a word about sex, of course. Nothing about her lesbianism, concealed by her public friendship with Sartre. During this time, Guibert's narrator is getting penetrated in every orifice, gobbling every cock that goes by, swallowing all the sperm. Sublime contamination. VD and I read and fuck, thereby producing a molecular communion between her book and mine. Bianca, who's wearing an enormous, realistic-looking strap-on dildo, is penetrating Violette anally, while the latter is licking Simone's clitoris. Violette likes both at the same time: getting it in the ass while she has her mouth on a pussy. And that is how, on a Sunday in 2006, gradually, but with a determined inevitability, Guibertian backroom sperm is poured over De Beauvoir's head, forming an unexpected turban.

T HIGH

Yesterday, I took my last dose of T. Today, I can feel the effects. No doubt about it. I'm having a Testo high. One of the first symptoms of testosterone lies in the sensation that the inside of my body is a fibrous and flexible mass that can spread itself through space in any direction; you could call it an organic conviction, the feeling that muscular intentionality can grab hold of any object, the certainty that any obstacle at all can be gotten the better of. But in addition, there is slightly more oily skin, sexual excitement, sweat. I want most of the effects of testosterone, but I can't stand my own sweat when I'm on it. A smell that isn't coming from somewhere else, from any other body, but from my skin, and from my skin directly to my pituitary gland and then toward my brain. I'm in T. I have become T.

Today, with this last dose of T, I tell myself that things are progressing. VD loves me; my projects are taking shape; we're on a train to London. These are the last days of winter. I'm mad about her. We go through the English Channel tunnel. Underground. She's sleeping next to me. Waking, she tells me that she dreamed that our friend Sextoy was taking us for a ride in her sports car, and that you, GD, were with us. We have some Clipper tea. Now it's my turn to fall asleep. Deliciously. While I'm sleeping, dozens of illegal immigrants are clinging to the chassis of the trucks holding merchandise, as a way of getting over the border. I dream that when we reach customs, I get arrested for trafficking testosterone. When they open my suitcase, they find only two balls of hash, additive-free American Spirit cigarettes, and two dildos. I go down for two years. In the dream, the idea of prison is reassuring: it will be like a detox from T.

We're like two deer on ice, she tells me, a few hours later, as we're walking in the frozen streets of London.

BEHEADING PHILOSOPHY

Years ago, I asked a Buddhist and Jesuit teacher what philosophy was and how I'd know someday if I was capable of philosophizing. The answer is a fable: A fledgling philosopher is climbing a mountain with his aged master. They take a torturous, steep route, go along a mountain, and find themselves at the edge of a precipice. The master has promised his pupil that, before reaching the summit, he will offer him the probability of wisdom and the opportunity to embark on the task of philosophy. He has warned him that the test of endurance will be difficult. But the disciple has insisted. The ascent is arduous, and the young man begins to lose hope. They have been walking for hours and are on the point of arriving at the highest point, when suddenly, the master takes from his backpack a spinning blade and, with a flick of his hand, sends it into the air. The propeller-like blades diminish into the distant clouds, then grow larger as the object comes back in the direction of the two men, its sound intensifying, until it slices off the head of the master with one perfect cut. The blood spatters the disciple's face as he watches, astounded. The cleanly severed head, eyes open, rolls to one side of the mountain, while the body, the arms of which are still wriggling, slides to the other side, toward the precipice. Before even having time to react, the disciple wonders if he should run to the side of the mountain to retrieve the head, or to the other, to collect the body. Sever your own head. Take some distance from your own body. Experience separation. In the West, until the current time, we had believed that philosophy was a thinking head (the presupposition of a cis-male, who, assuming he was putting his body aside, created an economic system, and whose cock was able to assume a universal position). But in the Buddhist fable, the second alternative is as valid as the first: running to the side of the body and, like Artaud, forcing the body to produce text. Two irreconcilable paths: an automatically typing head, which needs no hands to write, or a decapitated body that produces, as if by discharge, an intelligible reflection. That is the challenge and the temptation of all philosophy: running after the body or after the head. And what if the answer was in the act of the master, the act itself? If the potential for philosophy lay not in the choice between head and body, but in the lucid and intentional practice of autodecapitation? At the beginning of this book, I took testosterone (instead of providing a commentary on Hegel, Heidegger, Simone de Beauvoir, or Butler); I wanted to decapitate myself, cut off my head that had been molded by a program of gender, dissect part of the molecular model that resides in me. This book is the trace left by that cut.

ETERNAL LIFE

Now you are dead and buried, rotting; you were opened, then closed up again; so, you were empty for a moment, then full of worms, enclosed forever in this box, free, as you had never been. And I am coming to say farewell to you, to salute you like a pharaoh, although it's impossible to know whether you're aware of my presence in this crowd of people. Your mother is speaking. It would be more exact to say that she is using language against us, against you. She doesn't read anything that you've written, not a sentence of yours. She is mumbling and isn't telling us anything about what you meant to us. Now you are in your last house. I wish that you were *dans ma chambre*.[9] I'm coming to say adieu.

Today, I'm supposed to do a drag king workshop in Bourges. When I informed the participants that I wouldn't be able to do the workshop because one of my friends had died, they moaned and asked me to stay. The fact of your interment didn't mean anything to them; what they wanted was to do the workshop. But I'm going to come to your burial. No, I'm not doing it for you, I'm not doing it to be good, not out of obligation. I leave King Victor in charge of the workshop and catch a train for Paris. This time it's you again who guide my fingers as I dial VD. She says that she'll wait for me at the gate to the cemetery in Montparnasse. I hadn't brought any clothes that are appropriate for an interment, so I arrive in black trousers and an electric blue T-shirt. I'm dressed like a schoolboy. I didn't even dare to come in king drag. When I get to boulevard Edgar-Quinet, I see VD from a distance. She has gotten ready for the occasion, and she's dressed like a woman in the Sicilian Mafia: a suit with a black skirt, a 1950s pocketbook, a black coat, black heels. I come forward to kiss her. My skin grazes the skin of her check. My mouth is less than an inch above hers. Our knees are exactly the same height, our groins exactly the same height, as she will tell me a few days later. The heat from her body reaches me, before growing cold again. I breathe in her breath directly, while she asks me, "You OK?" She's surrounded by people: Axelle, Ann,

9. *Dans ma chambre (In My Room)* is the title of a novel by the deceased French writer, Guillaume Dustan. —Trans.

her lesbian friends. But she's clutching my arm to follow the small group of people who have come to say goodbye to you. Where are your readers? Where are all those who masturbated while reading you? Why aren't they here, come to masturbate one last time with you? Cowards.

The bump showing in the material of VD's pocketbook leads me to think that she is carrying a 9-millimeter Luger.

She takes my arm and walks with me to the hole in which they're going to put you. Your casket, the ultimate sling in which you're going to let your ass be taken for eternity, glides into the ground. People come forward, alone or two by two, toward the mound of earth that they have removed to put you in—you. Now you're the one who will take the place of that earth, which is outside among us, the living, where you were before. VD walks with me to the edge of the mound. Your casket has been lowered as deep as it can go, but it would still be easy to jump onto it and stay there, standing; it would still be possible to pull out a hatchet to make an opening and get you out of there. But no one moves. People have brought flowers, especially white roses, a few red, which are thrown onto the lacquered wood. But no one has brought a hatchet. Nor have I. That same morning, before your body was covered with earth forever, before it became invisible, I buried the DV minicassette titled *The Day of Your Death* in the park of swamps in Bourges. I put it in a large box of matches, the kind you use to light a fire, and on it wrote your name—your names: William, Guillaume, Dustan, Baranes—twice. I made a hole in the soft, muddy earth along the river with my hands, just as I had when I buried a bird that had fallen from its nest, which I'd wanted to save when I was six years old, and which I'd suffocated by feeding it sandwich bread half soaked in milk.

If you were still alive, you'd certainly hate us, VD and me, with a hot hate that was as silky as the skin of a cock that doesn't get hard, because you'd know what she and I are together, like the revolution on the move. That is why you'd mourn your gonadic heroism and would choose us as sacred wolves to carry on your AIDS-infected legacy. VD is standing next to me, in front of your grave. When I feel her right arm against my left side, I realize that, in this crowd of people, she is my future widow. VD, the Lady of Black French Letters, is my future widow. Your burial is our marriage. You, and no one else, will be the officiating ghost who will seal the alliance between your death and our love under the earth.

As we walk away from your body, which has already begun to ferment among the flowers of Montparnasse, I promise you that we will come to rub our bodies against your grave, that we will come to leave the traces of our bodily fluids on the slab; like a pack of mutating wolves, we will sleep on your earth, warm your bones; and like vampires, we will come to quench your thirst for sex, blood, and testosterone.

The Feminist Press is an independent, nonprofit literary publisher that promotes freedom of expression and social justice. Founded in 1970, we began as a crucial publishing component of second wave feminism, reprinting feminist classics by writers such as Zora Neale Hurston and Charlotte Perkins Gilman, and providing much-needed texts for the developing field of women's studies with books by Barbara Ehrenreich and Grace Paley. We publish feminist literature from around the world, by best-selling authors such as Shahrnush Parsipur, Ruth Kluger, and Ama Ata Aidoo; and North American writers of diverse race and class experience, such as Paule Marshall and Rahna Reiko Rizzuto. We have become the vanguard for books on contemporary feminist issues of equality and gender identity, with authors as various as Anita Hill, Justin Vivian Bond, and Ann Jones. We seek out innovative, often surprising books that tell a different story.

See our complete list of books at **feministpress.org**, and join the Friends of FP to receive all our books at a great discount.

THE FEMINIST PRESS
AT THE CITY UNIVERSITY OF NEW YORK
FEMINISTPRESS.ORG